STRATEGIES AND PRACTICE IN LAW FIRM MERGERS

Alan Hodgart

LEGALEASE
PUBLISHING

ISBN: 1-903927-49-8

Published by Legalease Publishing, Kensington Square House, 12-14 Ansdell Street, London W8 5BN

Printed and bound in Great Britain by Latimer Trend, Plymouth.

© Legalease Ltd 2005

www.legalease.co.uk

PREFACE

My aim in writing this book was to make available the experience I have gained over the years in law firm mergers, but also to provide a set of guidelines and principles for those who see merger as a possible option in the strategic development of their business. I also wanted to address the many misguided views about whether mergers can create value or not. I hope that I have achieved my aim and trust that this book finds a space on the bookshelves of many, as a valuable resource for the long term.

No book of this type is the work of one person and I received considerable assistance from a number of people. First I would like to thank Michael Evans, Lucy Morris and David Hurst at Legalease who were patient with me when I was writing and tough with me in the editing process. Also thanks to Maggie Braithwaite, my assistant, who typed the manuscript and Per Jansson, my research assistant, who did much of the analysis.

Finally I would like to thank Miguel Valdez Moreno for his continuing support and help with the planning process and the book that followed.

Alan Hodgart, London, September 2005

ABOUT THE AUTHOR

Alan Hodgart is a leading consultant in the field of law firm mergers. He has nearly 20 years' experience advising on the strategic and organisational development of the legal profession. His client base includes firms of all sizes and, over recent years, Alan has worked with a significant number of leading law firms throughout Europe and the US.

He is a regular speaker at conferences and writes articles on strategic issues that confront law firms.

Contents

Chapter 1: Introduction

Put the issue of a merger on the table at a meeting of partners of a law firm, stand back and watch the reaction. Some partners will adopt an open mind and express a desire to understand the pros and cons. Others will express views that are more emotive:

> 'People will think we can't run our own firm.'
> 'I don't want to become an anonymous cog in a large machine.'
> 'Mergers don't work, do they?'
> 'I don't see what it would do for me. I've got my clients and enough work.'

All of these issues can be legitimate concerns, but should not be taken to be objective generalisations about mergers. There have been some very successful mergers of law firms in the UK, USA and elsewhere. A merger that has a clear, strategic logic tends not to create the impression that a firm is 'giving up'. A merger will, of course, result in the new firm being larger than the antecedent firms, but good partners are rarely 'anonymous cogs'. A merger must be seen in terms of the benefits it brings to the whole firm and not through individuals' eyes.

Strategic logic

As with almost any business issue, there can be good outcomes and bad outcomes. The quality of the decision-making leading up to the merger, and the quality of the integration processes post-merger, are more often the determinants of good and bad mergers than anything else. Some poor mergers were clearly the result of a bad decision – it is hard to see any strategic logic in them, and they should never have happened. There are others that do not appear to have produced the promised benefits. The issue with those is more about a failure in post-merger integration than the decision to merge. Our experience of a vast number of merged firms is that the problems are more often due to integration issues than to the initial decision to merge.

The fundamental issue in any discussion about merger, be it about a tangible proposal or on a more conceptual level, is to see the merger as a means of implementing a strategy, rather than as a strategy in itself. The actual combination of two (or more)[1] firms simply provides the opportunity to create value that will make the new firm more competitive than either firm could be individually pre-merger. It should also result in benefits being attained more quickly than they would have been without merger. An effective merger therefore provides a base from which a firm's strategy implementation can be better achieved. The crucial issue is that it usually requires a considerable effort post-merger to transform the strategic opportunities for creating value that can flow from a merger into tangible competitive benefits – it does not 'just happen'.

The essence of an effective merger is its strategic logic, and it can take two forms:

(i)   both parties to the merger compete better within their chosen strategic position as a merged firm than individually; or

(ii) both parties will achieve a significantly enhanced strategic position to which neither could have aspired to without the merger, and which takes them to a different strategic direction.

A merger can be effective when either type of logic applies. There might even be cases where both types of logic apply. By this we mean that a firm could achieve an enhanced strategic position within an existing market focus that would not have been possible without a merger.

A decision to pursue merger as a means of implementing a strategy is a choice – there are often other options available (but not always). A strategy directed at achieving specific goals that either result in, or require, significant growth within key practice areas, might be available through a judicious use of aggressive recruitment of individuals, lateral hiring of teams and organic growth. A merger is simply another means of implementing a strategy – it is not a strategy in itself.

There are, however, particular strategies where the desired market position and the time available to achieve it might suggest that merger is the only sensible option. A firm in one jurisdiction wishing to pursue growth at the top end of another jurisdiction, where there is already significant consolidation at the upper end of the market, is likely to find merger a more viable way of achieving its objectives than the much slower path of lateral hires and organic growth. In a market that is consolidating

---

1 Whilst we recognise that there are mergers that involve more than two parties, we shall refer only to two-firm mergers throughout the book for ease of reading (unless otherwise stated).

rapidly, time might be of the essence, and relying on other means of growth might mean that the firm never achieves its desired market position.

Likewise with strategies that see a firm developing into new industry segments, new client types, and in practice areas where it has little to no capability at present. A merger, the 'right' merger, can be an attractive means by which to develop these capabilities, and a firm will do so much faster than if it chooses the lateral hires and organic growth routes.

There are, of course, pitfalls with the merger option, which is why we referred to the 'right' merger. However, there are pitfalls with all options in implementing a strategy, and merger does not necessarily raise any more issues than other options. The primary purpose of this book is to demonstrate how to decide whether merger is the best option, and to then make it work.

Economies of scale

We recognise that, in practice, there are mergers that are driven more by cost-saving reasons than by any major strategic logic. However, the important issue here is that few mergers can be driven, even primarily, by economies of scale. In most mergers of law firms, it is a merger of two partnerships, and most of the partners usually remain in the merged firm. Most of the associates remain too. It is rare for any firm to have such a level of spare capacity that it can absorb the clients of another firm without also taking over most of its fee-earners. Even though savings can be made in overheads because, for example, there is no need for two finance departments, depending on the size of the merger, the management of the 'new' firm will tend to be larger than that of either of the antecedent firms.

The 'new' firm itself will also be larger than either firm prior to merger, and clients will start to make competitive comparisons with other firms based on the firm's new size. The merged firm might need to increase its cost base in order to meet the service delivery and marketing capabilities of its new competitors. In other words, a change in size can result in a perception that the firm has changed market position, and clients' expectations of the firm will change accordingly.

There are circumstances where a merger might be justified on the grounds of economies of scale alone. One is where the merger leaves the 'new' firm in the same band of competitors that at least one of the antecedent firms was in before. There are two situations in which this can occur:

(i) A merger between two small firms where the change in size post-merger still leaves the firm in the same band of competitors. For example, two firms of 20 fee-earners each could be competing within a band of competitors of up to 50 fee-earners in size; a merger between them so that they now have 40 fee-earners will make little difference to their market position.

(ii) A merger between two firms, where one is very much smaller than the other, could leave the market position of the 'new' firm unchanged. For example, a 250-fee-earner firm merging with a 50-fee-earner firm is likely to leave the 'new' firm competing with the same or similar firms as before.

The second situation is where the firms proposing to merge are focused on a volume-driven, price-competitive sector of the market where significant economies of scale are achievable with greater volume (bulk personal injury litigation is an example here).

We are not suggesting that mergers of the type in the examples given above might not have a strategic logic that will change the market position of the new firm. All we are saying is that mergers such as these could be driven only by economies of scale. However, some attention still needs to be given to the business issues as well, because it is very important that the business strategies of the merging firms are complementary, but this could be a secondary consideration. We comment further on this in **Chapter 6**.

Christopher Honeyman Brown, chief executive of ASB Law, commented that:

'Those who don't save money by merging don't know how to structure a firm properly. Sure there are costs associated with a merger, but there are also savings.'

The senior partner of William Sturges & Co, Ian Gavin-Brown, made an even stronger statement:

'Merging is hugely expensive. One reason for doing it is the saving in overheads and costs. If you're not going to do that, there has to be some other very good reasons for merging.'

In contrast, the managing partner of Berwin Leighton Paisner, Neville Eisenberg, remarked that the merger between Berwin Leighton and Paisner & Co was not about cost-cutting:

'Our merger was never about cutting people or costs. It was about achieving more, through a better position in the market, than either firm could achieve separately. Some mergers might be about cost-cutting, but that was not our strategy.'

Mark Jones, managing partner of Addleshaw Goddard, took a similar view:

> 'Sure we saw some opportunities for savings, but that wasn't the driver of the merger, or an important part of it. The merger was driven entirely by the ability of the new firm to reach the market position to which both previous firms aspired, more quickly than either could separately. Cost savings were more of an ancillary issue, and helped to balance out merger costs.'

Undoubtedly, there will be some mergers that are primarily cost-driven (ie where the main rationale behind a merger is to achieve a lower cost-to-revenue ratio, and where the other competitive benefits are minimal). However, this is only justifiable in the situations noted above.

Firms undertaking a merger often claim that the merger will result in savings in overhead costs, and the 'new' firm should be able to be more competitive on price, and be more profitable. This seems logical, and is certainly appealing to partners when a merger is first mooted. The comments made by Christopher Honeyman Brown and Ian Gavin-Brown above follow this line of thinking.

However, the critical issue that firms should consider is what the merger is intended to achieve. Is it to attract more of the same clients and more of the same work, with the 'new' firm remaining in a similar market position to that of the two previous firms, or is it to improve the firm's market position by winning better-quality clients and work than before?

If it is the former, then the issue of cost saving is crucial. However, firms in this situation should also consider whether merger is the best way to achieve this – the other option is to remain a smaller firm but to operate more efficiently, and this option should be explored alongside that of merger.

What we often find is that the real reason for merger is to increase critical mass in specific practice areas. In other words, the merger is an act of defence for one or both of the parties, as a failure to have greater strength in depth will lead to a decline in market position. Hence, the primary reason for the merger is not cost savings and economies of scale, but the need to build critical mass in order to avoid a loss of market position. Cost savings, whilst important, are actually the secondary reason. (This was the point Mark Jones makes above.)

Cost savings could be the primary reason for merger where a larger firm wants to 'bolt on' to it a smaller firm. The merger, or, in reality, takeover, has no significant impact on the size of the larger firm or on its position in the market (although it does acquire additional clients (and therefore might be able to increase revenue) and additional direct costs, but no overheads (particularly if there are no additional property costs)).

The most difficult situation to justify is where two firms of a similar size seek to merge, and give cost savings as the primary reason for it. As we noted earlier, from the two firms' perspective, the logic of this seems unchallengeable – a larger revenue with a reduced cost base must result in the 'new' firm being able to price work more competitively, and to raise profitability. Post-merger, the firms consider any generation of extra revenue from existing clients, and any increase in profitable work as a result of attracting new clients, more as a bonus.

However, there is a very real danger in this logic in that it ignores the external (ie market) perceptions of the merger. Any merger of two comparable-sized firms results in a merged firm significantly larger in size than either of the antecedent firms. If the merging firms' existing or potential clients perceive the 'new' firm to still be within the same peer group of firms, and have similar competitive capabilities, as the previous firms were or had prior to merger, then the logic is sound. However, in today's legal market, this is rarely the case. Two firms of around 20 fee-earners which merge to create a 40-fee-earner firm, might not alter market perceptions too much. However, when two firms each averaging 200 fee-earners merge, the 'new' firm is much more likely to be perceived as being in a different market position than the two previous firms were.

One reason for this is that, whilst the merged firm will usually try to reassure clients that 'nothing will change', it will nevertheless be promoting the fact that the merger has resulted in it being able to improve services, offer a better range of experts, etc. Therefore, without realising it, the 'new' firm is implying to its clients that it is now more competitive, and clients then expect that to be the case.

Secondly, and independent of what the merged firm says or does, the more sophisticated clients will intuitively expect improvements in service as a result of a merger. For example, clients might not expect a 100 fee-earner firm to have the sophisticated delivery systems of a 400 fee-earner firm, but when a smaller firm increases to that size through merger, client expectations change. Over time, they expect the merged firm to perform at the same level as other firms of a similar size, and will take work away from the firm if it fails to achieve the higher standards of firms in its new peer group. This is where any argument about longer-term cost savings runs into the sand because improvements in competitiveness, especially in a higher level of market position, cost money rather than save it. The exception to this is where a firm is perceived to be a 'commodity firm', which is competing in the low-margin part of the market, and price is the primary competitive weapon, not service quality.

Along with this is what we call an infrastructure step-change, which occurs as a firm grows, be it through merger or otherwise. As a firm increases in size, the cost of its overheads tends to rise in steps, rather than in line with the size increase. This is because there will be certain points during a firm's development when it will need to increase its support infrastructure significantly simply to accommodate the new size. The firm can then increase revenue with a much lower growth rate in overheads for some time after it crosses that threshold need for infrastructure support. The process will, however, repeat itself as a firm grows. This is illustrated in **Figure 1.1**.

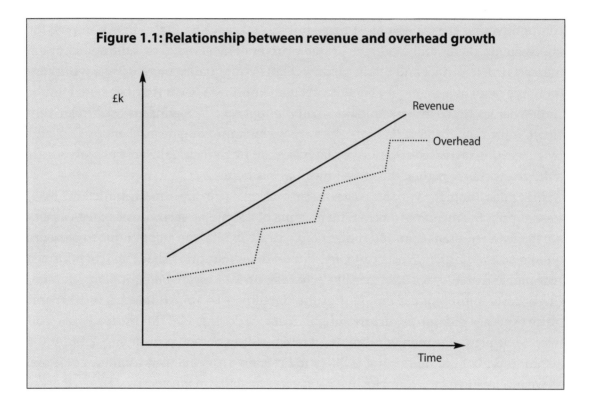

Figure 1.1: Relationship between revenue and overhead growth

For firms seeking to raise their quality of clients and work, the need to increase the quality of service as the size of the firm increases, and the need for greater infrastructure support, inevitably leads to an increase in cost per lawyer. These are made up of the costs incurred as a result of additional management time it takes to operate a larger firm, improved support given to fee-earners in order to improve delivery of service, new technology and related systems, and expanded finance, HR, marketing and administration departments (and without including any additional property costs that may be required).

There are, of course, situations where a firm has already expanded its infrastructure support in anticipation of future growth, which could result in considerable cost-saving (eg the acquisition of additional property space prior to a merger). In one recent London merger, a 200 fee-earner firm was able to absorb an additional 50 fee-earners without any overhead cost increases, as the larger firm had gone through a step-change in its infrastructure development just before the merger. In this merger, cost saving was not the driver. The business case focused initially on the potential for client development, and the increase in critical mass in key practice areas. Cost savings were a bonus.

In summary, as a result of the current state of legal markets, where increasing competitiveness means that most firms have to improve their ability to compete for good-quality clients and work, the primary driver of most mergers is the ability of the merged firm to attract and retain quality clients with quality work. Cost savings are therefore more of a secondary benefit, albeit an important one if they can be achieved.

What is often overlooked is that the potential for cost savings is often relatively small. A firm can increase its profitability more by improving its market position, and by generating increased revenue per lawyer, than by reducing the cost per lawyer. (If a firm can achieve both at the same time, that is a bonus.)

For one thing, the variable costs in a professional firm are actually quite low. Take, for example, the merger of a firm with revenue of £20m. The salary costs of fee-earners are likely to represent £7m, and if the profit margin is 33%, the amount due to partners will be £6.6m. Property costs can vary, but on the assumption that the firm occupies reasonable rented space, they are likely to take up 10% of revenue (or £2m). In total, these 'costs' represent £15.6m. Out of the remaining £4.4m, secretarial and general office expenses plus infrastructure support from marketing, HR, finance teams, etc will need to be paid. The merger might therefore result in one-off cost savings of £2m (or 10% of revenue) but this saving is likely to be eaten up as the firm continues to grow, as we discuss further below. However, a merger focused on improving a firm's market position could generate an additional 10% of revenue per lawyer in each of the three to five years following the merger; a significantly greater addition to profitability.

The cost-saving argument often focuses on the fact that the merged firm will not require two sets of infrastructure support. Whilst this is generally true, it is also the case that the 'new' firm will still need to have more infrastructure support than either of the antecedent firms did previously. (The exception to this would be the 'bolt-on' situation noted earlier.)

Hence, in the majority of mergers, the actual cost savings, especially when balanced against the costs of merger, are small to insignificant. Whilst the argument might be that the cost savings will continue beyond year one, evidence suggests that if the merged firm continues to grow, these savings will soon disappear. In the event that the merger does not generate improvements in revenue per lawyer through other competitive gains, the profitability of the merged firm is likely to decline over a three-to-five year period.

An analysis of the higher-profit and lower-profit UK firms indicates that high profitability is more a consequence of improving revenue generation than cutting costs. Excluding the Magic Circle firms, the most profitable firms have an average of £174,000 in cost per lawyer compared with £103,000 for the low profitability firms – a difference of 69%. On the other hand, they have revenue per lawyer of £255,000 compared with £127,000 for the low profit firms – a 100% difference. Put another way, the firms with highest profitability also have a higher cost base than many others but generate more revenue per lawyer.

This is shown in **Figure 1.2** (overleaf) where the most profitable firms earned a profit per lawyer of £81,000 compared with £24,000 for the low profit firms, a difference of 238%. Having a low cost base does not generate higher profits. Higher profits tend to come from having good quality clients with higher value work on which a firm can charge above average prices, thereby generating a strong margin. (We recognise that leverage has a role here, but the high profitability firms also achieve better leverage than the lower profit firms.)

Figure 1.3 (on page 11) demonstrates a second and related point. The group of firms which constitutes the higher profitability group is the same as in **Figure 1.2**. This group tends to carry out more higher value work than less profitable firms. The second group has a somewhat smaller share of higher value work compared with the top group, and earn mid-level profitability. The cost per lawyer for the second group is 17% lower, on average, compared with the top group. This indicates that there is a higher cost base required to service work in the higher value segment than in lower value segments.

A firm that is merging to improve its market position can expect to see a significant rise in overhead costs as its business develops. The firms operating in the higher-value sector of the market have a much higher cost per lawyer than those at the lower value end. On the other hand, firms operating in the higher value work sector have a much higher revenue per lawyer, resulting in a significantly better profit per lawyer than the average mid-to-lower-value focused firm. For the reasons we noted above, it costs money to make money, and no firm entering a merger should be under any illusion that, if the merger is to improve its market position in terms of client and work quality, then costs per lawyer are likely to rise, not fall, over the first few years post-merger. In

	Revenue per lawyer £k	Cost per lawyer £k	Profit per lawyer £k	Profit per equity partner £k
Higher profitability				
Macfarlanes	291	167	124	735
Herbert Smith	233	158	75	700
Ashurst	276	187	89	521
SJ Berwin	321	217	104	510
Berwin Leighton Paisner	259	198	61	425
Group average	255	174	81	576
Lower profitability				
Morgan Cole	80	66	14	68
RadcliffesLeBrasseur	163	144	19	100
Penningtons	121	96	25	136
Freethcartwright	160	128	32	146
Clarke Willmot	149	125	24	172
Group average	127	103	24	132
% difference	100	69	238	336

Figure 1.2: Relative revenue and cost per lawyer for higher- and lower-profitability UK firms

Source: Legal Business 100, 2004

addition, other than in exceptional circumstances, the actual cost savings from the average merger are small relative to the revenue base, and these can disappear simply by a firm growing in size, even without any improvement of its market position.

Of course, if a well-managed firm merges with a badly-managed firm, there will be a real opportunity to improve effectiveness and create efficiencies, and therefore to generate more profit from the poorly-managed firm's business than before. However, the question as to why the partners in the poorly-managed firm were not capable of doing this themselves should always be asked. In our experience, poorly-managed firms usually also have a number of other serious problems, and are not ideal firms with which to merge.

	Revenue per lawyer (£k)	Cost per lawyer (£k)	Profit per lawyer (£k)	Profit per partner (£k)
Higher profitability				
Macfarlanes	291	167	124	735
Herbert Smith	233	158	75	700
Ashurst	276	187	89	521
SJ Berwin	321	217	104	510
Berwin Leighton Paisner	259	198	61	425
Group average	255	174	81	576
Mid-level profitability				
DLA	218	174	44	475
Lawrence Graham	223	144	79	416
Richards Butler	219	158	61	415
Norton Rose	189	119	70	405
Nabarro Nathanson	202	132	70	344
Group average	207	148	60	414
% difference	23	17	35	39

Figure 1.3: Relative revenue and cost per lawyer for selected UK firms

Source: Legal Business 100, 2004

ASB Law's chief executive, Christopher Honeyman Brown, commented earlier that mergers can result in cost savings. He also noted that some of the savings come from better utilisation of people, and the ability to manage work better. A small, well-managed firm, with an appropriate strategic focus, should be able to save money just as well as a larger firm in the post-merger phase.

Honeyman Brown also noted that the merged ASB Law was much better equipped to compete for much larger engagements and clients than any of its three antecedent firms. This suggests that the merger had another strategic driver parallel to that of reducing costs. It also suggests that, as it rises up in the marketplace, ASB Law will follow the path of other merged firms, and will face an increase in cost per lawyer as it grows further in size and improves the quality of its delivery of service. Hence, it will need to ensure that it raises revenue per lawyer (or increases the ratio of partners to other fee-earners) if the added profitability from the cost savings is to be sustainable.

In fact, ASB Law's costs do appear to have increased in the years following the merger so any savings as a result of the merger have been outweighed by other expenditure. According to the Legal Business 100, ASB Law's cost per fee-earner rose from £63,000 to £81,000 from 1999/2000 to 2002/2003. Unfortunately, the 2003/2004 numbers are not on a comparable basis. The cost per equity partner increased from £529,000 in 1999/2000 to £850,000 in 2003/2004, although part of this at lease was due to no growth in equity partner numbers against an increase in revenue of over 50%.

Merger and the importance of size

This leads to an issue that requires discussion before we address the main subject matter of this book and this is the importance (or not) of size within the strategic logic of a merger. Merging two firms will result in a firm that is larger than either of the two constituent parts.

An increase in size results in many incorrect assertions being made about the intention behind a merger. These assertions can be either positive or negative. It is important that we dispel the myths associated with merger and size in this introduction in order to avoid repetition in later chapters.

Increase in size: consequence or strategic benefit of merger?

An increase in the overall size of a firm is a consequence of a merger (unless a major divestment programme occurs immediately post-merger) rather than a strategic benefit of a merger. Achieving a competitive depth of resources in one or more practice area (ie critical mass) is a strategic benefit. Where a firm uses merger to build critical mass in a number of practice areas, the firm will increase in size, but that increase in size is a by-product of the merger rather than a strategic aim in itself. Becoming larger overall is therefore not a strategic benefit, and does not add to a firm's competitiveness. The strategic aim is achieving a competitive critical mass in specific practice areas.

Increase in size: reaction of partners

Concern about being part of a larger firm is a real issue to some people. Others, however, will express concern over an increase in size purely as a way of trying to avoid a potential major change that will threaten the comfort zone in which they operate. We look at issues associated with the latter group of people in **Chapter 4**, but the key point here is that not all objections to merger on the grounds of the consequent increase in size are, in fact, objections to change. There are some people whose cultural values just fit better with a small organisation than a large one. This must be acknowledged in any merger discussion. It must also be recognised that at least some of these people will leave if the merger goes ahead (and this is probably best for everyone).

It is therefore critical to separate those who have a genuine concern about the size of firm to which they wish to belong from those who are really just concerned about change. Whilst a merger might offer some critical strategic benefits, there could be a strategic downside if several 'heavy hitters' in one or both firms leave post-merger due to cultural issues. (We distinguish here between people who object to a merger because of issues in the specific business case and people who object to a merger due to personal and cultural issues associated with size. The former group is more open to debating the issues and to carrying out further analyses, whereas the latter group is almost un-persuadable because their concern is about any merger whatsoever, not a particular merger.)

The main issue for those whose cultural values are suited more to a smaller than a larger firm is the potential strategic trade-off. A firm might need to become larger in order to realise its strategy, so if the partners want to resist growth, they will then need to redefine their firm's strategy. Partners often fail to realise this. The issue is that, as competition increases, it is essential that a firm ensures that it has a competitive strength in depth in all of its core practice areas. In order to do so, it needs to measure itself against peer group competitors or those firms against whom it will be pitting itself in the future if the strategy is successful. It also needs to take into account client perceptions.

There are still many lawyers who fail to understand that having critical mass is so important, and these are often people who dispute the need for a firm to merge.

Critical mass: practice area requirements

There are some areas of practice where a firm must have large numbers of lawyers simply to be able to do the job. One example is a huge and complex M&A transaction taking place across several jurisdictions and involving extensive due diligence. Another example is a large and difficult litigation case that might require the involvement of a significant number of lawyers leading up to trial.

Critical mass: clients' perceptions

There are also other areas of practice that do not require a large team of lawyers but where critical mass is still a key competitive capability, for example, employment law.

Example 1.1

Two mid-sized firms are pitching for the employment law work of a large company.

Firm A has two partners and two associates. Firm B has six partners and 14 associates.

The issues that the client would consider are:

- What if Firm A suddenly wins several big matters? Could they cope? Would our work suffer?

- With 20 lawyers to sustain, Firm B must do a lot of this type of work. Therefore, the body of experience within the group at Firm B must be far larger than that at Firm A where there are only four lawyers.

- Firm B must be good if it can attract a volume of work that supports 20 lawyers.

- If we go to Firm A and one partner does our work, what do we do if that partner suddenly falls ill or resigns? There would then only be one other partner at Firm A to pick up the work whereas at Firm B there would be five other partners to do so.

Hence, clients do see the size of a group as an important distinguishing capability.

Many lawyers fail to realise that clients see the size of a practice group as an important distinguishing feature amongst law firms. We illustrate the problem in **Example 1.1**.

It is not just the size of the firm but the size of a specific group that can matter. This does not mean that a smaller group of brilliant lawyers with an excellent track record cannot compete with a much larger group of second-grade lawyers, but when two groups are head to head, and there is very little else to distinguish them, critical mass will be important. Equally, a very good relationship between a partner in a small group and their client will allow the smaller group to fight off bigger competitors, at least for a time.

The type of client also matters. Small businesses which are irregular users of legal services will be less concerned about critical mass and more interested in the personal relationship with the lawyer. More sophisticated buyers, however, will usually take critical mass into account, albeit with differing degrees of importance.

Critical mass: size range

The other issue about critical mass is that a firm does not have to be exactly the same size as its peer group competitors. Critical mass is more about a size range than an absolute number. As we noted before, there are projects where a firm will need to have a large number of lawyers, and will be ruled out if it cannot convince a client that it has the resources. Where a project will involve, for example, 50 lawyers, a firm will need to have sufficient resources to devote 50 lawyers to the task and still carry out the other work in the group. One client might see the need for the group to include at least 150 lawyers, whereas another decision-maker might require at least 200 lawyers in the group. The short-listed firms will therefore tend to be those with a range of at least 150 to 200 lawyers within the practice group; a firm with only 80 to 100 lawyers in the practice group would be excluded unless it had some other, very compelling, competitive capability.

In other areas of practice, where the client's work requires one partner and an assistant only, the scale will be set more by the competition. In our example earlier, Firm A, with four lawyers, will be hard pressed to win if it is up against firms with 20 to 30 lawyers in the group and which have excellent reputations. Another firm with 12 lawyers in the group and which also has an excellent reputation could still be in the running because it is large enough to answer most of the client's concerns about critical mass, even though it is somewhat smaller than the other contenders.

It is hardly surprising that there is confusion about the concept of critical mass. It is, at least in part, defined in relative terms between competitors, and this can vary depending on the existing market position of the firms involved. There is no one precise measure for critical mass in terms of any practice area – it is definable only within a range, and that range is determined by a number of variables including the type of client that is buying the service.

Critical mass: argument for or against merger?

It is important to grasp these essential features of critical mass in order to understand many of the issues associated with merger. The need for 'critical mass' has been used to justify many mergers, but without any clarification as to what was meant by the term. We have seen merger prospectuses which contain statements about building critical mass and then go on to show what the number of fee-earners in each practice area would be post-merger. What is lacking in most of those cases was any assessment as to whether having the increased number of fee-earners in each of the practice groups would make the firm any more competitive. If the target client base does not see critical mass as important, then it is invalid to invoke critical mass as a reason for merger. In another case we have seen, a firm needed to build critical mass in order to compete for certain types of work, but the merger prospectus failed to identify what critical mass was, and a subsequent examination of the size of the practice group post-merger indicated that the merger did not in fact achieve it – bigger, yes, but that does not mean it passed the critical mass test.

Ironically, critical mass is also invoked as an argument against merger where partners deny the need to build up the size of a practice group, claiming it already meets the critical mass test, and seek to refute the business case for merger.

In most cases, the term is used as a concept, when it is, in fact, a potentially powerful competitive capability in many situations. But if it is to be used to either justify or refute the need to merge, then those using it should be prepared to put some measure on it, even if only by reference to competitors. During merger discussions between two law firms some years ago, the corporate practice group of both firms felt that a merger would result in them being considered for M&A transactions much larger than those that either firm regularly competed for at the time. We conducted a survey of a limited number of clients who had used either firm for M&A work in the past, and who had instructed other firms for much larger deals. Told about the proposed merger (in confidence), there was unanimous agreement that, given the reputation of the two firms, the clients would consider instructing the merged firm on transactions twice the size that they were being given pre-merger. We carried out the same exercise in another proposed merger. In that case, however, clients did not think that the increased size of the practice group post-merger would result in the merged firm moving out of the market position that both firms were in pre-merger. The general view was that the practice group would need to be 50% larger again to satisfy the critical mass requirements at the next level up in the 'food chain'.

Critical mass: strategic issue

Critical mass is a fundamental strategic issue. The particular strategy of a firm (which involves the firm defining the type of clients who are seen as the future core client group and the type of work that the firm wishes to do for these clients) will determine broadly the likely peer group of competitors in the future. From this can be drawn some idea as to the size that each core practice group will need to attain in order to be perceived as competitive.

Mergers – client-driven?

The issue of competitive capabilities is embedded in the view that mergers should be 'client-driven', but this term is often misunderstood. As a consequence, when partners are asked about the possibility of their firm merging, the reply is often 'our clients aren't asking for it'. The simple truth is that clients very rarely ask a firm to merge. There have been cases where firms are facing declining competitiveness, and, in discussions with key clients, the need to consider merger as a way of strengthening the firm and retaining the clients' work has been raised. But this is not a common situation, and even when it has arisen, it was usually as a result of a discussion initiated by the firm. Yes, mergers need to be client-driven, but this is not the same thing as clients saying 'Go merge!'.

There have been situations where firms have discussed with a particular client how it can obtain a type of work that was at the time going to another firm, or how it can receive higher-value work in areas that it is already providing to the client. Clients will spell out the competitive capabilities the firm needs to build in order to get the work, but rarely will they tell the firm to merge. If the firm decides that the best way of building these capabilities is to merge, then that is a client-driven strategy. It is a strategy driven by wanting to meet clients' needs, not by the fact that clients said the firm had to merge.

Firms have also created new market positions by merger that did not exist previously, and for which there was no explicit client demand. An example of this is the development of multi-jurisdictional firms particularly, but not only, in Europe. Major clients with needs across a number of jurisdictions, in the main, already had a 'stable' of good law firms in each jurisdiction. When asked in surveys whether they wanted a firm that could meet their needs in a number of jurisdictions, the initial response was lukewarm. When asked what a multi-jurisdictional firm would need to offer by way of benefits over a single jurisdiction firm in order to achieve client switching, many clients articulated the same things, one of which was a competitive critical mass in core practice areas in each jurisdiction. Hence the need for firms seeking a multi-jurisdictional position in the market to build critical mass quickly, and an obvious way to achieve this was through local mergers. Clients did not ask for it – they simply articulated what would lead them to consider a multi-jurisdictional firm over single jurisdiction firms, Even though it was not requested by clients, it was still client-driven, albeit focused on the identification of latent client needs.

Client-driven does not mean that clients are asking a firm to merge nor that they are threatening to take away work unless the firm merges. The latter situation is only likely to happen when a firm is declining in competitiveness but, even then, clients usually need to be asked for their opinion as to whether merger would correct the problem.

When lawyers say that clients have not asked them to merge, the immediate question to ask them back is whether clients have been asked what competitive capabilities a firm will require in the future given its strategy, and whether a firm's strategy is sufficiently clear to enable them to ask the question. It is not about asking whether or not the firm needs to be bigger, but whether its strategy will require a build up of strength in core practice areas, one way to achieve which is merger.

So where is the synergy?

Devoted readers of management literature will undoubtedly be asking themselves at this stage 'so why hasn't synergy been mentioned'. Be prepared – this is the only section of this book where the 'S' word is used.

The primary reason for avoiding the use of the word is that it has been so mis-used in the corporate world that it is now seen as cliché; a word used to justify any merger without any substance behind it.

In fact, the substance of this chapter is all about synergy, but it is a complex subject not easily summed up in one word. In his book,[2] Mark L Sirower writes: 'Synergy must imply gains in competitive advantage – that is competing better… [than either party did before].' Whilst he is referring to corporate acquisitions, the same applies to law firm mergers. That is the point being made throughout this chapter. There is little point in merging two firms unless the end result is that all partners in the combined firm are in a better competitive position than they were in pre-merger, and such a position is one that they want to be in.

Synergy between two firms starts with the strategic vision of both – without that it is not possible to decide whether synergies exist. The issues posed in this chapter are dealing with the issue of synergy. What is it about this combination that will enable the merged firm to be more competitive than either of the antecedent firms could be independently? The answer to this question determines whether synergies exist or not. Hence, we have dealt with 'synergy' by looking at the strategic logic of mergers, albeit avoiding the use of the term. The means by which synergies can be created are discussed below.

Mergers – partner opposition

As we noted earlier, there are lawyers in many firms who are more culturally attuned to a small firm environment than that of a large firm. What is often not made apparent is that in opposing merger because of their cultural discomfort, they are, in effect, asking the firm to adopt a new strategy. Part of this is because of a lack of understanding about the importance of critical mass. Another aspect is that partners often adopt strategies that lack any clarification on the implication of pursuing such a strategy on the size of the law firm. The strategies of many firms articulate a desired position in the market but, too often, fail to quantify what this means in terms of the future size of the firm, given the need to build critical mass in core practice areas. Hence, partners are able to

---

2 *The Synergy Trap* (New York: Free Press, 1997), p77.

agree a strategy without any sense as to what might be required in terms of growth. When a merger proposal is presented as the way to achieve the size required by the strategy, partners reject the merger in principle while still clinging to the strategy. Where a strategy requires a significant size increase in a relatively short period of time, merger is almost the only way to achieve this. Partners who have voted for the strategy but oppose any merger are either disputing the need for the size increase (which should have been debated before agreeing to the strategy) or, in effect, asking for a revision of the strategy to one that does not carry the same size implications. (There can, of course, be valid strategies that require little, if any, increase in size, but if this was the existing strategy then merger would not be on the table.)

Some would say this analysis is too black and white, and it is, but it makes the point. There will, of course, be situations where a firm could achieve its strategy by organic growth or by merger. It rejects merger and is able to pursue organic growth quite effectively. Our point still stands. The firm will still need to be considerably larger in order to achieve its strategy and those who favour a small firm environment will, at some point, start to express discomfort. All a merger proposal does is speed up the process of reaching the discomfort level.

Hence, it is firstly very important that partners have some sense as to the likely resulting size of their firm if a particular strategy is to be pursued successfully. Secondly, it is equally important that those who oppose creating a larger firm say so at the time the strategy is agreed and not when an implementation step (ie merger) is under way. Thirdly, if there are enough 'small firm believers', then a firm might be better to abandon a strategy that will lead to a much larger firm and develop a more constrained strategy. On the other hand, if the 'small firm believers' are an insignificant minority, then the firm should pursue its strategy, even if its includes merger, and allow (or even help) the 'small firm believers' to go to a firm that better suits their cultural values.

Mergers – individual versus firm-wide perspective

This leads to the requirement to view a merger proposal, first from a firm-wide perspective, second from a departmental or practice group perspective, and third from an individual perspective. This is one of the most difficult issues in any major partnership decision. A decision to merge is a very big one indeed, and it is only natural that people think instinctively '… but what will happen to me?' when the issue of their firm merging is first broached. By nature, a high degree of professional people are relatively insecure, and any decision that might shake up their position and status within a firm can set off 'the wobbles'.

But a decision to merge by a firm must be seen from the whole-firm perspective. A merger might leave 20% of the firm unchanged, doing what it has always done with the clients it has always served. The other part of the firm might be offered huge opportunities to win better-quality clients, undertake better value work and attract superior people, all of which will raise the reputation and profitability of the firm as a whole. Even those in the unaffected 20% are likely to eventually see some positive spin-off from such a merger.

It is harder to take a firm-wide view when a merger means that the practice group of a partner will be completely absorbed by a much larger and better performing group of the proposed merger partner. Partners in this situation do often feel that if they vote for a merger they are really 'turkeys voting for Christmas'. As a partner in this situation once said:

> 'I can see all of the benefits to the firm, but I'm going to be eaten alive and then spat out by the other lot. No thanks!'

As we discuss in **Chapter 11**, management cannot simply gloss over these fears. They must be addressed if a merger is to succeed. It is vital that partners enter a merger feeling very positive and motivated by its possibilities.

There are several issues to consider where a partner or partners feel threatened by merger. There are cases where partners are underperforming; they know it but they have escaped attention from within their existing firm. However, they can see that their underperformance would surface in a merged environment, and they fear the consequences. Regardless of the fact that a merger is being considered, these people need to be identified and helped, either to improve or to find another job. There is also the situation where a certain practice group is underperforming compared to the rest of the firm. A merger will address some of that group's competitive capability issues, enabling it to raise its performance to an acceptable level.

It is vital that management works through these issues with such partners as part of the business case for the merger. The fears of underperformers should not be a reason for avoiding a merger that has potential strong strategic benefits.

Often, there are partners who are excellent performers but simply feel threatened by a merger. They can see the benefits to their department and to the firm, but feel they will lose status, respect, influence or position as a result of the merger. These people are the hardest to deal with because the problem is one of trust. Good performers will come through in any firm. As we say to these types of partners, the new firm would be crazy to suppress good performers. The merger will be successful only to the extent that it nourishes the better performers, no matter which antecedent firm they came from.

The same point applies to a partner who is department head in their firm and thinks it is likely that they will not be the department head in a merged firm. If they were good at managing the department then they might get the job in the merged firm, if not at the outset then later on. If they were not good at it, then it is best that someone else takes over and that the partner goes back to fee-earning.

While it is natural that people will think of their personal situation in the event of a merger, it is crucial that management focuses on the benefits to the overall firm, but also then works with those partners who can see the benefits to the firm but feel threatened either as a group or personally. In some cases, it will be better to allow a partner to leave the firm either before or at the time of merger. In other situations, efforts must be made to show how the firm-wide benefits can trickle down and across the firm.

Everybody in a firm will feel a tremor of nervousness about the impact on them of a merger at some stage in the process. What management must seek to ensure is that a very high percentage of people go into the merger feeling that it is right for the firm's core practice areas and, therefore, right for the firm. In this case, it will also be right for the people in the firm, provided they continue to perform well.

Competitiveness

This brings us back to competitiveness. A merger that does not enhance competitiveness should not be undertaken. Competitiveness in this sense has two meanings. The first is whether a merger will make a firm more competitive in its existing market position. The second is whether the merger projects the firm into another market position and, then, whether the merged firm has (or can build) the competitive capabilities required to compete there.

Set out in the box overleaf are issues which should be focused on when considering a merger in order to determine whether the merged firm really will become more competitive than either of the two antecedent firms could have become without a merger.

While there will be many other issues to consider, our experience is that where a strong business case is developed around the issues set out overleaf, many of the other problems that arise during merger talks are easier to address. If people can see that significant benefits to the business can arise from merger, they are more likely to have the will to overcome problems that might otherwise become deal-breakers. Equally,

---

Issues that need to be addressed at the outset of any merger discussion to determine resulting competitiveness of firm

- Will the additional size of the merged firm provide competitive advantages not otherwise available?

- Does the merger provide critical mass in core practice areas, and who are the competitors it is being measured against?

- Will the merger allow existing core clients to be serviced to a level not possible without the merger?

- Will the merged firm be in a position to attract new clients and core practice area work that could not be attracted without the merger?

- Will the merged firm be attractive to the type of lawyers it wishes to recruit, and does it allow it to raise the 'gene base' over and above what could be done otherwise?

- Does the merger allow the building of a higher-quality infrastructure than could be done otherwise?

---

where it is not possible to develop a compelling business case, then it is probable that further discussions should cease and no more time should be wasted.

Do mergers work?

Having said all that, it still leaves a key question up in the air. Do mergers work? An oft-repeated statement is that 70% of mergers do not work, and yet most of those who use it have no idea of the evidence which supports the statement or of its origins.

One source lies in some work carried out by KPMG in 1999, when it estimated that only 17% of major global M&A deals enhanced value for shareholders. Furthermore, they estimated that 53% destroyed value, and 30% were neutral. By 2002, however, their estimates were that 34% enhanced value, 31% destroyed value, and 39% were neutral.

It is important that the methodology used in these studies be understood. Whilst we are not supporting or decrying the methodology, it does make a difference to how the results might be interpreted. For one thing, the study was based on major global corporations, not professional firms. Furthermore, the primary measure as to whether value was enhanced, destroyed or neutral was the share prices of the companies pre-deal and then approximately one year later. This was put into relative context by comparison with the industry segment change in price. The question that goes unanswered is the impact of measuring the post-deal price two or three years later, given that it can take up to three years before the benefits start to accrue.

Hence, while the KPMG study is a useful piece of data, it certainly does not lead to the generalisation that 70% of mergers fail. Even if only a minority of M&A deals enhanced value within a year, the rest might still have turned out to be effective mergers. Furthermore, we do not know what would have happened to the share prices of the two companies if the mergers had not taken place.

Other studies have revealed contradictory data. Booz Allen Hamilton's survey *Making Acquisitions Work: Capturing Value After the Deal* (1999) estimated that 51% of corporate M&A lost value, and 49% gained in value. Again, the timeframe measured was one year, which could suggest that over a longer period, more would be seen to add value.

The survey also argued that, of the M&A where value had declined, the issue was more about poor post-merger execution than the strategic logic of the decision to merge. McKinsey, in various publications about the value of M&A, make similar points.

When we look at the UK legal market there have been mergers that appear, from the outside, to have been very successful. The most obvious was the 1987 Clifford Turner/Coward Chance merger that created the springboard for that firm's development into a leading global transactions practice. Other notable mergers would include the Dibb Lupton Broomhead/Alsop Wilkinson merger in 1995, Addleshaw Sons & Latham/Booth & Co in 1998 followed by the Addleshaw Booth/Theodore Goddard merger in 2003, and Berwin Leighton with Paisner & Co in 2002. CMS Cameron McKenna is a merged firm, as are Denton Wilde Sapte, Lovells, Beachcroft Wansbroughs, Hammonds, Eversheds, Nabarro Nathanson and Cobbetts. Notable cross-border mergers include Clifford Chance, Linklaters, Freshfields Bruckhaus Deringer, Norton Rose, Ashurst, Mayer, Brown, Rowe & Maw, SJ Berwin, Jones Day and Taylor Wessing. In fact, of the top 50 firms by size in the Legal 500 (2004), 25 have had a merger or brought in a group which is equivalent to a merger, either domestically, internationally or both.

While there will undoubtedly be differing views about the degree of effectiveness of these mergers, most of these firms have performed well over recent years, certainly within the relative trends of their market segment. There have been, of course, some mergers that appear to have done less well. The mergers into the legal arms of the major accountancy firms were all somewhat difficult even before other forces created problems. Morgan Cole has not exactly prospered since its merger, and there have been a number of de-mergers. The merger between Withers and Crossman Block resulted in a eventual de-merger.

Nevertheless, the evidence in the legal market against the proposition that mergers per se are bad, and that a high proportion do not work, is overwhelming. Of course, we cannot say what would have happened if the merger had not occurred. Would Clifford Turner and Coward Chance have each earned an average profit per equity partner (PEP) in excess of £600,000 per annum over the last five years or so? We cannot say for sure, but it is unlikely if they had stayed as they were whilst the legal market changed the way it did. Likewise with Addleshaw Booth & Co. Its PEP went up in the years after the merger, well above what the two antecedent firms had earned previously, and it has continued to rise in its new form of Addleshaw Goddard. The latter announced a PEP of £405,000 in the year ending April 2005, whereas in 2002 Addleshaw Booth & Co's was £275,000 and Theodore Goddard's was £350,000.

How much of these additional earnings were due to the merger, and how much were due to market changes, we cannot say. What is evident, however, is that a number of the firms mentioned above could not have seized the opportunities that arose from changes in the market in their pre-merger state. To achieve the post-merger levels of profit without the merger that they undertook would have required another, comparable merger or a major strategic development programme, requiring enormous change.

The fact that a significant number of larger law firms have improved their market position and profitability post-merger leads to the conclusion that merger can be very beneficial. We can only conjecture now what would have happened in the absence of merger. They did merge, they have not fallen apart, their market position has been enhanced, and their profitability is higher than prior to the merger.

Another critical point, often overlooked by those who invoke evidence from the corporate sector to suggest that mergers between professional firms are not likely to add value, is the very different market structures that apply in many industries. A number of the well-reported corporate mergers that appear to have damaged shareholder value (eg Time Warner/AOL and Hewlett Packard/Compaq) were in industries that were already highly consolidated. In contrast, legal markets throughout the world are still very fragmented. Whilst the very top end of the legal market has undergone some consolidation, there is still a long way to go further down in the sector.

For example, taking the size (in terms of fee-earners) of the largest 500 firms in the UK, the table opposite illustrates the extent to which this market is still highly fragmented.

Figure 1.4: The UK's largest 500 law firms

Size band (no of lawyers)	No of firms
1,000+	6
700-999	5
500-699	9
400-499	7
300-399	17
200-299	27
100-199	100
99 and below	347

Source: Legal 500 (2004) – refers to UK lawyers only

Not only are there more strategic opportunities available in a fragmented market, the merging of two small organisations is much more manageable than merging two corporate behemoths of the size of Hewlett Packard and Compaq.

Hence, for those with a clear strategy, and the ability to implement it effectively, we see the prospect of many more successful law firm mergers in coming years.

The evidence overall is that law firm mergers can work.

Approach of this book

Within this book we have used nine mergers between UK law firms (although one merger involved three firms) as case studies, and readers can decide for themselves the extent to which these mergers have worked. Set out in the table overleaf are details of the merged firms.

This book is directed at the management of law firms as well as other partners and any third parties interested in the topic. It is a book based on both principles and practical experience. While there are some that see principles as only theory, it is true that 'there is nothing so practical as a good theory'. Principles underlie almost every aspect of business but, at the same time, principles are guides and not something to be followed rigidly. It is critical, however, to know if a principle is being broken, and why, rather than to act in ignorance. We seek to provide that level of guidance.

In each chapter, we discuss the principles along with what people actually did in their merger situations. What did they do to address the issues that arose? How did

Figure 1.5: Case studies featured in this book

Name of merged firm	Names of antecedent firms	Date of merger
Addleshaw Goddard	Addleshaw Booth & Co Theodore Goddard	May 2003
ASB Law	Argles & Court Burstows Stoneham	November 1999
Berwin Leighton Paisner	Berwin Leighton Paisner & Co	May 2001
Blake Lapthorn Linnell	Blake Lapthorn Linnells	May 2003
Brabners Chaffe Street	Brabners Chaffe Street	January 2002
Denton Wilde Sapte	Denton Hall Wilde Sapte	January 2000
Kidd Rapinet	Kidd Rapinet Steggles Palmer	February 1997
TLT Solicitors	Trumps Lawrence Tucketts	May 2000
William Sturges & Co	Chethams William Sturges & Co	July 2000

they arrive at key decisions? To what extent was it a 'hearts' or a 'minds' merger? These, and many other issues, are discussed.

What will become clear is that there is no template for undertaking a merger. On the other hand, there are a number of processes that do need to be carried out. The order in which these are carried out might vary, and the way in which they are carried out might differ, but they all are an essential part of the merger process and should not be omitted.

26

CHAPTER 2: WHY FIRMS MERGE

We noted in **Chapter 1** that merger is (mostly) an option. It is not a strategy in itself, but rather a means of implementing a strategy. Firms can choose to implement a strategy by organic means or through merger (and, often, both). The underlying rationale for choosing the merger path is that it is perceived to be the optimum way of sustaining competitiveness in terms of a firm's desired strategic positioning. A firm with a strategy that does not require significant growth is unlikely to find merger a real option, but it is an option in any growth strategy.

Merging two firms is never a simple exercise, although some mergers are simpler than others. From a business viewpoint, there are a substantial number of issues to address in merging two firms, and, when dealing with the merger of two law firms, there is also a need to integrate two partnerships, which raises a whole set of other issues.

However, organic growth can be difficult too. A strategy which requires an increase in size in a firm's core practice areas, by taking on individuals and teams from a variety of different backgrounds, brings with it a host of problems. Integrating people with different histories, from different cultural environments and who have differing expectations, is complex. Ensuring that an increase in size is profitable is another major headache associated with organic growth. Lateral hires often do not result in an immediate transfer of the individual or team's previous clients, but they do result in costs being incurred from day one.

In addition, organic growth tends to be relatively slow. If a firm wishes to demonstrate increased critical mass in a practice area, organic growth means that it takes a significant amount of time before the desired size is achieved, by which point, the market might have changed yet again, resulting in even greater size being required. Merger, on the other hand, can provide an overnight increase in critical mass, and, while it might take a little time to bed down, can be promoted to clients very soon post-merger.

A simple way of looking at it is that a merger is a quicker way of achieving what organic growth can, but both approaches bring with them their own problems. No rules can be laid down as to whether merger or organic growth is better. The answer will depend on both the situation at the time, and the cultural perceptions within the firm. Some firms are culturally averse to merger, whereas others are quite open to it.

One key point that came out of our case studies is that none of those firms interviewed said they would never merge again, which is certainly a rebuttal to those who believe mergers are not an effective way of implementing a strategy. Michael Brabner, managing partner of Brabners Chaffe Street, noted that, whilst his firm is not actively seeking a merger, it will consider one, if necessary. Jonathan Lloyd-Jones, partner of Blake Lapthorn Linnell, was not quite so open to merger, but did not rule it out as an option in the future. Neither did Christopher Honeyman Brown, chief executive of ASB Law.

Neville Eisenberg, managing partner of Berwin Leighton Paisner, was quite adamant that merger was a growth tool for the future, as was Mark Jones, managing partner of Addleshaw Goddard, Ian Gavin-Brown, senior partner of William Sturges & Co, and Virginia Glastonbury and Mark Andrews, partners of Denton Wilde Sapte. The interviewees at Kidd Rapinet also saw merger as a future option for the firm. Only David Pester, managing partner, and Robert Bourns, senior partner, of TLT Solicitors considered a future merger unlikely, although that was partly because their firm's merger had occurred in the last three years. However, they did add 'never say never'.

One reason, therefore, as to why firms merge is that experience indicates that it 'ain't all bad'. Certainly, the apparent success of many mergers has made other firms more open to the idea of it as a means of implementing their strategy. Of course, the strategic logic to merge has to exist, but more and more people are realising that, despite the complexities, a merger is as valid an implementation process as organic growth. Those who oppose merger on the basis that 'it doesn't work', are on shaky ground.

Firm culture

There are, of course, other reasons for a firm not wanting to merge, even if a strong business case for merger exists. However, apart from situations where the business case for organic growth is even stronger than that for merger, the only valid reason is cultural. There are firms with a huge aversion to merger, as they believe that their internal culture is strong and a competitive advantage, and that any merger would weaken it. Whether they are right or wrong does not really matter. What matters is that they believe it and, to that extent, they are right to avoid merger. Should they have ever merged with a like-minded firm, they might have found that that their culture would be shifted but not weakened, but that is hypothetical. A firm's belief about its culture can therefore be a valid and powerful driver in shifting its focus towards organic development and away from merger. Apart from that reason, merger should be retained as an option by every firm that is seeking to implement a clearly defined strategy requiring growth.

Hence, the first answer to why firms merge is that it is perceived to be the best means for implementing a growth strategy, preferable to the other option of organic growth. Therefore, firms should not countenance the idea of merger until they have a clear, strategic direction.

Strategic direction

A clear, strategic direction is one that contains a good understanding of the level at which the firm is seeking to compete in the legal market. This requires articulation of the desired core clients that the firm wishes to attract, and the desired core practice areas in which genuine competitive strengths can be built. In addition, it is essential that the strategic direction takes into account the geographic region (or regions) that the firm sees as its marketplace, and the competitive capabilities that it will require to succeed in that targeted market position.

Only when a strategic direction is articulated in this amount of detail, is it possible to identify the necessary characteristics of a potential merger partner, should merger be the route chosen for the strategy's implementation. The examples on pp30-31 illustrate this point.

If nothing else, it often pays firms considering merger to have an outsider carry out a 'health check' on the business case that has been developed to support the pursuit of merger. It is very easy to fool oneself that some broad statements of intent constitute a strong business case, when all that might lead to is a merger that does not create the value required to achieve the potential of the initial firm.

A key point here is that there are quite a number of law firm mergers that were put together without a structured approach, and that are not failures in the sense that they resulted in a de-merger, but nor are they successes. One cannot point a finger at those firms and say 'what use was that?' Their profitability is at their market average, they have good people and clients, and growth is satisfactory. What the mergers have not done, however, is move those firms into a more competitive market position with better clients, people, profitability and reputation. The mergers have left them as a bigger version of what they were before, but not any more competitive. They are, therefore, a failure in terms of enhancing competitiveness even though the antecedent firms are not necessarily worse off than before.

This crucial point is made very clear in our case studies. In every case, the firms that merged had a strategy, and this guided them towards a merger partner that met

2. Why firms merge

Example 2.1

Firm A's strategy included the objective of building a strong finance practice, with a focus on bank lending, asset finance and acquisition finance. It was estimated that the firm had to at least double in size in these areas of practice in order to be recognised as a serious, mid-market competitor. On separate occasions, several very good firms approached Firm A with a view to a merger, but none had a strong finance practice. Firm A considered whether a merger with such firms would assist it in building a finance group by lateral hires post-merger. The view was taken that it was most unlikely, so Firm A examined the market and identified three firms whose profile satisfied its need for a finance practice, and which also met other strategic requirements. Firm A eventually merged with one of these very successfully.

Firm A could have merged with one of the other 'suitors', which were good firms, but it was not clear how the strengths of those firms could move Firm A forward. It is almost without doubt that, in the absence of a clear, strategic direction and clarity about its objectives, Firm A would have merged with one of the firms that had made the earlier approaches. Whether the merger would have eventually been successful is not a prediction we can (or should) make, but it is clear that the eventual outcome would have been quite different to the one that Firm A's chosen strategy was leading it towards.

---

their strategic needs more closely than many of the other merger opportunities that were available. As we noted in **Chapter 1**, a merger is not about being bigger – a large firm with no strategic focus is just as vulnerable as a small, unfocused firm. A merger is about achieving specific objectives in a firm's strategy and, unless these are articulated clearly, there is a real danger that the merger will simply create a larger firm that is no more competitive than either of the antecedent firms, and which could even be less so.

Case studies
Addleshaw Goddard

The merger between Addleshaw Booth & Co and Theodore Goddard demonstrates this very clearly. Addleshaw Booth & Co was based in Leeds and Manchester and had a small London office. It was focused on building its mid-market corporate and finance capabilities (including private equity) and increasing its real estate and litigation strengths. Its client focus was the FTSE 350 company segment, but it was constrained geographically. It was clear that its success in the north of England would not necessarily lead to rapid growth in its chosen strategic focus area, because London was the largest market for its client and practice area focus.

Example 2.2

Firm B gave as one of the key reasons why it wanted to merge the need to 'grow corporate'. We explored this objective with it by taking into consideration the strategic position in the market that it was seeking and the type of clients it saw as core. We discussed with it what it meant by 'grow corporate'. It transpired that it had been successful in winning a large number of companies which were among the leading businesses in the firm's region as clients. It had done this by targeting real estate transactions for those clients.

Firm B wanted to become the 'upper mid-market leader' in its region. In effect, it wanted to provide larger companies in the region with high-value, specialist advice, as well as carrying out higher value real estate transactions for them. Research showed that there was a gap in the market for this. At the time, the larger companies in the region were using London firms for certain services and larger, regional firms for other work. However, they were quite happy to offer Firm B deals worth up to £100m, but only if it had roughly double the number of corporate transaction lawyers than it had at the time, and it had a reputation in the corporate market. The companies were quite happy that Firm B had the competitiveness in other practice areas that was required to support that level of deal. The companies' higher-value deals would go to London firms or large, regional firms with strong London offices.

Market research also showed that many of Firm B's clients were in the private equity market, and would also be happy to instruct it on mid-sized deals, if Firm B had the necessary competitiveness.

By the time we had gone through this exercise and analysis, it was clear to everyone that 'grow corporate' had a specific meaning. It meant that the firm had to double the size of the corporate group, that it needed lawyers with a reputation for working on deals worth around £100m and, if possible, that it had a private equity team.

In the six months prior to our consultation, Firm B had held merger talks with three local firms. It was clear from the analysis that we undertook that a merger with any of these firms would not have achieved Firm B's goals. None had a corporate group of adequate size, and a merger with at least one firm would only have increased Firm B's corporate department by 4%. None had a reputation for handling £100m transactions. None had any capability in private equity. All that a merger with any of them would have achieved would have been to create a larger firm, but not one which could create additional value in terms of Firm B's desired strategic positioning.

Theodore Goddard had a strong 'City' reputation, ie a reputation in corporate and finance work, albeit at the mid-market level. The firm had fallen behind many of its competitors in terms of size and there was a risk that its better-quality clients would move to firms with greater critical mass.

The strategic logic for the merger therefore came from the client and practice area focus of each firm, plus the geographic reach required by Addleshaw Booth & Co. By merging, Theodore Goddard achieved critical mass in its core practice areas and also gained additional clients of its core type. Addleshaw Booth & Co gained a strong London practice and also strengthened its corporate and finance teams. It also took on additional capability in other practice areas such as real estate.

ASB Law

The three firms (Argles & Court, Stoneham and Burstows) which merged to form ASB Law were based in the south-east of England. Prior to the merger, no one firm was dominant in the region, and no one firm could offer a comparable coverage across the region. Each firm was looking to grow its business in similar areas and to attract similar types of clients. Each firm had, however, strengths that were complementary to those that the other firms brought to the merger. Competition was, however, fierce and the firms could see that, over time, there would be threats to growth.

The three firms had already worked together in an alliance-type relationship in the past, so they knew each other well. Their merger created a firm that could service the whole region, not only enabling it to look after the needs of its existing regional clients better, but also to pursue other regional clients and to drive up the quality of work. This, in turn, made the firm more attractive to better quality lawyers. The merger also combined the particular strengths of each firm under one roof.

The strategic logic of this merger was, in effect, extending the geographic reach of each firm, but also had a strong client and practice area focus. By extending its geographical reach, the merged firm was able to attract larger, regional clients that none of the antecedent firms could have hoped to individually, and it also was able to achieve critical mass in all of its core practice areas.

Berwin Leighton Paisner

The merger of Berwin Leighton with Paisner & Co also had a clear strategic logic, driven, primarily, by the need for both firms to build critical mass in key areas. Both firms were London-based, without international offices, so geographical issues were less important here. Berwin Leighton, the bigger of the two firms, wanted to build critical mass in its corporate group and to achieve a better balance between its core practice areas (pre-merger it had a strong real estate focus and it wished to position corporate and finance alongside this strength within the firm). It also knew the type of corporate work it wanted to attract. It wanted to be considered as a more 'heavyweight' firm in London in order to attract better quality clients for the type of work it was targeting in its strategy, particularly in the area of corporate and finance.

Paisner & Co had a strong corporate focus in the mid-market and a strong client base, together with good real estate and technology practices. It was aiming to develop greater critical mass in the corporate field in order to avoid being squeezed out of good mid-market work. Whilst not seeking a merger at the time, it found it an attractive option once raised.

The merger, therefore, satisfied the needs of both firms' strategies. Berwin Leighton achieved more balance in its practice areas overall, as the new corporate group was of a competitive size and comparable to the size of the other groups in the firm. This also satisfied a similar need in Paisner & Co's strategy and provided it with more strength in a range of practice areas. The 'new' firm had more depth and breadth and a larger 'footprint' in the quality mid-market than either firm had had previously. The 'new' firm was able to make strong lateral hires, attract quality clients, build a stronger finance practice and assemble the resources to enable it to start looking at international expansion.

Paisner & Co also achieved an indirect benefit. Its strategy pre-merger required it to build up its support infrastructure, which would have required a significant investment. Berwin Leighton had already developed its infrastructure significantly, so the merger saved Paisner & Co having to do the same.

Blake Lapthorn Linnell

The merger of Blake Lapthorn with Linnells was driven more by geographical needs. Both antecedent firms were seeking to grow their businesses and improve the quality of clients and work. Both could see constraints emerging in their local markets. Whilst neither firm had reached a limit on expansion, they could both see that their ability to keep growing within their chosen client and practice area focus was going to be more difficult in the future.

As Walter Cha, the former managing partner of Blake Lapthorn, noted:

'It wasn't saturation for us on the south coast, but our reputation was well known. We found ourselves in a position where we were conflicted out of work from time to time… It was an imperative in our point of view to go north from the south coast… our catchment area was only 180 degrees – the rest was water and fish.'

Linnells had the same issue. An Oxford-based firm, it had tried to grow through satellite offices, but this approach had proved unsuccessful, and the offices were closed down. It felt that, given the nature of the marketplace, lateral hires and growing larger in Oxford was not the answer. Instead, merger with a similar firm in another region, thereby providing greater critical mass and a wider catchment area for work, seemed the best way to develop its strategy.

Hence, there was a client and practice area growth driver, but there was a geographical constraint imposed by the market. Growing within their pre-merger markets would require moving away from their focus as the local markets were not large enough to sustain the required growth. Widening the geographical market and achieving greater breadth and depth would allow the 'new' firm to service clients with wider regional needs, and to move up to the next level of client and work. In other words, it would allow it to break out of the strategic constraints imposed by size, both in terms of firm and market.

Brabners Chaffe Street

Brabners Chaffe Street was created for a number of strategic reasons, but underlying them was a strategic decision by Brabners to build up its corporate and commercial work. This also required the development of a new type of core client. The firm was based in Liverpool, and could see that the reduction in shipping work and clients (associated with the decline of Liverpool as a major port), required it to develop a new direction. At the same time, Manchester, 31 miles away, had become the commercial centre of north-west England. Manchester was a somewhat parochial city, and businessmen wanted their professional advisers to be local. In addition, commercial clients of Brabners expected the firm to have a Manchester office, and were surprised to find it did not.

Brabners had been looking at opening an office in Manchester for some years. However, given the strong Manchester business culture, it did not feel that opening a 'greenfield' site was an option it wished to take. It preferred the merger route, which brought with it a client base.

Brabners 'merged' with a corporate and commercial team from Lace Mawer, and then with the Manchester firm of Chaffe Street. The corporate and commercial group wanted to leave Lace Mawer, and was attracted by Brabners' strategy. Chaffe Street had some profitability problems and had started to split. It too liked the strategy of Brabners. In addition, both mergers fitted comfortably with Brabners' culture.

Denton Wilde Sapte

In the Denton Hall/Wilde Sapte merger, the two sides had differing strategic reasons for merging. Wilde Sapte had a strong finance focus, and the finance industry had become more international over time, and larger transactions tended to be multi-jurisdictional. Wilde Sapte's strategy was to build an international capability that would help secure major clients for high value work. Given the competition, remaining London-focused was not an option for a firm that wanted to retain the higher value end of finance work.

Denton Hall, like Berwin Leighton, wanted to 'beef up' generally, feeling it was a little below the level of many direct competitors, which affected its critical mass in a number of areas. Its strategy also included the development of a much stronger finance group.

Denton Hall provided Wilde Sapte with a merger partner that had an extensive international network that met its needs. Wilde Sapte provided Denton Hall with a strong finance group, and enabled the merged firm to match the critical mass that its competitors had in a number of other practice areas.

Kidd Rapinet

Kidd Rapinet's merger with Steggles Palmer in 1997 was driven by the need to bolster its commercial department. Steggles Palmer saw the need to have a bigger litigation capability, which Kidd Rapinet could provide.

Kidd Rapinet believed that merger, rather than organic growth, was the better option for developing its commercial department. The key issue was critical mass. Without it, it would be difficult to attract the type of work the firm was seeking. Clients need to see that a firm has the resources and experience to handle a certain size of transaction. As noted earlier, it is very slow trying to achieve critical mass by organic means and lateral hires – merger does it overnight.

TLT Solicitors

The merger between Trumps and Lawrence Tucketts came out of the strategic need facing both firms, which was growth. Competing in the South West's mid-market brought both firms head to head with much larger firms which were still growing. Neither Trumps nor Lawrence Tucketts could allow the size gap to widen for fear of being pushed further down the chain in terms of the value of work they could win. As David Pester, managing partner of Lawrence Tucketts, said:

> 'The numbers game was important. We were not perceived as large enough. The referrers of business were happy to use us but were worried that we didn't have critical mass to handle a job over a certain size.'

There was no one practice area that drove this merger. Lawrence Tucketts had a good corporate finance group, along with a strong reputation in real estate and planning. The tax group was developing, as was that of reconstruction and banking litigation, but the firm struggled to recruit high-quality people in these areas.

Trumps was somewhat weaker in corporate finance, but wanted to develop this area. It had good real estate and tax work. Both firms had shared their ambitions with each other some years before, and had kept in contact. They both realised that they were moving into a similar market position, albeit from differing starting points. This merger was more about what the two firms could build together, rather than about achieving an overnight transformation of either.

William Sturges & Co

William Sturges & Co merged with Chethams in 2000. Chethams saw the need for growth: 'We felt we were too small to service our client base. … It was an advantage to merge into a larger firm.' Chethams also had a property lease on its offices that was coming to an end, and this drove it towards merger rather than organic growth. Furthermore, Chethams was wary of lateral hires: 'Lateral hires are terribly tricky things… good lateral hires are like gold dust.'

William Sturges & Co was approached by a third party about a possible merger between it, William Sturges & Co and Chethams. Merger was not actually on William Sturges & Co's agenda, although it was open to considering it. It saw some immediate advantages in the link-up – a much stronger litigation practice, better critical mass in a number of areas and some substantial overhead savings. William Sturges & Co also had spare capacity, and all of Chethams' employees could move into its building. The merger would also result in a shedding of support staff so the overhead cost per lawyer would drop.

Client-driven or not?

These case studies also highlight a point made earlier in **Chapter 1**. Not one of these mergers was driven by clients saying that the firm had to merge. Mark Andrews, former senior partner of Wilde Sapte, noted:

> 'Clients were saying what they always tend to say in mergers. If this will make it easier for you to give us a better service then do it… All they are interested in is the impact of the merger on your ability to deliver services.'

Christopher Honeyman Brown, chief executive of ASB Law, saw the merger as a way to tap into a regional market that existed but which had no regional firm servicing it. Clients were not asking for a merger (no other firm offered this benefit), but there was clearly a latent demand to be met. The same was true for Berwin Leighton Paisner. Its clients did not drive the merger decision, but both antecedent firms sensed that they could move up the value chain with some of their better quality clients.

As we noted before, Brabners had some clients who were surprised that the firm did not have an office in Manchester, but none of them said 'you should have'. On the other hand, its lack of a presence in Manchester might have meant it was missing out on work. Denton Hall was in a similar position. Its weaker finance practice pre-merger probably meant that existing clients gave finance work to its competitors. When merged with Wilde Sapte, it had a more competitive 'footprint' with major clients. Virginia Glastonbury (then of Denton Hall) said:

> 'There was something very sellable to clients… we could go to our clients and say we have
> a stronger finance capability and Wilde Sapte could demonstrate to its clients that it now
> had a strong international network. This was very obvious then and very tangible.'

The Kidd Rapinet and Steggles Palmer merger achieved client-related objectives but clients did not 'drive it on'. Both firms were aware that their clients had work that they would not instruct them on pre-merger because they felt that the firms lacked the necessary size and depth of expertise, and also because, sometimes, they were not acceptable as legal advisers to the financial institutions involved.

We are aware of instances where law firms have been told by a client that they will lose their business if the law firms does not merge. In every case, it involved a firm that was undergoing some decline, but which had very loyal clients who were willing to discuss the situation with the firm. These clients were aware that, if they simply moved their work without warning, the firm could collapse, and they did not want this to happen. In one sense, they were really telling the firm to build critical mass and to do it quickly, and that merger was the only way to do this.

As the case studies also show, effective management in a law firm usually results in the firm having a sense of what clients are thinking. As Paddy Grafton Green, previously senior partner of Theodore Goddard, stated: 'We had a good client base with clients that were growing. If we didn't grow with them then we'd lose them.' Good client managers are also aware of work that a firm might be missing out on from key clients. There are many situations where clients will pass work at one level to a smaller firm but, above a certain level (of size, complexity or both), work will be given to a larger competitor with greater depth. It is vital that a firm has a good sense of the cut-off point in such situations so that it can decide whether a particular merger will achieve the critical mass required or not.

Merger versus organic growth

The other important issue that emerged in the case studies with regard to drivers of merger was the choice of merger over organic growth and lateral hires.

In the case of Addleshaw Booth & Co, Blake Lapthorn, Argles & Court, Stoneham and Burstows, and Brabners, their mergers all involved geographical reach – each was seeking to build outside its home location. In Addleshaw Booth & Co's case, it had opened a London office but knew that it had to have in excess of 200 lawyers in London in order to be competitive within its strategic focus. Organic growth would have been too slow, and the investment that it would have required exceeded the cost of the 'right' merger. Others reached a similar conclusion. Brabners saw particular difficulties trying to break into the Manchester market. Argles & Court, Stoneham and Burstows' whole rationale was to extend market reach quickly in order to be ahead of the competition. Blake Lapthorn saw the need to expand to the north, and it considered it best to do so by merging with another firm that had clients and profits rather than by adopting a 'greenfield site' approach, and then using lateral hires.

Theodore Goddard chose merger over organic growth because of timing. The London market was increasing rapidly in competitiveness, and other firms were developing ahead of Theodore Goddard. It felt the need to acquire the extra critical mass quickly. To do so through organic growth ran the risk of clients defecting before the firm had reached the appropriate strength.

Wilde Sapte chose merger primarily because to build its own international network would be costly and would take a significant amount of time, during which competitors with already established international networks would have eroded its client base. This was a very similar situation to that of Theodore Goddard, except that Theodore Goddard was London-focused and Wilde Sapte was internationally focused.

With Berwin Leighton and Paisner & Co, the issue was one of timing. Both firms had growth strategies in a London market where competitors were developing in breadth and depth. They ran the risk of taking too long to 'beef up' their practices to a competitive level. They also saw the opportunities that could be exploited by increasing size immediately.

Kidd Rapinet and Steggles Palmer chose merger over organic growth because they felt that they had to reach critical mass quickly. Otherwise, the 'glass ceiling' would keep rising, and they would never be able to get to where they wanted to be. Hence, timing was the issue again. Similar issues were involved in the creation of TLT Solicitors. There was a need for both antecedent firms to make a 'level change', which would require a significant investment. Lateral hires were costly, and the larger competitors attracted the best candidates due to better profitability, so both firms felt merger would achieve an increase in size to a level where they could compete more effectively for quality work and good lateral hires. By merging, the investment costs per lawyer were less, and improved profitability was more likely to be achieved than by each 'going it alone'.

Lessons

Several key points emerge from these case studies that reinforce our opening comments. All of these mergers had good strategic logic even though this was not always apparent externally. As David Pester, managing partner of TLT Solicitors, noted:

> 'The reasons for our merger weren't always clear to the outside world. When we did merge a reaction was "well, what will that do?". What we had recognised was each other's ambitions.'

All of the mergers discussed here had a strategic logic based around client development, practice area competitiveness (especially critical mass) and geographical reach. Some were more obvious to outsiders. The logic of the Addleshaw Goddard merger and the Denton Wilde Sapte merger was recognised almost immediately. So too was the logic of the Brabners Chaffe Street merger and the ASB Law merger. Each of these mergers was transformational in its own way in that it was clear that the parties to the merger were gaining something quite significant in terms of competitiveness over and above what either party had prior to the merger.

Other mergers, such as TLT Solicitors, William Sturges & Co, Kidd Rapinet, Blake Lapthorn Linnell and Berwin Leighton Paisner did not attract the public's attention in the same way. To quote David Pester, people said: 'What will that do?' These mergers are development-based rather than transformational. The logic and benefits of these type of mergers tend to emerge over two to three years. Transformational mergers tend to achieve some large gains almost overnight, although there is still a lot of work to be done to bring the merged firms together and to consolidate the immediate benefits.

Managing partners contemplating merger often ask: 'What will people think?' Our answer is always: 'It doesn't matter what people think. What is the strategic logic and what are clients saying?'

Whilst there are differences between a transformational and a development merger, one is not better than the other. Yes, it is desirable to be described by the press as 'having pulled off an eye-catching merger'. No, it is not desirable to be on the receiving end of an article that implies 'This is a stupid idea! How could they do it?' But, bury the ego and focus on the fundamentals.

Similarly, when choosing to develop a strategy through merger or organic growth, one way is not inherently better than the other. The issue reverts to timing and particular needs. Paisner & Co was not looking to merge, but realised that a merger with Berwin Leighton was better than going it alone.

In other situations, where firms are trying to build critical mass, the real option to merge is more about narrowing the focus than pursuing organic growth. Addleshaw Booth & Co faced an uphill battle to develop critical mass across a broad range of practice areas in London. The same was true of Blake Lapthorn in Oxford and both Trumps and Lawrence Tucketts.

Critical mass within markets changes over time as firms grow and clients 'up the ante'. A firm that is below critical mass today might never achieve it by organic growth alone. One option is to become more specialised and narrow down the firm's overall size, dispose of some practice areas, and build critical mass in only a few. This might be possible with organic growth. On the other hand, such a strategic shift in a 'full service' firm is very hard to achieve because it is, in effect, a break-up of the partnership and can be quite traumatic. It has happened (eg the break-up of DJ Freeman and the creation of Kendall Freeman), but it can be very unpleasant.

Hence, for firms that are below the critical mass level in core practice areas, that want to remain (broadly) a full service firm, and that aspire to compete at a level or more higher in the market, merger is often not just an option but an imperative. The only other option is a fundamental shift in strategy which is ruled out by endeavouring to remain full service.

We noted at the start of this chapter that there are firms which are averse to merger for cultural reasons, and this is not to be dismissed provided it is a valid reason and not used to avoid difficult discussions and decisions. What is critical for any firm that declares itself to be against merger, is to recognise the strategic consequences. It might well be that, by remaining 'independent', the firm cannot sustain its critical mass across enough practice areas, and will start to lose ground to larger competitors which have greater depth and comparable quality.

An interesting point to note is that the largest 30 firms (by revenue) in the London market (excluding the Magic Circle firms) in 2004 are all full service (in business law at least), and the mean average is 648 (*Legal Business* 100, 2004). In 1998, the same group (not the same firms) had an average size of 365. This shift in size is not just about being bigger, but is driven by building critical mass in core practice areas, as we noted earlier. Neville Eisenberg, managing partner of Berwin Leighton Paisner, commented: 'Another driver was to distinguish our profile by being bigger and having a better platform for quality growth… ', but he was clear that this was not simply about increasing the workforce without any strategic logic. Paul Lee, senior partner of Addleshaw Goddard, made the point that:

> 'By being bigger we have more resources, we cover more territory, we have more people out in the market drumming up work, and we have much more experience and knowledge to sell. But we must be competitive in everything we do or our size is wasted.'

This is the challenge for those firms which want to remain around a certain size and feel that a merger would destroy many of the good things about the firm. They might well be right, but they must also keep the other side of the ledger open ie to remain successful whilst not merging might require a fundamental strategic shift.

The same point applies to firms that operate in one location, especially a relatively small geographic market, and focus on better quality work and clients. In any geographical market, there tend to be more firms seeking to attract better quality clients and work than actually exists. Clients may grow and new clients may emerge; the better value legal requirements might also increase. But at any moment, other than during a major economic boom, the target growth rate of firms seeking a higher value market share outstrips the growth of the market itself.

Some firms out-perform others and move into a 'leading position'. Unless the market is very large, even these firms will run into growth problems eventually. By maintaining that rate of growth, dictated by a number of factors including growth in partner numbers, they start to reach the limit of market share within their strategic focus on clients and practice areas. They can move outside of this focus, which usually means going down the value chain and risking declining profitability, or they can stay in their focus and move into another geographical market. This was the approach of Blake Lapthorn in moving north and, to some extent, the three firms that created ASB Law.

As Blake Lapthorn, Brabners and Addleshaw Booth & Co found, in order to develop in a new geographical market, it is often better to merge with an established and profitable competitor in that market than to build through a 'greenfield site' approach.

To quote from *The Leopard*: 'If we want things to stay as they are, things will have to change.'[1]

This approach is something that every firm must have at the head of its strategy. Pursuing a particular strategic focus in highly competitive markets will, over time, require a firm to change internally in some quite dramatic and fundamental ways. Even market leaders go through significant internal adjustments to maintain this leadership. Firms that wish to avoid significant internal changes will need to adapt their strategic focus over time to one that matches this desire. Markets change, competitive conditions change, and critical decisions need to be made. Maintaining a strategic focus in the long term will place the emphasis of change more internally; focusing on maintaining an internal environment in the longer term will put the emphasis on change to the firm's external positioning.

---

1 Giuseppe Di Lampedusa, *The Leopard* (London: Folio Society, 1988), p17.

Chapter 3: The dating game

There are three stages in finding a merger partner. The first is the identification of potential merger candidates (Identification Stage). The second is initial discussions with firms selected from those identified (Initial Discussion Stage). The third is in-depth discussions with the preferred candidate (In-depth Discussion Stage). In this chapter, we cover the Identification Stage and the Initial Discussion Stage, and we discuss the In-depth Discussion Stage in **Chapters 4**, **5** and **6**.

Parties to most effective mergers have gone through each of these stages. However, there have been occasions where one firm has been approached by another to see whether it would be interested in undertaking merger discussions, and that firm has then gone straight to the Initial Discussion Stage without any further consideration about whether that firm is a suitable merger partner for it. Although some successful mergers have occurred this way, as we note below, this is a somewhat risky approach.

The move through the Identification Stage and the Initial Discussion Stage can be informal or formal (or a bit of both). There are situations where a firm is pursuing a specific strategy, and is aware that the 'right' merger could speed up the implementation of that strategy, and even enhance the firm's strategic position. Whilst it may not draw up a list of merger candidates, the firm does, over time, note that certain firms have some of the characteristics that would be required from a potential merger partner and later holds Initial Discussion Stage talks with them. The firm might not have a clear-cut plan to merge, but it is an option that senior management is keeping open.

What is often forgotten, is that in places like London, New York, Paris, Frankfurt and other major cities, the leaders of many firms know each other, and can even be very good friends. They see each other regularly and many dine together from time to time. As William Perlstein, the co-managing partner of Wilmer Cutler Pickering Hale and Dorr, said recently:

'What's interesting about the legal profession is that we are often both competitors and friends at the same time. We do talk a lot but, of course, there are areas that we don't go into. We often know each other from law school or previous firms so naturally we stay in touch.'

As a consequence, when firms start to think about merger, they are not always starting with a blank sheet of paper – even at a general level, some sifting through potential merger candidates will already have gone on. The informal approach is not, therefore, necessarily without strategic logic. We will discuss this later on in the chapter.

The Identification Stage

Specification

The formal approach to identifying potential merger candidates starts with a firm identifying the specification of an 'appropriate' merger partner. This specification covers the characteristics and attributes required in a partner and will include 'hard' and 'soft' criteria. An example of the 'hard' and 'soft' criteria identified by one law firm when seeking a potential merger partner is given below.[1]

Example 3.1

'Hard' criteria

In addition to being located in the same city, the potential merger partner should:

- have a strong private equity practice, with a good relationship with leading funds;
- have a good mid-market M&A practice, with experience of transactions valued around £100m to £200m;
- have a commercial litigation practice that matches its corporate practice in terms of reputation and quality; and
- have a top 50 client base that includes a high percentage of FTSE 500 companies, along with similar institutions and other businesses (including private companies).

These 'hard' criteria were in line with what the firm's strategy was designed to achieve. In seeking a merger partner that either possessed these already, or was well advanced in developing these, the firm hoped to speed up the implementation of its strategy.

The firm had a second set of 'hard' criteria. These were attributes the firm possessed and which they perceived a target firm should want in a merger partner.

The potential merger partner should:

- require a finance practice comparable in terms of reputation and quality to the corporate market position (particularly in debt finance, asset finance and property finance);

---

1 A summary guide of the questions to be considered in identifying merger candidates is also set out in **Appendix 1**.

Example 3.1 (continued)

- require a significantly stronger real estate transactions capability; and
- seek to benefit from additional strength in employment, IT, IP and EU/competition.

'Soft' criteria

The potential merger partner should:

- be well-managed, in a consensual manner;
- have a flexible partner remuneration system with a strong performance element; and
- have a performance management system that is effective and efficient.

The firm also identified behavioural and cultural criteria, which required the potential merger partner to:

- have a very strong team-based approach;
- have high levels of respect throughout the firm;
- be transparent and open;
- be performance-driven (but not at the expense of everything else); and
- employ people who accept responsibility for what the firm agrees to do.

Need for flexibility

Clearly, the characteristics and attributes chosen in the above example are very specific. This raises a key issue in the search for a merger partner, which is the need for flexibility. It is highly likely that any potential merger partner will not meet the exact specification of a firm. To a degree, there will therefore be a need for compromise. One issue that firms should address before trying to identify any potential candidates is to identify the criteria which it would be prepared to compromise on, and the extent to which any such compromise could deviate from the criteria of its 'ideal' merger partner.

Generally, we find that firms are prepared to compromise more on the 'hard' characteristics than the 'soft' at this stage, the view being that if the 'soft' characteristics and attributes are close to what the firm requires, then the 'hard' characteristics can be achieved over time. However, firms will shy away from a merger if there is a significant cultural gap between it and the prospective partner (although the culture of a firm is the hardest thing to identify when researching potential partners – see **Chapter 10**).

The other point to make about the formal approach is that the first stage of identifying potential candidates usually happens in several steps. One might start, for example, by listing firms which broadly appear to meet the 'hard' characteristics, and then narrow down the list by introducing the other criteria. In one merger exercise we were involved with, we started with a list of over 100 firms which generally met the 'hard' criteria. We then applied the criteria that dealt with the benefits that the merger would bring to the other party, and very quickly whittled the list down to 20 or so firms. Another round of analysis reduced this to a shortlist of seven firms. The interesting point was that many of the firms eliminated were firms that a lot of partners considered to be good merger candidates, and, should an informal merger process have taken place, almost certainly would have been included in Initial Discussion Stage talks. The use of the formal, structured approach demonstrated to these partners why their 'favourite' was not, in actual fact, a good, strategic fit.

The key point we are making here is that, whether or not a formal or informal approach is used, it is essential to base the initial selection process on the strategic requirements of the firm making the selection, and on the perceived benefits that the merger could bring to the potential merger partner. This goes back to the need for clarity about the firm's strategic direction, along with what needs to be done to achieve it. Identifying the 'gap' between where the firm is today and its desired future position, makes apparent the areas of the firm that need to be developed (ie 'filled in'). The most appropriate merger candidate is one that helps the firm to achieve this, and, at the same time, benefits from the strengths of the merger. (We noted in **Chapter 2** that there are also instances where, once the two firms start talking, they find they can achieve a strategic position significantly above that which either firm thought it would be able to achieve, but the need for strategic complementarity still exists.)

The division of the 'hard' criteria into 'what benefits do they bring to us?' and 'what benefits do we bring to them?' is a crucial point to think about. It is surprising how many firms approach other firms about a possible merger on the basis of the first question alone. These firms entirely ignore what the other party might be looking for in a merger partner, and whether they can provide it. On numerous occasions, one firm has approached another to 'talk merger' and, whilst the firm making the approach might be a good firm, it may bring very little in the way of strategic benefits to the firm it has approached. It is obvious what the approaching firm would achieve by the merger, but much less clear what the one being approached would achieve. Too often, it is assumed that simply being bigger means being better, but that is not always the case, as we discussed in **Chapter 1**.

An objection that is often raised to the formal, structured approach is that it is too rigid and too focused on finding the 'ideal' candidate and, therefore, is likely to exclude every firm from consideration. The rationale behind this argument is that if an ideal firm is unlikely to exist, it is pointless to start with the ideal firm as a goal. Supporters of this approach believe it is better to start by simply canvassing names of good firms and to go from there. The contrary view, which we support, is that the identification of potential candidates is more effective when one starts with a very specific set of criteria than with a very broad approach. The criteria should define the 'appropriate' rather than the 'ideal' firm, and will quickly eliminate firms with some general appeal but which would bring little strategic benefit to a merger. By starting with a large number of candidates, it also provides some assurance that a suitable merger partner will not be overlooked. By then applying a second set of stricter criteria, a firm can quickly recognise the firms which are more likely to have the characteristics and attributes required.

At this point, the need for flexibility kicks in. In every case, no candidate will fit the specific criteria exactly. The process of whittling down to a shortlist (of no more than ten firms, preferably less) for talks at the Initial Discussion Stage requires a considerable amount of analysis and thought. What we are arguing here is that, from a process point of view, it is always more effective to have a clear guideline, and then assess the acceptable degree of deviation from that guideline, than to start with a vague indicator and then try to develop tighter guidelines as the process unfolds. What can happen with the latter approach is that the final selection will contain the 'best of the bunch', but will actually be a significant distance away from what is required for a merger to be really effective.

Another practical point about the formal process is that, as the list of candidates gets smaller, the difference in benefits between the shortlisted firms also narrows. In the example given on pp44-45 above, one candidate had a stronger M&A practice than other firms. Another candidate had a private equity practice that met the criterion but an M&A practice that did not. A third firm had an almost ideal corporate practice but also had a major weakness in the commercial litigation field. None of the three firms were perfect, but they all would bring particular strengths to the merger, albeit of a different type. On the surface, it is hard to say that one was better than the other. Each candidate met one of the practice area criteria, but was weaker on the other two. The firm, in the example above, will therefore need to review its criteria and see if it can decide whether one is more important than the other. This process forces the firm to be even more specific as it moves to choose a candidate. In the event that it decides all three practice area criteria are of equal importance, it will need to rank each firm in terms of its relative strength on all three, and make a choice based on a composite assessment. Basing the identification of candidates on quite specific criteria forces management to think through its priorities, and even to make priorities within the priorities. Put another way, the formal approach tends to be much more rigorous than an approach which starts out with a very broad (ie vague) brush approach.

In summary, the critical issue that is being highlighted here is that, as a general rule, whether an informal or formal process is used to identify potential candidates, the firm should be very clear about the specific criteria that a merger partner needs to meet, and the benefits that each firm could gain through a merger.

Timing issues

For timing reasons, some firms might elect to pursue a formal process because they see a need to merge within a defined time period or else abandon a particular strategy and accept a somewhat lower future market position. Others might feel less pressure in terms of timing, and therefore decide to adopt a more informal approach. It is highly risky, in either situation, to have merger on the agenda without also having identified the specific set of criteria that the ideal partner should meet.

Culture

Before moving to the Initial Discussion Stage in the merger process, it is important to discuss further the issue of culture (we also come back to this in **Chapters 9** and **10**). This is an issue of prime importance when identifying a merger partner and, indeed, is the one area that many firms are not prepared to compromise on as much as it would with the 'hard' criteria. As we noted earlier, the formal process involves identifying firms that meet the 'hard' criteria, and then introducing the 'soft' criteria in order to whittle down the shortlist. To many, this is contradictory – if the cultural criteria are more 'rigid' than any other, then surely the identification process should start by applying them before the others?

The basic problem with culture as a criterion in the search for a merger candidate is that the real culture of a firm is rarely apparent from outside. It is not even immediately apparent when one has access to a firm. For this reason, it is very difficult to ensure that two firms have compatible cultures, especially at the Identification Stage of the merger process. Even if both firms articulate a similar set of values, it is difficult to know whether these are values that a firm espouses, but are not practised, or values that really do guide behaviour and provide an ethical basis to the firm. One of the problems is that if they really are values that guide behaviour, people from the firm find it hard to articulate what those values are – they are taken for granted, and are considered to be 'the norm' to such an extent that no one can actually identify them.

Of course, many firms demonstrate their culture through their behaviour and through the type of structure and systems they have in place, and this is all that firms can rely on in the early stages of identifying merger candidates. An example of this is DLA Piper Rudnick Gray Cary (previously Dibb Lupton Alsop), which at one stage in the 1990s articulated a set of values that were very aggressive, and which were demonstrated in practice. At that time, there were very few (if any) firms that would put it on their list of merger candidates, no matter how close it appeared to fit their 'hard' criteria. Whether they were right or wrong to do so is not our point. The DLA culture appeared, at that time, to be unacceptable to many partners in other firms, and no amount of further analysis about the suitability of DLA as a merger candidate would convince them otherwise. This attitude among many firms continued well beyond DLA changing its internal environment and becoming much more cohesive. DLA has changed internally over the last decade while retaining a high level of competitiveness in the market, but there are still partners in firms today who would strike it off any list of merger candidates because of past perceptions about its culture.

The same point can be made about other firms. The way they behave in the marketplace and are structured and managed is usually taken as an indication of their cultural norms. Two Magic Circle firms are a good example of this. Were Slaughter and May to ever contemplate merger, it is highly unlikely that it would be with Clifford Chance, purely on the basis of what would be seen to be significant cultural differences. While it might be incorrect to assume this, all of the external evidence generated from the way these two firms behave in the market, and reach decisions, indicates that they operate with a major difference in culture. (We are not suggesting one is better than the other, only that they do appear from the outside to be very different.)

Hence, in putting together the initial list of firms, and using the 'hard' criteria as a guide, it is quite common to prepare an interim list and then filter it. Where the perceived culture of a firm appears to be so far from what is required that there is little point in it remaining on the list, it should be removed. This is where an outside adviser can play a role. People inside a firm might have an outdated or biased view about a particular firm, and may want to eliminate it as a potential merger partner at the outset. An outsider, however, might be more aware about the changes that have occurred within that firm which, whilst not yet apparent, are leading to a shift in behaviour that will make it a closer fit with the other firm in terms of culture. In two actual merger situations recently, the eventually very successful merger partners would have been eliminated at the outset on cultural grounds but for the intervention of an outside adviser who was able to show that the perceptions about culture were not accurate.

Another way is to talk to people who have left a particular firm, although, depending on their reasons for leaving, one might not get an unbiased view about the firm's culture.

When is an informal approach to the merger process applicable?

As touched upon earlier, the informal approach can be effective in two situations:

(i)   where the selection criteria results in a small 'pool' of easily identifiable candidates; and

(ii)   where a possible merger is on the agenda but there is no pressing need for it.

Small pool of candidates

This arose in a case where a firm in a medium-sized regional location saw the chance of moving up a level in its local market by increasing critical mass in a couple of core practice areas by way of merger. To be effective, however, the merger partner had to be a local firm. It did not require a lot of analysis to identify the small number of potential candidates, and they were well known to the firm seeking the merger. The formal process set out above would have been overkill in this situation. The Lawrence Tucketts/Trumps merger is an example of this. However, where a firm is seeking a merger partner in another region, the formal process would be more applicable. This would be particularly so if law firms from several regions were being considered. The Blake Lapthorn/Linnells merger is a case in point here.

The selection process can also result in a small group of easily identifiable candidates when the primary criterion of the merger partner is a highly competitive strength in one distinct practice area. This could, for example, be in an area such as high-value private equity deals, or in top-level acquisition finance transactions. The more restrictive and specific the requirement, the more likely it is that the potential candidates will be virtually identifiable by that alone. There is therefore no need to produce a large list and whittle it down by assessing firms against a range of criteria.

The merger between Denton Hall and Wilde Sapte comes to mind here. In such a situation, firms searching for a merger partner are usually aware of the candidates without too much assistance, and may have even already had a discussion about merger with them. Mark Andrews (formerly senior partner of Wilde Sapte) commented that this was the case with Denton Hall. Both firms had quite specific requirements, knew the other firm and did not look further.

Again, the exception to this is where a firm is seeking a merger partner which has quite narrow and specific capabilities, but which is located in another geographical market about which the firm has no detailed knowledge. A common example of this is when US firms are looking for a possible merger partner in the UK. Their criteria are often quite specific, but they might lack in-depth knowledge of the UK market, in which case the more formal approach to the merger process is better.

No pressing need for merger

The informal approach can be effective in a second situation where a firm sees merger as a useful means of moving its strategy forward but has no urgent need to pursue such a step. An approach by a suitable firm that does have a more urgent need might move the former firm to take this quite seriously, even though it has not gone through a formal process of identifying candidates.

A variation on this is where a firm has carried out a formal assessment of candidates, but sees one as clearly head and shoulders above the rest. Instead of moving through the process of shortlisting firms, it approaches the prime target and proceeds. So the formal process becomes more informal.

A third variation is where two firms know each other very well, and might have floated the idea of merger in a vague way every now and then, but nothing happens because it is not a pressing issue for either firm. At some point, one or both firms decide they should merge, and they turn immediately to their 'close friend' without any search process coming into play.

Which approach?

The formal approach is more appropriate where, for a variety of possible reasons, there is a need to make reasonable progress in securing a merger partner, and the selection criteria appears to result initially in a wide pool of candidates. As the process progresses, the number of candidates is reduced down, and this occurs within a timeframe that management has set. It is an effective approach to finding the right candidate, because it starts with almost, if not every, firm that could possibly meet the criteria, and so no possible candidate is overlooked. Addleshaw Booth & Co, Theodore Goddard, Linnells, Steggles Palmer and Chethams are examples of firms that started off with a large pool of candidates. As we have shown, there are also situations where an informal approach to the selection of a merger candidate is appropriate. As we note elsewhere, however, the informal approach is risky where a firm has not thought through its strategy, has not thought about merger as an option, and lacks knowledge about firms which might generate real strategic benefits in the event of a merger. As always, there is no one way to approach this issue – it will depend on the particular situation.

The Initial Discussion Stage

Whether the formal or informal process is used, there will be a point reached at which one firm appears to best meet the selection criteria, and the approaching firm decides an initial discussion could be worthwhile. Under the informal approach, the Identification Stage and the Initial Discussion Stage tend to occur firm by firm. With the formal approach, the shortlist of firms is identified and initial discussions are then held with each one. The two stages are therefore more distinct.

There is no one way to approach the Initial Discussion Stage talks, and, to some extent, it depends on the existing relationship between the two firms.

Relationship between the firms

As noted already, senior or managing partners already know each other in some cases, and the initial discussion occurs over lunch, dinner or coffee in a very informal way. The prime purpose is to see if the other firm would even be interested in contemplating merger discussions, and if so, what might be the key criteria that each firm is looking for. In markets like London and New York, meetings such as these are a regular occurrence.

In situations where the two firms do not know each other well (or not at all), the search firm[2] might not feel that a brief informal meeting would provide sufficient opportunity for it to best explain why merger discussions might be in the best interest of both firms. The firm that has been approached might be willing to meet, but the 'casual chat over lunch' type of meeting might not be enough for an unknown firm to convey its strengths and to develop a real interest in the target firm.

---

2 We use the term 'search firm' to denote the firm actively seeking a merger partner (not a consultancy that specialises in search, be it for individuals or firms).

One has to remember that this meeting is as much a 'go/no-go' decision meeting for the search firm as it is for the target firm. The search firm might have identified a firm as a potential candidate by carrying out an analysis from an external viewpoint. However, whether or not that analysis actually reflects reality is a different matter. Significant changes might be under way in the target firm that are not yet apparent to the outside world, and those changes might result in effectively removing the firm from the search firm's list of potential candidates.

Therefore, when the two firms know each other reasonably well, a lunch between the two senior or managing partners might be enough to clarify the 'go/no-go issues' for both firms. On the other hand, a 'cold call' by the search firm requires it to take a different approach, and we discuss this in more detail below.

First contact between search firm and target firm

When a search firm first makes contact with a target firm, particularly where there has been little or no contact between them previously, and where the target firm operates in a different geographical region to the search firm, it is essential for the search firm to overcome an initial response of: 'Why would we want to talk to them?'[3]

If this is the reaction of the target firm, the search firm must convince it that, even if it was not contemplating a merger, a discussion about it would be worthwhile for both parties, even if it does not amount to anything. At least each firm will have learnt something about the other, and it might just lead to something.

Whilst the approach will vary depending on the circumstances, there are some general rules to follow.

Initial telephone call

Initial contact is best made by telephone. A telephone call provides a more personal touch, and allows the caller to identify the key points at the outset in order to grab the attention of the target firm. It also enables the caller to better gauge the initial reaction of the target. If the target's response is questioning and/or cool, the caller can then elaborate further as to why setting up a meeting to discuss a potential merger would be worthwhile.

It is often more beneficial if the initial call is made by an outside adviser, particularly if the adviser is well regarded by the target firm. One advantage of this

---

3 This is not always the response. In one situation known to the author, it transpired that each firm had, unbeknown to either, targeted the other. The initial response to the 'cold call' was: 'I was trying to work out how to contact you!' This is, however, extremely rare.

is that the adviser can discuss the merger proposal with the target without divulging the name of the search firm. If the target firm does not then express an interest in the idea, there is no risk of the fact that the search firm is 'in the market' for a merger becoming public. This is an important issue to consider if the search firm intends to have initial discussions with a number of firms in one location – word can soon spread, and this can then devalue the initial contact that the search firm makes with other potential candidates. Another advantage of using an adviser who is well regarded by the target is that the firm is more likely to assume that it would not have been approached unless the adviser saw some value in it for the target firm.

Initial meeting between search firm and target firm

No matter who makes the call, the purpose of it is to set up a meeting at which the business case for merger can be discussed in outline, although with sufficient detail to allow both firms to be able to identify the potential benefits and note any major impediments to a merger between them. It is important that this meeting is not merely a 'general chat' between the two firms. As one managing partner noted recently:

> 'Firm X asked for a meeting which I assumed would be about merger. We spent over an hour talking generally about our firms, nothing too specific, but at no stage did they raise the "M" word. It was all a bit strange really. I left with only a hazy outline as to what a merger would do for us.'

The most effective approach to the initial meeting is to:

- make it clear that the topic to be discussed is whether a merger between the two firms might be mutually beneficial;

- set aside three hours or so for the meeting;

- not exchange too much detail – it might look as if the search firm has already assumed that merger talks will go ahead or is trying to build up competitor information;

- structure the agenda so that the search firm is able to decide after the meeting whether or not to pursue the target firm further;

- include a discussion, in broad terms, about:

  - each firm's strategy and general view of market trends;
  - what would be required for a merger to be beneficial to both firms;
  - the potential advantages and disadvantages of a merger; and
  - the compatibility, in a general sense, of the two firms in terms of structure (both at an organisational and partnership level), compensation, management philosophy, technology, etc; and

- put a confidentiality agreement in place.

An initial meeting along these lines not only allows both sides to consider the 'tangible' issues surrounding merger, with no obligation or commitment, but also opens up a dialogue between them that allows each side to get a better sense as to how the other side approaches issues. After a recent initial meeting between two firms that barely knew each other (and between participants who had never met), the managing partner of the target said:

> 'That was extraordinary. As the meeting progressed, it felt more and more as if we were discussing the issues with fellow partners.'

Of course, there is a balance to be achieved at the initial meeting. Whilst the target might be the one firm that the search firm wishes to pursue, if there are a number of other firms on its shortlist, it is best if the search firm is up front about this, and makes it clear at the start of the meeting. Whilst this might inhibit certain aspects of the discussion, it is a more honest approach, and could prove to be more beneficial for the search firm in the longer term.

For example, if the search firm decides to continue to the In-depth Discussion Stage with another firm, but that does not result in a merger, it might want to re-open merger discussions with one of the other firms on its shortlist with which it held an initial meeting. If, however, a target firm thought that it was the sole contender for a merger with the search firm, and then found out it was not, it might then be unwilling to re-open merger discussions with it.

It can be difficult enough to go back and re-visit merger discussions – if a target firm feels that the search firm was not being open at the outset, it is even more difficult.

Final candidate

Assuming that the search firm had several firms on its shortlist, there is then one more step to be taken before it can proceed to the In-depth Discussion Stage, and that is to decide which firm it would like to hold in-depth discussions with. It also has to consider whether that firm is likely to agree to a merger.[4]

We are often asked whether In-depth Discussion Stage talks can be held with more than one firm. Even if the two firms are in different jurisdictions, this is difficult. As we note in **Chapter 4**, discussions at this stage are best undertaken with some degree of intensity, and it is difficult to keep more than one set of discussions running at the same time.

Furthermore, it is usual for firms to sign agreements in regard to exclusivity at the In-depth Discussion Stage, which is difficult to do if talks with other firms are going ahead, particularly if a merger with only one firm is intended. (We comment in **Chapter 4** on the situation where a firm wishes to merge in a number of jurisdictions, and therefore has parallel discussions taking place.)

Finally, if the candidates are in the same location, there is a real danger that one or more of the sets of discussions will become public knowledge (especially in the UK), and, should this happen, the outcome is likely to be that none of the firms will wish to continue.

Of course, the search firm might decide that none of the target firms with which it held initial discussions are suitable, or that none of those firms would be willing to proceed to the In-depth Discussion Stage. In which case, it can either decide to go 'back to the drawing board' (ie the Identification Stage) or abandon the merger search for the time being.

The critical point is that a decision to proceed with one firm must be made before moving to the In-depth Discussion Stage.

Moving from the Initial Discussion Stage to the In-depth Discussion Stage is, in terms of the merger process, a 'crossing of the Rubicon'. While not a commitment to merge, it demonstrates a serious intent.

Viewpoint of target firm

We have approached this chapter so far from the viewpoint of a firm that is actively seeking a merger partner (either on an informal or formal basis). We will now deal with

---

4 Of course, one or two follow-up meetings to the initial meeting might be required before a decision is taken as to which firm is to be the final candidate, but we see this as forming part of the Initial Discussion Stage rather than part of the In-depth Discussion Stage.

the point of view of the target firm that may not have merger on the agenda, but receives a 'cold call' from a firm seeking an initial merger discussion.

The first point we would make here is to echo what we said in **Chapter 2** – any ambitious firm in today's competitive market should, at some point, have engaged the partnership in a discussion as to whether merger is an option that should be pursued, left open or closed off. Other than situations where cultural reasons are a major inhibitor, a strategic view is that merger should at least be an option, even if it is not actively pursued.

Target firm has already considered merger as a potential route

If a firm has considered merger as an option, we would also suggest that management (at least) should have discussed in some depth the type of merger partner that would be beneficial in achieving the firm's strategic objectives, and, at the same time, identified potential merger candidates, or at least the type of firm with which it might merge. Even if consideration of a merger goes no further than this, management should review its 'merger policy' from time to time (around twice a year), and should update the thinking about merger, as well as the potential candidates.

If this has been done regularly, a firm that becomes a target is well placed to respond to a 'cold call'. The target firm might be approached by a firm that is not on its potential candidate list but, having considered the type of firm that it could usefully merge with, it is in a good position to judge whether the caller seems to 'fit the type', and to react quickly. We also find that firms which have been through this type of strategic thinking about merger are more confident in the initial meeting. They are also more likely to agree to hold an initial meeting, unless the approach is from a firm that is so different from their identified type of potential merger partner that it is clear that a meeting would be a waste of time.

A firm that has thought strategically about merger as an option, and which agrees to an initial meeting when approached, will still need to do further research before agreeing to proceed to the In-depth Discussion Stage. The firm that approached it might be within its identified merger partner type, but might not appear to be a really strong candidate. The approach we recommend in this situation is a condensed version of the analysis that firms should carry out at the Identification Stage to identify a shortlist. In other words, having been approached and found the initial meeting positive, the firm should put itself in active search mode: 'If we are to merge, is this the prime candidate, or are there others which will bring greater benefits to a merger with us?'

Whilst this will inevitably cause a delay in any response by a target firm to a request from a search firm for an Initial Discussion Stage meeting, the work already done as a part of the strategic thinking about merger will speed up the process. There is also a need to be open with the firm that has made the approach, and which now wants to proceed to Initial Discussion Stage talks. Should the target decide it wants to stand back and carefully analyse its options within a certain timeframe, given that the search firm has already had the opportunity to do this, our experience is that a keen 'suitor' will not be deterred (although perhaps a little frustrated, but this is not necessarily a bad thing as being frustrated could indicate that that the intentions of the suitor are true).

Target firm has never considered merger as an option

For a firm that receives a 'cold call' approach but has not carried out any in-depth analysis of merger as an option, the decision whether to proceed to the discussion stage or not is a different type of decision. Our advice is that, unless there are some very clear reasons not to proceed, there is more to be gained than lost from an Initial Discussion Stage meeting.

At the initial meeting (or even before), the target firm should be open about the fact that it has not previously explored merger as an option, and, therefore, should the meeting result in both parties seeing value in taking discussions to an In-depth Discussion Stage level, that it will need to set aside time to seriously consider the proposal. If the initial meeting demonstrates that merger could bring some major benefits to the target firm, it should then undertake a 'crash analysis' of whether there are more suitable potential merger partners that it should be pursuing instead.

It is a very difficult position to be in. On the one hand, there is a prospect of merger that appears, on the surface, to be attractive. On the other hand, no analysis has been done to see if this is a 'high priority' prospect or one of a lower order. Even with a 'crash analysis', there might still be some doubt as to whether the search firm is the most suitable option. At that point, a business decision will need to be made as to whether to proceed on the basis that there appears to be significant benefits in merging with the search firm and, therefore, that it is worth pursuing, or to pass up the opportunity. However, prospective merger candidates, especially ones that are actively searching, are not likely to give the target firm the luxury of time to explore all its options and to decide if the search firm is the best merger partner for it. This is why we recommend that any firm that has not ruled out a merger should have done the required thinking in order to be able to react quickly, if approached.

Last-minute nerves

This touches on the final point for this chapter. In narrowing down firms to a shortlist, and in making the final choice of merger partner, partners of the search firm will often question whether the firm would be better off to defer any merger decision, to re-visit some of those firms that were excluded earlier on, or even to analyse firms which never made it onto the initial list. Many partners have an innate cautiousness when it comes to making big decisions about their firm, particularly ones as huge as a decision to merge. Comments that flit around at this time include: 'Have we missed something?'; 'How can we be sure we have made the best choice?' and 'Maybe there'll be a better candidate next year.'

There is also a tendency at this stage for many partners to point to their 'ideal' candidate. Unrequited love is painful, but there are times when partners need to be told that there is very little likelihood that their ideal firm will merge with theirs. Everyone wants to marry up, and no one down. Choosing an appropriate merger partner means choosing one that will provide the search firm with the required strategic benefits, but which will also recognise the significant gains that it would receive from a merger with the search firm. The more benefits from a merger there are which flow to both parties, the more likely it is that a candidate is appropriate (whether it wants to merge is another matter).

It is therefore important that management demonstrates its leadership as well as taking into consideration the firm's concerns. There is a risk that a further analysis by the partners about whether or not the prospective merger candidate is suitable could continue until the target firm loses interest. Equally, deciding to commence merger discussions without keeping partners informed will not result in enthusiastic support from those partners should a proposal to merge then be put forward. If the initial analysis covered a wide spectrum of firms, and partners were informed about why firms were rejected during the whittling-down process, it is easier to persuade them that it is highly unlikely that a better choice exists.

It is at this stage that the formal process has an advantage over the informal process. The informal process is less structured, and is usually carried out on a somewhat ad hoc basis over a lengthy period of time. Partners do not necessarily get the sense that 'the market has been explored', nor are they always clear why particular firms have been rejected. Indeed, it is quite possible that they are unaware that any discussions at all have taken place with some firms. Therefore, when management has adopted the informal process, and when it puts forward a proposal to commence In-depth Discussion Stage talks with a merger candidate to partners, it also needs to set out in some detail what has led it to that choice of firm. We have seen situations where management in many firms has created considerable tension within the partnership by proposing merger talks without demonstrating to partners how it came to settle on one particular firm over others. Extolling the virtues of the final candidate is not enough. Partners will want to know why the virtues of that candidate are superior to those of others. Management should therefore include a discussion of this within its proposal.

The involvement of an outside adviser who knows the market can also be helpful at this point. The adviser is often able to explain why certain firms have been excluded, and why others were not even on the initial list. An outsider is sometimes seen to be more objective in the merger process than management. As one partner noted during a discussion about whether to proceed to merger discussions:

> 'It's not that I don't trust management or even think that they have steered us to "their" choice. It's more that they have their own bias about other firms like all of us and I just don't know if that has got in the way of an objective decision. Having an outsider involved gives me more confidence that it is probably the best choice.'

The same point applies in the situation where management agrees to a merger proposal without the partners being aware of it. Whilst uncommon, there are a number of cases where partners have agreed that a merger should be ruled out, only to then open a brown envelope on their desk some time later which contains notice of an actual proposal to merge with Firm X on which they will need to vote within ten days or so. This might be an appropriate approach in very specific situations, but it should not generally be adopted. (This approach has been used in at least two cases where management was concerned about competitor reaction, and wanted to complete the deal as quickly as possible and without a leak to the press. The danger, of course, is that in 'bouncing' partners into a decision in these circumstances, it loses the vote.) It is therefore again important that management not only discusses the proposal to hold in-depth merger discussions with a particular firm with the partners, but also why Firm X is the best choice out of all other possible candidates. A failure to do so can lead to partners objecting to the proposal, not because a good business case for Firm X did not exist (and it might even be that a very strong one does), but because they are not clear about the options the firm might have otherwise had, and why Firm X is the best choice. In other words, they might vote the proposal down based purely on the way in which the process was handled, and not on the quality of the business case itself. A number of potentially very good mergers never got off the ground because management in one of the firms involved misread the attitude of the partnership on the issue of merger.

Case studies

We have set out above the processes that should be followed in finding a merger partner, but do firms actually follow them in practice?

Of the 19 firms involved in the nine case studies used for this book, nine followed a version of the formal process, and ten were more informal in their selection of merger candidates. Of that ten, seven were target firms and three were search firms. Six of the 19 firms used an outside adviser to assist in the identification of a potential candidate, and five of these advisers made the initial approach. (In a couple of cases, the other party was also actively looking at merger as an option, and, in one case, had an adviser.) Eleven of the firms involved in the case studies knew their merger partner(s) reasonably well prior to initial contact. Two firms, which were the target firms, did not use an outside adviser at the Identification Stage, nor did they know the other firm prior to the approach being made.

Addleshaw Goddard

Addleshaw Booth & Co and Theodore Goddard both undertook a formal process at the Identification Stage and at the Initial Discussion Stage. Theodore Goddard had an initial list of 70 potential candidates which was then reduced to a shortlist of nine. Addleshaw Booth & Co had an initial list of 68 firms. Both firms had the other on its final shortlist.

Theodore Goddard held initial discussions with four US firms and five UK firms. These discussions led to a decision to abandon the idea of a US merger, which had been favoured by some partners, because of the difficulties these talks threw up. Addleshaw Booth & Co reduced its shortlist to 17 firms, 12 of which had a turnover of less than £30m and five of which had a turnover greater than that. Both firms used a very structured approach to the selection process, working through a set of criteria that a candidate had to meet in order to make it onto the final shortlist. In both cases, cultural compatibility was an important part of the selection.

As Mark Jones (previously managing partner of Addleshaw Booth & Co) noted:

'Addleshaw Sons & Latham and Booth & Co… knew each other well and that counted a great deal in the success of that merger. We had to be sure that the next merger would be between two firms that had a close a fit culturally.'

Paddy Grafton Green (previously senior partner of Theodore Goddard) echoed a point made above about the early meetings:

> 'What did I know of Addleshaw Booth & Co pre-talks? Absolutely nothing! We wanted a merger partner with good business synergies, a quality reputation, aspirations and a track record of treating people well. Addleshaw Booth & Co demonstrated all of these in our first meeting and, frankly, this came as a surprise to me. First impressions, in other words are crucial: get that first meeting right. If the chemistry doesn't work in the first meeting then the whole deal won't work.'

Berwin Leighton Paisner

At noted earlier, Berwin Leighton initially took a formal approach to identifying candidates, but then adopted a more informal approach to the subsequent selection of a merger candidate. Its strategic review had identified the criteria that a merger partner should meet. Neville Eisenberg (previously managing partner of Berwin Leighton) said:

> 'We identified a number of potential merger partners and we spoke with some – about five firms, a real mixture. We didn't have a formal list but chatted to a number over a period of time.'

Its merger with Paisner & Co resulted from a chat between Eisenberg and Harold Paisner (previously senior partner of Paisner & Co).

Paisner & Co was not actively seeking merger, but was a candidate on Berwin Leighton's list. Once approached, there was excitement about what the merger could offer it, and the firm did not look elsewhere. There had been, for a long time, a view amongst management that if the firm was to consider merger, then Berwin Leighton would be a good candidate.

Blake Lapthorn Linnell

Blake Lapthorn and Linnells both followed a somewhat formal process in that they both identified a shortlist of firms, and held initial discussions with a number of them. When Linnells contacted Blake Lapthorn, the latter had already decided that Oxford was a suitable location for a merger partner. Linnells had drawn up a shortlist of firms based on a set of merger criteria, but a number of the initial discussions had not amounted to anything due to 'wrong practice areas' and 'the wrong time in our development', but Blake Lapthorn took up the contact. Within a couple of meetings, the discussions moved to an In-depth Discussion Stage level.

Denton Wilde Sapte

Both Denton Hall and Wilde Sapte had a clear set of merger criteria that emerged from their respective strategic objectives. They both knew the type of firm they were seeking as a merger partner. The possibility of a merger between the two emerged when Mark Andrews (previously senior partner of Wilde Sapte) was having dinner with James Dallas (previously Chairman of Denton Hall). As Andrews noted:

> 'It is difficult to say who made the approach. The management of both firms knew each other very well. The possibility was raised when James Dallas and I were having dinner. The subject came up, and it seemed to us that it was something worth looking at. One tended to have these meals from time to time with contemporaries just to talk about a wide range of issues.'

Kidd Rapinet

Kidd Rapinet was aware that of some areas of its practice required strengthening, although it was not actually in the market for a merger. Steggles Palmer had decided to pursue the merger route and, using the more formal process, identified a number of firms, including Kidd Rapinet. From initial discussions, Kidd Rapinet appeared to it to be the best choice, and Kidd Rapinet saw that Steggles Palmer would meet many of its requirements. Both firms had identified their strategic objectives. Whilst Steggles Palmer had adopted a formal approach to the search, Kidd Rapinet was not actively searching, but had identified the criteria that a future merger partner might fulfil.

William Sturges & Co

The merger between William Sturges & Co and Chethams was similar to that of Kidd Rapinet and Steggles Palmer. Chethams had identified that a merger would be beneficial, and was clear about the criteria a potential merger partner should meet. It used a formal process and approached William Sturges & Co. William Sturges & Co did not have merger on its agenda at that point, but saw the attraction in it because it was clear about its strategic objectives.

ASB Law

The merger to form ASB Law emerged out of a more informal process on the part of all parties. The three firms involved, Argles & Court, Stoneham and Burstows, were all located in different parts of south-east England, and had worked closely together through an alliance-type relationship. Hence, when the idea of creating a larger regional firm came up (initiated by Burstows), it was natural that it would involve the existing alliance members. No other search for a merger candidate was carried out by any of the firms.

Brabners Chaffe Street

The merger that resulted in Brabners Chaffe Street involved a mix of semi-formal and semi-informal processes. Brabners had identified some years before the need to be in Manchester, and saw merger as the only real option. Whilst it did not draw up as rigorous a set of criteria as Addleshaw Booth & Co and Theodore Goddard, it was clear as to what it was seeking.

The search process was, however, quite informal. Brabners approached a number of firms, including Chaffe Street, about a potential merger in the 1990s but nothing came of this. Chaffe Street had acted on the other side of a deal involving Brabners. It liked what it saw, and approached it when a decision to merge was made. Robert Street (previously senior partner of Chaffe Street) met with Michael Brabner (previously senior partner of Brabners) and suggested they hold merger talks. As Street remarked: 'We were attracted by Brabners' culture and its practice strength.'

TLT Solicitors

The merger of Trumps and Lawrence Tucketts was the result of a mainly informal merger process. Neither side listed a set of criteria or identified prospective merger candidates. Both firms did, however, have a clear idea about their evolving market position, and where they wanted to be within that market. They knew each other reasonably well and, at one point, had practically been neighbours. As David Pester (previously partner of Lawrence Tucketts) noted:

> 'As Trumps developed, the opportunity became more obvious… what we recognised was each other's ambitions. We'd actually kept in touch, off and on, over five years but on a low-key basis: we didn't want to send any hares running in the marketplace given Bristol is a small market.'

Lessons

The overriding lesson from these case studies is that there is no one way to go about identifying and approaching a merger partner, although circumstances will likely dictate the best process to be followed.

As we noted in **Chapter 2**, the key issue was that all firms, in their various ways, had a reasonably clear, strategic agenda, both in terms of what they were trying to achieve in their market and what their market was, together with the gaps in their arsenal that needed to be filled in order to succeed. This is one of the strongest messages we wish to convey throughout this book. Our case studies are about mergers that have been successful – not necessarily world-shattering – but mergers which have enabled the parties to achieve more strategically, and to be more competitive, than either firm could have done or been without merger (or at least, not for a much longer period of time as an independent firm). It is no coincidence that each of the firms possessed a degree of clarity as to its strategic issues.

Our experience has also brought us into contact with many 'not so successful' mergers. It has become clear that a factor in a number of these was that one or both of the parties had only a fuzzy idea about what the firm was trying to achieve, and what the implementation priorities were. They were in the 'let's grow corporate' category of firms, but did not fully understand what that meant, so much so that almost any firm with a corporate group would have met the criteria. Being clear about what a firm's strategy really means is fundamental to selecting a merger partner that is truly appropriate. We will comment further on this.

Some firms cast a wide net in looking for a partner. Addleshaw Booth & Co, Theodore Goddard, Berwin Leighton, Brabners, Linnells and Steggles Palmer are examples. Others identified a partner relatively quickly, in each case because they already knew the firm. This was so for Denton Hall, Wilde Sapte, Paisner & Co, Argles & Court, Stoneham, Burstows, Chaffe Street, Trumps and Lawrence Tucketts. In the cases of William Sturges & Co and Kidd Rapinet, they were approached as part of a more formal process undertaken by the other parties, but immediately saw the strategic logic in a merger when they took into consideration their own strategic ambitions.

Again, there is an important lesson to be drawn from this which goes back to a comment made earlier in this chapter – if a firm wants to make sure that a merger candidate is a good choice, it should not set out in search of 'the holy grail', ie its ideal candidate, which may or may not exist, or if it does exist, does not want to merge with that firm. Mark Jones (previously managing partner of Addleshaw Booth & Co) made this point:

> 'We didn't come up with ideals [when looking at possible London merger partners]. For example, would we merge with Allen & Overy? The real question is would they merge with us? Unlikely, so we set out from the start to look at the art of the possible.'

Where two firms know each other, have observed each other's development over time, see strong complementarity between the two businesses, and similarity in what they are seeking to achieve, there is a lot of sense in regarding the other as a serious merger prospect. Even in such a situation, a firm should look at other potential partners (albeit briefly) to ensure that the firm that it knows is appropriate. However, unless a really 'hot' prospect emerges from this search, it is better to proceed with what is on offer rather than canvassing widely and over a long period of time in order to ensure that the first choice is indeed best. Trumps and Lawrence Tucketts are good examples of this, as are Brabners, Chaffe Street, Argles & Court, Stoneham and Burstows.

On the other hand, Addleshaw Booth & Co, Theodore Goddard, Berwin Leighton and Linnells did not have one obvious candidate in mind at the outset. There was nobody 'next door that they had grown up with and felt pretty comfortable about'. Whilst this was the case for Addleshaw Sons & Latham and Booth & Co at the time of their merger, it was not with the merger of Addleshaw Booth & Co and Theodore Goddard. They were therefore absolutely right to stand back and take a bigger picture view, and to start with a set of specific criteria and a wide list of candidates that met some initial criteria, and then to narrow the list down by working through the rest of the criteria. By simply putting a pin into one name out of 60 or 70, these firms might have struck lucky or, more likely, not.

The importance of culture is another lesson that comes through here. As we noted in **Chapter 1**, firms need to carefully consider what another firm's culture might be. Where firms know each other already, they are likely to have a subconscious idea of some of the elements of the other's culture, although some probing will still be required to ensure that their initial feelings are correct. Where the merger search includes firms whose internal environment the search firm has little knowledge of, culture is a harder criterion to understand. Firms may have strong views about certain other firms and, rightly or wrongly, decide there is little point including them on the initial list of merger candidates. Other firms might be complete unknowns, and so the search firm will have no idea about their culture. That is why the exploratory meetings at the Initial Discussion Stage are important. Those meetings are often the best way to assess possible cultural compatibility and can result in a firm feeling that 'this is a firm with whom we can do business'. Paddy Grafton Green's quote on page 62 supports this.

The use of advisers to identify a merger partner varied throughout the case studies. Both Addleshaw Booth & Co and Theodore Goddard had outside advisers, as did Chethams, Linnells, Steggles Palmer and Burstows (although in Burstows' case, an adviser was used to initiate discussions with the alliance partners). We noted earlier that an outside adviser can be helpful in certain situations, although it is instructive to note that, of the nine case studies, advisers were only used at the Initial Discussion Stage by six firms for five of the mergers. Our view is that an outside perspective can assist any prospective merger, even if it is only to cast an eye over the process, and to provide comfort to partners that they have made the right decision. However, that is a choice that each firm needs to make at the time. Berwin Leighton, for example, did not have an adviser, and instead left the issues in the hands of the in-house team, but in this case the identification of potential firms was not a complex process (see **Chapter 5**).

Once a firm believes it has selected the appropriate merger partner, the next step is to put this decision to the test.

CHAPTER 4: IN-DEPTH MERGER DISCUSSIONS – THE FIRST MEETING

We noted in **Chapter 3** that there were three stages in finding a suitable merger partner:

(i)   identifying potential merger candidates (Identification Stage);

(ii) holding initial discussions with the more promising candidates (Initial Discussion Stage); and

(iii) in-depth discussions with the favoured candidate (In-depth Discussion Stage).

We discussed the Identification Stage and the Initial Discussion Stage in **Chapter 3**. In this chapter and **Chapters 5** and **6**, we deal with the In-depth Discussion Stage.

At any stage of merger discussions, there is usually a point at which one or both firms realise that this feels 'right'. This happens in the Initial Discussion Stage meetings, although more based on previous perceptions and 'chemistry' between the firms in the meetings. It is this that usually moves the process to the In-depth Discussion Stage. It happens again at the In-depth Discussion Stage, although this time based more on hard evidence, and much more detailed interactions between people in the two firms. In every merger with which we have been involved, there is suddenly a point when everyone knows it is going to happen (or not). As a rule of thumb, the longer it takes to get that feeling at the In-depth Discussion Stage, the less likely is the merger.

To reiterate a key message of **Chapter 3**, personal relationships are very important in the early meetings at the In-depth Discussion Stage. Rightly or wrongly, the impression that each firm gets about the other from those meetings is an early indicator of the culture of the other firm, and how people from it behave. As the senior partner of a firm that went through a failed merger discussion said:

'I should have called it off after the second meeting. The other senior partner and I hit it off, and the broad business case looked good. But there was a highly abrasive attitude that permeated the other firm. We thought it was just the attitude of a couple of the partners who were involved in the discussions. Eight weeks later, and after a huge effort had gone into it, we felt on our side that we could never be in the same firm as them. It was an attitude that ran through everyone – I really do kick myself for not having the courage of my convictions much earlier.'

As we discuss later, firms will generally pick partners that they see as 'role models' for the firm to take part in the merger discussions. It is therefore not unreasonable for those around the discussion table to be seen as typical of the rest of the firm.

Agenda of the first meeting at the In-depth Discussion Stage

Having taken the decision to discuss a potential merger seriously, the process is more effective if the first meeting[1] is used to agree upon the planning and structuring of the subsequent discussions than to launch straight into the merger talks themselves. The issues below (see box on p71) are some of the more important ones that should be discussed and agreed upon by each side in the first meeting.

Going through these issues in the first meeting not only structures the process, but it helps to avoid serious misunderstandings further down the line that could undermine the trust between the two firms. In one case of which we are aware, merger discussions between two firms almost came to an end at the second meeting when it emerged that one of the firms had informed all its partners and staff that it was involved in merger discussions. The firm had a general policy of complete transparency in all matters, and therefore did not think it unusual to do so. The other firm had not told its partnership, let alone its staff, and could not understand why the other firm had been so public about it. The issue was resolved, but there was high tension in the room that day.

The communication process

The confidential nature of merger discussions is something that worries the management of most firms. Whilst partnership mergers do not have the external implications of public company mergers, they do still involve some very significant communications issues.

---

1 The use of the term 'first meeting' in this chapter refers to the first formal discussion. There will have been one or more initial discussions of the type referred to in **Chapter 3** prior to this, at which very little information is likely to have been exchanged.

Agenda for the first meeting

- The communication process (internally and externally):
  - when should the partnership be told;
  - dealing with the press and handling leaks.
- How the discussion process should be managed:
  - use of core negotiating teams and task forces.
- When to broaden out discussions to involve a wider audience:
  - how much should be divulged?
- Composition of the negotiating team.
- Confidentiality agreements:
  - are they required?
- Potential deal-breakers:
  - what are they?
  - how should they be handled?
- Exchange of initial information
- use of outside advisers
- agenda for the discussion meetings

As a number of people from firms in our case studies have confirmed, it is hard to negotiate a merger in the public spotlight. It simply puts pressure on everyone, and, of course, the press is always looking for an angle to the story, one that can be negative or at least sceptical about the merger.

The merger discussions between Addleshaw Booth & Co and Theodore Goddard attracted considerable press attention, which put enormous pressure on the discussion participants, especially those from Theodore Goddard. Theodore Goddard had been through two previous merger attempts, both of which had attracted a great deal of publicity. The firm had also seen a number of partner departures, particularly after its second merger attempt. An impression was being built up in the marketplace, and echoed in the legal press, of a firm in trouble, and finding it hard to retain partners.

Then came the start of the merger talks with Addleshaw Booth & Co. The legal press got wind of these discussions very quickly because a disaffected employee at

Theodore Goddard began leaking stories and documents. More partners left during these talks, and this received further headline publicity. What the press failed to appreciate was that these resignations came as no surprise to Theodore Goddard, and had, in fact, been accepted prior to the commencement of the merger discussions with Addleshaw Booth & Co. The press, however, maintained a picture of a firm in trouble.

Needless to say, this put enormous pressure on the merger process. Addleshaw Booth & Co felt obliged to carry out due diligence on Theodore Goddard in order to establish whether it was indeed a firm about to implode. The press coverage was also very destabilising for the partners of Theodore Goddard. Lesley Jackson (one of the partners on the merger negotiating team for Theodore Goddard) said:

> 'It's awfully upsetting to pick up the legal press and read some of the things it was saying about us which we knew weren't true. It also creates a huge amount of internal tension amongst people outside of management.'

Paddy Grafton Green (previously senior partner of Theodore Goddard) said:

> 'We were pretty sure that there were not going to be any more partner resignations. We'd talked with everyone. But the unrelenting negativity of the press left us wondering each day if some partners would just decide to chuck it in and go somewhere else. And then the deal could have collapsed. The press can create a very unstable state inside a firm, often based on gossip and rumour. It was a very unpleasant experience.'

Like Theodore Goddard, Wilde Sapte had been through a failed merger attempt (with the legal arm of Arthur Andersen), and had suffered from some very negative press coverage during and after the merger discussions. It also lost partners before and during the merger talks, but, like the partners at Theodore Goddard, they had resigned much earlier. However, their departure enabled the press to build up a story of a troubled firm that was struggling to retain its best people. Mark Andrews (previously senior partner of Wilde Sapte) said:

> 'Press coverage on merger discussions can be very damaging, and I'm not sure the press knows how bad it can be. The moment it gets out, most mergers are finished. So keeping it out of the public eye, keeping complete confidentiality, is incredibly important.'

A former partner of a firm that went through a failed merger attempt felt quite bitter about the press coverage the merger discussions had received:

'A disaffected partner leaked a biased account to the press. No matter what we said, the press treated us as if we were covering up problems that just didn't exist. Our prospective merger partner got "cold feet", and I didn't blame it. Some of the press comments were almost vitriolic, and damaging internally. We had staff who were completely demotivated and destabilised. Talk about being guilty before it's proven. The press hung us out to dry even though we had tried to co-operate.'

A number of firms in our case studies were more concerned about staff finding out that their firm was in merger discussions from the press than whether the press coverage was positive or negative. Neville Eisenberg (previously of Berwin Leighton) remarked:

'Any leak about discussions can be stressful. Staff wonder whether they will have a job or not, and this places pressure on management. There was a leak during our discussions with Paisner & Co, but we were able to get a memo out to everyone before the story was published in the press. It is far better that people hear the story from management than from the outside world, even if the press coverage is positive.'

Paul Taylor, senior partner of Kidd Rapinet, agreed:

'Word can get out. We weren't a big City firm, so it wouldn't have made the ITN news, but you do have to be a little careful if people hear it on the grapevine rather than from the managing partner. They'll start thinking about redundancies, and some might resign when you don't want them to do so.'

Virginia Glastonbury (previously deputy managing partner of Denton Hall) made this point very clearly:

'People underestimate the impact of reading about merger discussions in the press. As soon as they do, a lot of people are immediately frightened about their jobs.'

What came through strongly from those who have been through the merger process is the need to manage both internal and external communications.

Internal communication is particularly important when a smaller firm is looking to merge with a much larger firm. As a number of people in our case studies noted, the merged firm is not going to need two accounting departments, two marketing departments, etc, so those working in these departments can feel quite vulnerable. The rumour can often go round the smaller firm that, once the firms have merged, and the larger firm has secured the smaller firm's clients, the lawyers from the smaller firm will be axed. The logic of this rumour is hard to understand. Post-merger, the larger firm will need more lawyers to carry out the work – it is unlikely that it will have enough capacity to take on the new clients and be able to use its existing fee-earners to get the increased workload done (unless the smaller firm is, in relative terms, very small indeed). In addition, the staff of the smaller firm, particularly the partners, will have established good client relationships, and these cannot just be transferred to the larger firm overnight. There are very few (if any) mergers where this has been the intention of the larger firm, but the fact that it is a common rumour demonstrates the degree of internal destabilisation that merger discussions can create.

When the press is commenting almost weekly on the merger, especially if in a negative light, the task of management is extremely difficult. Not only is it charged with negotiating a merger, it also has to keep reassuring the people in its firm that they are not in imminent danger of losing their jobs, and that much of the press comment is based on rumour, not fact.

A critical issue, and one often underestimated by firms that have not been through serious merger discussions before, is the need to plan the communication process before in-depth talks begin, not when they are first contacted by the press. There are a few aspects to this communication process that need to be considered, the first being when the partnership should be told about the merger discussions.

When should the partnership be told?
The need for confidentiality

In some firms, serious merger discussions are not able to commence until all the equity partners have agreed to them. In some cases, this is expressly required in the partnership agreement, while in others, management feels that it needs such backing. As we discuss below, this immediately increases the likelihood of a leak to the press. For other firms, the merger discussions can progress quite far before they feel their partners need to be told. In either case, as a rule of thumb, firms should always assume that news of the merger talks will be leaked to the press, and that as soon as the whole of the partnership finds out, a leak will be imminent. We are not suggesting that partners are untrustworthy, simply that the more people who know about the merger discussions, the more likely it is that those discussions will become public knowledge (usually by accident).

Denton Hall and Wilde Sapte went to great lengths to retain confidentiality. The merger proposal went before partners on a Thursday, with the vote on it taking place the following Monday. It was therefore timed to fall between press publication dates. Mark Andrews (previously senior partner of Wilde Sapte) said:

'You just cannot conduct negotiations in the glare of publicity. The legal press don't understand that its own scrutiny can kill off merger discussions.'

Wilde Sapte was even careful about the choice of venue for the meeting at which partners were told. Andrews recalled:

'There was one tremendous piece of chutzpah, which was when we decided to tell all the partners. We had to bring them all together, and we decided that the most secret place to get everyone together was also the most obvious place to look for them. So we hired the Law Society's rooms. We got them all together one evening, and nobody spotted it.'

Other approaches

Other firms have taken a different approach to the communication process, usually due to the size of the partnership, and the importance that the marketplace will place on the merger.

Linnells had 20 partners, all of whom were kept informed throughout the merger process. Similarly, Kidd Rapinet told its partners on day one, and held weekly information meetings with them.

Ordinarily, Brabners would have told its partnership about the potential merger early on in the process, and would have trusted its partners to keep it confidential. Chaffe Street, however, had some difficult issues to deal with during the merger talks. Both firms therefore decided to keep it quiet until the deal was agreed. They told their respective staff at Christmas, with the merger taking effect on the following 1 January.

As Theodore Goddard was negotiating its merger in a blaze of publicity, there was no way it could keep it quiet, even if it had wanted to do so. A number of internal progress meetings were held with partners in the pre-merger discussion stage, and these continued as the negotiations progressed.

Berwin Leighton and Paisner & Co commenced serious discussions in mid-November 2000, and these continued through to mid-January 2001. The partners in both firms were informed, discussed the proposal in late January, and voted on it in early February. There was a leak to the press, and the firms informed staff two weeks ahead of the planned merger date (which was to be early February, after the vote).

The firms merging to form TLT Solicitors held the discussions between November 1999 and January 2000. The discussions were confidential to a small group until the business case had been developed. Meetings took place with partners in December, and staff were informed that merger discussions were being held soon after.

Merger not inevitable

An important point to make here is that, even when merger discussions have become serious, they could still collapse. What might appear to be a strong business case in outline can prove to be otherwise once the detail is filled in. Furthermore, due diligence can bring some insurmountable problems to the surface. One merger almost foundered when the due diligence exercise threw up a pension fund deficit on the part of one of the firms. Whilst this was eventually offset against some liabilities of the other firm, it did almost cause the talks to be called off.

Generally, management does not want discussions to become public knowledge until it looks likely that a deal exists. To go public, and then to announce that the deal is off, not only reflects badly on management personally, but can also tarnish a firm's image in the marketplace. Lawyers are trained to look for problems, and when merger talks are abandoned, the reaction is often: 'What went wrong?' It can therefore create difficulties for the firm in hiring lawyers in the future. Clients will also question what happened. A number of firms have suffered from this over the years, including Denton Hall, Wilde Sapte, Theodore Goddard and Richards Butler.

Common message and timetable

Ideally, the communication to both partnerships should be made at the same time and contain identical, or very similar, messages.[2] This is not always possible, of course, because of differing policies in communicating issues to partners. As we noted above, some firms keep their partners involved throughout the process, and others prefer to involve them later on. Brabners changed what would have been its normal timescale for informing its partnership about the merger in order to fit in with Chaffe Street's needs to keep it confidential. Whatever approach is adopted, our advice is to always endeavour to agree upon a common timetable of communication at the first of the In-depth Discussion Stage meetings.

---

2 We are aware of one amusing incident where this did not happen. Two firms had only recently entered into merger discussions. The partners in one firm were aware that these discussions were taking place, but the partners in the other did not. At a client meeting at which both firms were present, a partner from the first firm privately made a number of jocular remarks to a partner from the second firm. The partner from the second firm had no idea what the comments were about, and thought that the other partner was acting very strangely. Only later did it become apparent what the incident was all about. This situation is best avoided wherever possible.

Dealing with the press and handling leaks

We noted above that no matter how confidential the merger talks are, it is best to assume that there will be a leak to the press about them at some stage. Hence, another aspect of the communication process to agree at the first meeting is what to say if the press asks if merger discussions are under way.

It is not wise to deny everything. If a journalist has got wind of the merger discussions, they may well have some evidence to back their story up, and even if it is only a hunch, they will keep digging until they find some. It is not a good idea to issue a denial only to have a reporter produce evidence supporting the story a week later – management can look more than a little foolish. Furthermore, the press does not like being lied to. When the merger is eventually announced, if firms have issued a denial, annoyed journalists may exact revenge by affording the merger faint praise or worse. Whilst this is not the end of the world, positive press coverage can help to reinforce the message that the merged firm is trying to make to clients, partners and staff. A negative reaction by the press can make 'the sell' just that bit harder.

The critical point to remember is that the press is only doing its job. Whilst management might not always agree with the role of the press, and press intrusion can create major difficulties if merger possibilities have not been discussed internally, it is far better to try to manage the communication process, and to keep the press on-side. There are times when this will not be possible, but the aim should be to do so.

Press statement

The best approach is for both parties to agree at the outset to a statement that can be released should the press find out about the merger discussions. The actual wording of this statement will vary depending on the stage of the discussions. If at an early stage, the statement should acknowledge that a meeting (or meetings) between the two firms has taken place, but only in the context of meetings that firms have on a regular basis with each other in order to exchange views. The statement should also include a comment that neither firm is intending to merge at present, but should an opportunity to do so come along and be beneficial to both firms, it would naturally be considered. If the discussions are at an early stage, this statement will be true.

The only area where a firm might need to 'skate on thin ice' in the early stages of discussions is if a journalist asks the direct question: 'Are you in merger discussions?' If this happens, the firm can either come clean or answer along the lines of: 'We have discussions from time to time with firms we know, and the issue of merger is often raised. We are not, however, intending to merge with any particular firm at the moment.' The final sentence of this statement is a small 'white lie' – whilst a merger might not yet be agreed, the firms are at least considering whether or not to seek to merge. It is not, however, an outright denial.

Preliminary announcement

Some thought should also be given to when the firms would be prepared to issue a preliminary announcement about the merger should the press find out about it further into in the discussion process. As mentioned on page 75 above, Berwin Leighton Paisner pre-empted a press leak by making an announcement about the merger earlier than planned. When firms should make such announcement is a judgement call. However, a draft announcement should be prepared from the outset, and not just when it looks as if merger is a probability. Should a leak then occur, the best approach is to stall the press for 24 hours, and to circulate the announcement both internally and to major clients.

Public relations consultants

Public relations consultants are often criticised for being all 'puff and wind', but there are some who do really know what they are doing. Whether or not to bring a consultant on board is another decision that firms should make. Not only can consultants help plan the communication process should news of the merger discussions be leaked to the press, they can also reach deals with it to delay publication of the story until the firms involved are able to inform their staff. They are also very good at coaching management in how to answer questions from journalists without 'falling into a hole', and without creating difficulties that may arise later.

Appointing one spokesperson

Firms should also ensure that, no matter how many people in a firm know about the merger discussions, only one person from it deals with the press. Difficulties can arise when all the partners in a firm are aware of the merger talks. It is surprising how many lawyers are flattered by being contacted by the press, and end up unintentionally saying something that confirms the journalist's suspicions. (Even excellent litigators can lose their senses when contacted by the press.) Equally, it is also a dead giveaway when partners make 'no comment' statements. The rule must be that no one accepts or returns a call from a journalist. All calls should instead be referred to the appropriate spokesperson for the firm who will have been coached on how to deal with press queries.

A journalist told an amusing story about a rather inept approach at denying merger discussions. There were rumours quite some years ago of a merger between a major US and a major UK firm. The journalist called the senior partner of the UK firm, a very respected and sophisticated lawyer, who at first said: 'No comment.' He then paused and said: 'Well, we know them of course, and work with them.' He then paused again and said: 'What I'm saying is they would be someone we would consider if we were merging.' The journalist then asked: 'But are you in merger discussions?' He received the reply: 'No comment.' The merger never happened, and whether the two firms were in discussions or not is not the point. The key issue is that there must be a clear and agreed statement for the press, and not a flustered senior partner caught thinking (or trying to) on his feet.

How the discussion process should be managed

The first meeting should also be used to plan the scope of all future meetings (or, at least, the first few), how they should be conducted and by whom.

Some firms prefer to nominate a small, self-contained team to work through all the major issues and, effectively, to conclude the deal apart from a range of relatively minor issues (core team only approach). Others prefer to use a small negotiating team but to supplement it with a number of task forces, each dedicated to addressing specific issues and to making recommendations (or suggesting possible options) to the main negotiating team (task force approach).

Core team only approach

The core team only approach is more applicable where both firms are smaller, and where the negotiating teams will therefore have a good understanding of all aspects of their respective businesses. This approach was used in the merger between Brabners and Chaffe Street. Initially, the discussions were between Michael Brabner and Robert Street, senior partners of their respective firms. Michael Brabner then involved another partner, and subsequently set up a small team in order to go through the issues in greater detail. This approach was also used in the merger between Kidd Rapinet and Steggles Palmer, and between William Sturges & Co and Chethams.

There is an obvious reason why this approach is used by smaller firms, and this is the size of the partnership. In a partnership of 15 to 20, if several task forces are used in addition to the core negotiating team, more than half of the partnership is likely to be involved in the discussion process, and, therefore, those who are not involved would also then need to be told about it.

The core team only approach is also advantageous when a high level of confidentiality is required. For example, in the merger between Denton Hall and Wilde Sapte, there was a period of six weeks when only a core team of five people on each side was involved. These teams, made up of the professional managers of each firm, focused their efforts on issues that they had identified as potential deal-breakers, namely, profit-sharing, management structure, client issues and the name of the firm. Both firms had been through a merger process before, so the core teams knew the type of information that the other side would require, and were adept at assembling it. However, both firms involved their board once they felt they had a deal so there was also an additional group other than the negotiating team involved.

Task force approach

In general, however, when a merger is between larger firms, it is more difficult to run through the process using only a small, central negotiating team, and a task force approach is used. For example, Addleshaw Booth & Co and Theodore Goddard increased the size of their core teams quite quickly. The press was already aware of the merger discussions, so there was no use in trying to maintain confidentiality (other than about the specific details of the merger itself). The merger negotiations took around ten weeks. Each side had a negotiating team of two plus their finance directors but supplemented this with a number of task forces that reported back to them. The task forces were asked to examine particular issues and to make recommendations. They looked at items such as partnership agreements, leases, finances, employment contracts and policies. The core team instead focused on the major issues of strategy, the business case, management structure, partner remuneration and profitability. In addition, the various professional directors of both firms carried out specific roles in the due diligence process, and also reported back to the core team.

Which approach is best?

As with many aspects of the merger process, there is no one way to do it. Both approaches can work in particular situations. As discussed, the merger between Denton Hall and Wilde Sapte was a large merger that used the core team only approach (although, as mentioned above, they did supplement the core team with other assistance). The merger between Addleshaw Booth & Co and Theodore Goddard used the task force approach, although their core negotiating teams were smaller than those of Denton Hall and Wilde Sapte.

As we noted earlier, having a core team only can be quite effective in mergers of smaller firms because that team is likely to have a good grasp of the overall business, and to understand each practice area and what it does. It will be familiar with the major clients, will have a view about all the partners and fee-earners, and will understand the management structure, finances and operations of its firm. In small firm mergers, the core team tends to be made up of those already in managerial roles.

The potential danger of the core team only approach, even in small firm mergers, is that the negotiators may think that they know how things work, when the reality may be somewhat different. This might only be the case in respect of minor areas of practice, but it could also be so in respect of a major area such as the firm's internal environment. In one merger of which we are aware, the negotiating team painted a glowing picture of its firm as having an open, transparent and trusting internal environment and effective leadership. The reality was that this was only the view amongst the senior partners on the negotiating team. By others, the firm was viewed as secretive, authoritarian and tension-ridden, and without leadership. The senior partners genuinely believed their firm to be the way they had described it, but the reality emerged only after the merger. This caused enormous problems and difficulties for the merger partner, which did have an open, transparent and trusting internal environment. In the difficult integration process that followed, a number of excellent people from the merger partner left because of fears that the internal environment they were used to would be lost in the merged firm.

There is also the danger with a small negotiating team of 'group think' developing. The negotiating team puts forward a combined view in regard to particular issues, whereas in reality each member has some point of disagreement. The collective disagreements can in fact add up to a significant divergence from the view the group has put forward. No person, however, dissents from the combined view because, for each person, the difference appears small, and they do not wish to be seen disagreeing with colleagues over what seem to be minor issues. The feeling that the group should be united and speak with one voice results in the other side receiving a misleading message, albeit unintentionally.

These potential difficulties are not easy to resolve in a small firm merger. Sometimes, the due diligence process will facilitate a discussion between people outside the core teams, but again the problem of 'group think' can come into play. It is difficult for a person from one firm to be completely honest about their firm with a representative of the potential merger partner, particularly when it involves having to discuss negative issues, so everyone stays with the 'party line' rather than expressing their own opinion. Hence, not only might a misleading impression be given about an issue, there might also be a greater sense of cohesiveness transmitted than actually exists.

One way to overcome these problems is to involve an outside adviser in the negotiation process. We will comment on this further in **Chapter 5**.

Large firm mergers carry with them their own problems. As we noted earlier, the first is that of confidentiality. This tends to result in the need for a small negotiating team, usually with a limited amount of support. This therefore imposes a significant amount of work on the core team. As with a small firm merger, there is also the danger that the views put forward by the core team are not representative of the views of the partnership as a whole. Widening the group, however, can lead to the merger discussions becoming public knowledge before this is desirable.

Involving a larger number of partners in discussions does, however, have significant advantages, as the merger between Addleshaw Booth & Co and Theodore Goddard illustrates. Although the core negotiating team was quite small, the various task forces set up to conduct the due diligence involved a wide number of partners. By being members of a task force, partners (and others) from both firms were able to get to know each other, and to form a view about their potential colleagues. They were also able to get an insight into the culture of the other firm simply by observing the behaviour of the task force members. It is important to note here that core group members should consult regularly with the task force members about the behaviour of the other firm's members, and endeavour to see if a pattern exists. Do they always get lost in detail? Are there people who exercise leadership or not? Is the mood amongst the partners one of suspicion and lack of trust?

Where confidentiality is not an issue (or at least not a major one), the benefits of bringing in a significant number of participants to the process heavily outweigh the potential disadvantages of doing so. However, having ten, 11 or 12 task forces running at the same time requires good project management skills, and someone to monitor the process, in order to ensure that each task force addresses the correct key issues, and does so within the required timeframe.

When to broaden out discussions to a wider audience

There should be agreement at the first meeting not only as to when to inform the whole of the partnership about the merger discussions, but also when to broaden out communication beyond a core group. Each firm might take a different view on this. If task forces are to be used which involve people from both firms, this will mean telling both partnerships at the same time as task forces are developed. Clarification of this process and timings at the outset avoids misunderstandings later on.

Agreeing whether or not task forces are to be used is best done at the outset, because this decision might influence the timing of the communication to partners. This might be an issue in one firm and not the other. Some firms tend towards a centralisation of activities while others commonly use task forces to work on projects. (There can, of course, be a problem where one firm is much smaller than the other, and the use of task forces would involve a high proportion of partners from the small firm, but this is a specific issue that would require negotiation at the time. There are occasions where task forces are from one firm only, because both parties agree that there is nothing contentious that requires 'thrashing out', and a report on what exists in both firms may be all that is required.)

An ancillary question to all of this, which also needs to be agreed upon in the first meeting is, once the partnership has been informed, the extent to which it should be kept involved in the process. Addleshaw Booth & Co and Theodore Goddard held a number of briefing meetings with their partnerships during the merger discussions. Denton Hall and Wilde Sapte, on the other hand, only told partners about the proposed merger a few days before the vote. Berwin Leighton and Paisner & Co involved the partnerships about half-way through discussions, and proceeded to keep them informed. Neville Eisenberg (previously managing partner of Berwin Leighton) said:

> 'We agreed on what information was to be shared and given out. We gave them lots of time to think about it, and didn't put a lot of pressure on them.'

Aside from the issue of confidentiality (which is what drove Denton Hall and Wilde Sapte to keep their respective partnerships out of the loop until the last minute), our rule of thumb is that it is better to involve the partnerships as soon as is practicable, and to keep them informed at appropriate points throughout the merger discussions. This consultation process should involve face-to-face meetings between the negotiating team and the partnership, not just the circulation of written information.

The information divulged to the partnership should not necessarily include the specific details of issues being agreed upon (eg the exact amount of partner remuneration in the new firm), but should give the partners a sense of what the negotiating group's views on these issues are. In a number of the case studies, the core teams found it very useful to obtain the views of the partners on the main issues of the business case before they finalised the merger proposal. In some of these cases, partners raised issues that, had they not been dealt with at that stage, might have undermined the final proposal. In one merger, some tricky issues about the management structure needed to be worked out. The negotiating teams floated the options (including the advantages and disadvantages of each) to the partnerships at a couple of meetings, listened to the partners' concerns and were able to formulate a proposal that then received the backing of both partnerships. It is questionable whether this would have occurred without the core negotiating teams 'testing the water'.

As Michael Brabner, managing partner of Brabners Chaffe Street, remarked: 'You have to trust people, and generally they are pretty good at keeping the information internal.'

Benefits of having a wide involvement

Paul Lee, senior partner of Addleshaw Goddard, said:

> 'Unless there are very good reasons, it is important to ensure that partners are kept informed along the way. There will be difficult issues to resolve, and it is helpful to get an initial view on them from your partners. People are also usually more positive about things that will affect them if they've had a chance to think them through than where they feel bounced into them.'

This sums up the two major benefits of having a wide involvement of partners where possible (although we reiterate that this is not always appropriate):

(i) It allows the negotiating team to put forward ideas, proposals and options to the partners, and to hear their concerns ahead of the need to commit to a final merger proposal. The final proposals can then be developed with this feedback in mind.

(ii) It provides the partners with time to absorb ideas, to think them through, to ask questions and to come to a decision which, if the process has been handled sensitively, is usually a positive one. People do not like to feel that they are being pushed into an agreement on something important without time for reflection.

There is an additional benefit in widening the involvement in the discussions to include the rest of the partnership, and this is that it tends to 'flush out' those individuals who will be opposed to the merger, no matter what. These individuals tend to divide into two groups:

- In any merger situation, there will be a group of people who will be sceptical, even cynical (Group A). They have an inherent concern about the concept of merger, and, given the choice, would prefer not to do it. However, if they have been consulted by the negotiating team in the manner described above, they should come to see the business logic of the merger, and recognise the overall benefits for their firm (assuming they do exist).

- There can, however, be another group of individuals within a firm who are so fiercely opposed to merger that they will vote against it no matter how strong the business case is (Group B). This group is usually formed of two types of individual. The first type will oppose a merger if it appears to dilute or reduce their own power, position, status and/or influence (either personally or within the firm). The only type of merger to which they will agree is a takeover of another firm, as their position will not be jeopardised by such a merger. The second type is simply opposed to the strategic concept of merger. They tend to see mergers as always producing more negatives than benefits, resulting in failure, diluting the culture of the firm, and creating a firm which is bigger than they feel comfortable with. Some people in this category will realise that a refusal to merge might lead to the firm having to review its strategic goals, but they accept that compromise. Others believe that the firm can achieve its goals without merger.

If the partnership is only given a short period of time between finding out about the merger proposal and voting on it, Group B will be afforded the opportunity to appeal to Group A before the latter has time to think the merger proposal through rationally. As a consequence, Group A may vote against the proposal, not because they are against a merger *per se*, but because of the uncertainty created about it. Whilst a widening out of the discussions at an early stage could also result in Group B lobbying against it, management should have the confidence that the business case for merger would win over Group A. This comes back to the need to have a very strong business case supporting a merger proposal which management is prepared to back.

If there is fierce opposition to a merger, it is better to find this out earlier rather than later. Whether the opposition is rational or not, if management is aware of the feelings of the partnership at an early stage, it will be in a much better position to decide whether or not to proceed with the merger discussions, and, if so, how. Numerous merger talks have taken place based on management's belief that it understood the feelings of the partnership towards the idea, and thought it could obtain a vote in favour of it. The reality proved to be vastly different, and a lot of time, money and effort could have been saved had management brought the partnership into the loop much earlier on. Had it done so, it might have been able to persuade its firm that merger was the best course of action, and, even if not, could have abandoned the discussions much earlier on.

Some years ago, two international firms made at least one serious attempt to merge, but when it came to the vote, one firm voted against it. It was quite clear, in hindsight, that the management of that firm did not have the widespread support of its partnership, and, despite a strong business case for merger, the partnership did not completely trust what was being proposed. Partners had only been given the information a week earlier and what started off as a small opposing group ended up as a majority by the end of the week. Management had no time to counter the negative arguments made by the initial minority, and the mood of the partnership moved to reject the proposal.

When a successful merger can be concluded without a wider involvement

The management of both Denton Hall and Wilde Sapte kept the merger discussions within a tight-knit group until very late in the process. Mark Andrews (previously senior partner of Wilde Sapte) noted:

> 'The single factor that made it easier to do this merger the way we did was that both partnerships, the entire corpus of partners, had already bought into the desirability and the potential of a merger. Both partnerships were ready to go ahead if the right merger partner could be found.'

In the merger between Brabners and Chaffe Street, discussions needed to be kept very contained, and so partners were also told extremely late in the day. The partners of Brabners had, however, already agreed that its firm needed to be in Manchester (which could only come about as a result of a merger with another firm). Furthermore, management felt confident that Chaffe Street was an ideal candidate.

What these case studies show is that a successful merger can be concluded without substantial involvement of the partnership, provided two pre-conditions exist:

(i) the partnership has already agreed that merger is either the only or the best way to further the firm's strategic aims; and

(ii) the firm's strategic objectives are clear, as are the attributes that a merger partner should possess.

A qualification to this, however, is that the 'price' of the merger is not seen by the partnership as too high. By this we mean that issues concerning governance, management structure, profit-sharing and other matters deemed important do not unduly favour the merger partner. This is, of course, something that management needs to bear in mind when negotiating the merger. It could be management's judgement at some point in the discussions that although conditions (i) and (ii) have been met, it needs to consult the partnership well ahead of any vote because it is doubtful that some of the terms being demanded by the prospective merger partner will be accepted.

Composition of the negotiating team

The composition of the core negotiating team is a critical issue from two viewpoints - that of the firm itself and that of the prospective merger partner. No matter whether or not the discussions are broadened out to involve a wider audience, at the end of the day, it is the negotiating team that has to present the merger proposal to the partnership for it to vote on (or has to recommend or decide not to proceed with the merger discussions).

It is therefore important that the members of this team are people whom the partnership respects and whose judgement it trusts. Similarly, the prospective merger partner needs to feel confident that the people with whom it is negotiating carry the necessary authority to present a merger proposal to the partnership that will be accepted as the best possible deal that could have been negotiated. What must be avoided is the situation where the partnership regards the negotiating team as a conduit between it and the other side. If it does, it is likely to seek constant amendments to the issues that the negotiators have agreed upon, or alternatively, it will expect all major issues to be discussed with it before they can be agreed upon by the negotiating team.

Management involvement

For these reasons, some firms believe that negotiations should only be carried out by their management team (or a few members of it). Other firms prefer management to stay out of the negotiation process, and to concentrate on managing the firm, and instead, to appoint other, well-respected partners who have a strong overall understanding of their firm as the negotiators. In the latter situation, management still needs to work closely with the negotiating team. It would not be wise for a merger proposal to be presented to the partners that the firm's appointed management is not then prepared to back. Whilst this does create the need for an extra layer of internal discussion and interaction, it means that there is no risk of the day-to-day management of the firm suffering due to key figures being tied up with intensive merger discussions. The alternative, of course, is to have a mixture of members of management and partners without management responsibility involved in the negotiations.

In a firm of up to around 20 partners, the negotiations will almost certainly need to be conducted by management, as otherwise too high a proportion of the partnership would be involved.

The issue of whether or not to involve management is more one for larger firms to consider. In bigger firms, the management team tends to have a relatively full workload, and tying it up in merger discussions over an intensive two-month period might have an adverse impact on the firm's performance over that critical time.[3]

Criteria of the negotiators

Whatever the composition of the negotiating team, it is important that the people involved meet three criteria. The members of the negotiating teams of all successful mergers have possessed these qualities. They are:

(i)   to be respected by the partnership and trusted to put together a deal that is in the firm's best interests;

(ii)   to have a strong sense and understanding of the firm's strategic goals, both at the firm-wide and practice group level, so that they are able to exercise their judgement on the business issues effectively in the merger discussions; and

(iii)   to have an acute understanding of the dynamics of their partnership and its 'culture' so that they are able to assess what might and might not be acceptable to their partners in a merger deal.

In all of our case studies, the negotiating teams were made up of people from central management. Berwin Leighton Paisner's negotiations were handled by

---

3 Critical because a firm does not want to face declining performance levels in the run-up to a merger. Such a decline might not only influence the proposed profit-sharing arrangements of the new firm, but also lead to second thoughts by the other side about going ahead with the merger discussions.

management of both antecedent firms, with other partners becoming involved later on to deal with the integration issues. In the merger to form Denton Wilde Sapte, both firms also used central management as the negotiators (primarily for reasons of confidentiality, as discussed earlier). Central management was also used in the merger to create Addleshaw Goddard. Addleshaw Booth & Co fielded its senior partner (Paul Lee), its managing partner (Mark Jones) and its finance director. Theodore Goddard was represented by its senior partner (Paddy Grafton Green), its finance director and another board member.

Of the smaller firm mergers, ASB Law was put together mainly by the managing partners of the three antecedent firms. Similarly, in the mergers to form Blake Lapthorn Linnell, Brabners Chaffe Street, Kidd Rapinet, TLT Solicitors and William Sturges, the negotiations were all predominantly conducted by core management personnel.

Hence, whilst it is logically possible to separate the negotiating team from management, no firm in our case studies did so. Jonathan Lloyd-Jones (previously senior partner of Linnells) noted that:

'I kept partners informed throughout the process but I was the main negotiator on our side. Our partners were comfortable with this as they had seen that management was prepared to say "no" in the past. We wouldn't simply take any firm on board, and they knew we wouldn't take them down a path that was inconsistent with our strategy.'

In other words, the partners at Linnells trusted management to negotiate a deal that was in the interests of the firm as a whole.

Paul Lee gave another reason as to why his firm fielded its two most senior executives:

'The deal with Theodore Goddard was fundamental to our strategy, and we placed the highest importance on getting it done. Mark Jones and I both felt that we had to take full responsibility for its success or failure. In addition, we felt it would make for far more effective negotiations because we could agree upon many issues knowing that the rest of the management team, and the partnership, would not have a problem with them. Anyone else would have had to refer a number of issues back to management, and we didn't want that sort of delay.'

While all firms in our case studies used the same approach, we contend that there is no single correct way to carry out merger discussions, provided some key principles are met. In our view, it does not matter whether the negotiating team is from central management or not, provided it meets the criteria set out on page 88. In practice, a central management team should meet these criteria (unless the members are very new to their roles) and, provided the operational management of the firm is not undermined, it is likely to be the first choice to carry out the negotiations. In the event that the negotiating team includes people outside management roles, it will not matter, provided they also meet the criteria.

Initial 'chemistry'

Another reason why central management tends to be the main player in the negotiations is that the preliminary discussions leading up to the serious merger talks will almost always be conducted by members of it. Given that some rapport will have been established in these meetings (and, if not, it is unlikely that merger discussions would have got this far), it is often thought best not to jeopardise that relationship by passing the negotiations over to others.

There is undoubtedly some truth in this. The initial 'chemistry' between those involved in the early meetings should be preserved at all costs. Therefore, if a firm does not want its senior management to be caught up in intensive merger discussions, it needs to structure the early meetings to reflect this. Whilst senior management should be present at the early discussions stage in order to give the proceedings legitimacy, it should ensure that the focus at those meetings is on those people who will be driving the negotiating process forward.

Confidentiality agreements

The issue of confidentiality agreements is relatively straightforward. Merger discussions will require each side to exchange some very detailed and important information. In addition, firms will need to discuss some particularly sensitive internal issues that would not normally be discussed outside the firm (eg problem partners, professional negligence claims, etc).

A view held by some is that if two firms need to provide each other with confidentiality agreements then there is insufficient trust between them from the outset, and therefore that a merger is either unlikely to happen, or, if it does happen, will result in ongoing tensions.

The opposing view is that a negotiating team has a duty of trust to the other partners, and to not exchange confidentiality agreements would be irresponsible, no matter who the other firm might be. A partner who had been through a difficult series of merger discussions that eventually failed said:

'You have to be very frank with each other, and some of the issues discussed are things no one outside the firm knows. When merger discussions fail, there can be tension between the parties, and you don't want to have to wonder what might become of the information you've given them.'

Another partner commented:

'You can agree to give everything back, but what information might they have copied before that? And what about the confidential issues that were discussed? You must have written agreements no matter how well you trust them at the outset.'

Denton Hall and Wilde Sapte did not put confidentiality agreements in place. Virginia Glastonbury (previously deputy managing partner of Denton Hall) remarked: 'I think we had an understanding that, if it didn't work, we would give everything back.' Mark Andrews (previously senior partner of Wilde Sapte) went further:

'The lack of agreements was a consequence of the fact that, from day one, we were all convinced it was going to happen. The early evaluation was done quickly, and it looked such a good fit that we just got on with it.'

Addleshaw Booth & Co and Theodore Goddard had relatively straightforward confidentiality agreements in place from the outset, as did Trumps and Lawrence Tucketts. These agreements simply provided that any information that passed between the two sides was to remain confidential. The agreements also stipulated that certain information could not be shared with people outside of the negotiating team without approval from the other side.

The view that exchanging confidentiality agreements indicates a lack of trust between the parties that could jeopardise a merger's success, was dismissed by a number of people on the grounds that if firms do not know each well at the outset, no trust will be established. Mark Jones, managing partner of Addleshaw Goddard, remarked that:

'Confidentiality agreements are a sign of commercial good sense more than anything else. In addition, they just remind everyone of the confidential nature of the process, something which can "slip out of sight" during intensive negotiations.'

On balance, the general consensus is to put confidentiality agreements in place, albeit simple ones covering all the information to be exchanged (both written and oral), providing for the return of any documentation exchanged should the deal not proceed, and specifying whether or not certain information is to be withheld from the rest of the firm.

Potential deal-breakers

In-depth merger discussions occur in two phases. The first is where both parties are still uncertain as to whether or not a deal really does exist, no matter how good the preliminary discussions might have been (Phase 1). The second phase is where a deal is 'on the table', although there are still a few issues that need to be resolved (Phase 2). As we noted earlier in this chapter, there is a turning point that occurs between Phase 1 and Phase 2 at which the firms will realise whether or not the merger almost certainly will or will not happen. Whilst the timing of the transition from Phase 1 to 2 cannot be planned, it is possible for firms to identify in advance the indicators that mark this transition, and this should be done at the first meeting.

These indicators are usually of two types:

(i)   Issues that are deal-breakers or are not negotiable. The new firm's name, the partner compensation system, aspects of the management structure, and the handling of certain liabilities, are areas that can contain deal-breaking elements.

(ii) Issues that are not deal-breakers, but are important enough to warrant serious thought and discussion. This second type is often not given the respect it deserves. In general, firms think that if the deal-breaking issues are resolved, then the deal is done. What can happen, however, is that on a range of other issues, including systems, technology, people, billing arrangements, etc, one firm will insist on having its approach taken forward into the new firm. The other side can then start to feel that it is being taken over, not merging. It is therefore often the way in which a firm handles these issues that can become the deal-breaker, not the issues themselves.

Identifying the issues that fall into these two categories in advance not only allows the parties to visualise the transition of the discussions from Phase 1 to Phase 2, but it also provides a sensible agenda of points to be discussed in-depth. It is important to tackle these issues during the earlier meetings, as there is little point in spending weeks resolving the less important issues only to have the deal collapse as the parties cannot resolve an issue that they had earlier identified as a potential deal-breaker or a serious point for discussion. We discuss this further in **Chapter 6**.

An example of the first category is the name of the new firm. For one firm, not having its name in the merged firm's name will be considered a deal-breaker, even if that firm is much smaller than its potential merger partner. On the other hand, another firm might feel that the firm's name is a negotiable issue. For instance, it might only be concerned about the length of time its name remains in the new firm's name. It might, for example, want it to be there for at least two years. In this situation, the name of the firm is an issue that falls into the second category.

The most common issues that are deal-breakers (under either category) are governance and management, profit-sharing, liabilities, professional negligence claims, potential departing partners, premises, client conflicts, substantial merger costs that outweigh the benefits, and the name of the merged firm. Another issue that crops up from time to time is whether all the practice groups of both firms will be brought into the merged firm. We discuss these issues and how they might be resolved in more detail in **Chapter 6**. The point to make here, however, is twofold. First, it is better to start the merger discussions knowing what each firm's particular sensitive issues are. Secondly, by identifying the issues at the outset, the firms then have an agenda of things that should be discussed at the subsequent meetings as they will be issues that need to be resolved reasonably early on.

An important factor influencing how the potential deal-breakers will be handled is the strength of the business case for merger. It is not unusual to find that once this is developed in full, and both parties recognise the extent of the benefits, issues that were once regarded as potential deal-breakers can actually become more easily negotiable. It is important not to assume that the business case will have been fully developed in the preliminary discussions, and that the in-depth discussions will only deal with how to achieve the merger, as this will rarely be the case. However, it is generally true that the more superficial the business case at the first meeting when the potential deal-breakers are identified, the more likely it is that those issues will prove to be insurmountable. Conversely, the stronger the business case in the early discussions stage, the more likely it is that both sides will be able to resolve the difficult issues. Paul Lee (who was involved with the merger of Addleshaw Sons & Latham and Booth & Co, and subsequently Addleshaw Booth & Co and Theodore Goddard) noted:

> 'The business case for doing both of our mergers was so compelling to both parties that we knew we had to find a solution to everything else. And we did!'

Hence, firms should not leave the first meeting without making clear what the potential deal-breakers are, and without deciding how the business case that was discussed in outline at the initial discussions will be further developed.

Finally, some discussion should take place in the first meeting about how the parties will resolve deal-breakers that do appear to have become critical issues. If both parties see the benefits of a merger from the business case perspective, it is important that all efforts be made to resolve those issues. Firms might therefore want to consider the need to retain outside advisers. Denton Hall and Wilde Sapte had a consultant on hand in case problems emerged, and other firms have done the same. Whilst intelligent and logical thinking on the part of the firm will resolve many issues, some problems may require the involvement of a third party who has different skills and experience, is completely objective, and who can help to reach a solution that is acceptable to both sides, and one which the negotiating parties would never have been able to achieve on their own. We deal with the involvement of outside advisers in more detail in **Chapter 5**.

Exchange of initial information

At the first meeting, it is also important for the parties to agree on what information will be exchanged at the initial stages at least. We say initially because, if the discussions proceed, an enormous amount of information will need to be exchanged and reviewed. There is, however, some that, if not already exchanged in the preliminary discussions, should be exchanged prior to the first in-depth negotiations meeting. This information is listed below (see box).

At this stage, most of the information should be in summary form but should contain sufficient detail to allow the other party to identify the areas that it may wish to explore further.

Sometimes firms are not keen to exchange all of this information, particularly given the sensitive nature of a lot of it, until they are sure that the business issues have been addressed, and that a strong case for merger exists. If this is the case, the firms should still exchange items (i) to (vii), with the rest to follow once it is agreed that the merger has a strong business case underpinning it.

Exchanging this information in advance results in more productive meetings at which the participants can explore and identify the key issues. It also facilitates the exploring of various options and addressing of problems. If this information is not exchanged in advance, the meetings can become rather tedious, with each side explaining its structures, policies, systems and approaches, rather than getting to grips

Initial information

(i) A summary of the firm's strategic objectives and strategy, detailing any particular focus on client types, practice areas, industries and locations.

(ii) A discussion on how the firm considers the merger will help it to achieve those objectives (or assist it in achieving significantly enhanced strategic objectives).

(iii) Summary information on the firm's core clients (eg top 50 or 100 in terms of revenue and profit generation (the number depending on the size of the firm)) over a three-year period, preferably to include:

- the name of each client and the revenue generated (broken down by each main practice area or work type) in each of the last three years;

- the relative percentages of revenue and absolute amount generated by these clients in groups of ten (ranked by total revenue) eg clients 1 to 10, 11 to 20, 21 to 30, etc;

- some assessment of the profitability generated by each core client, if possible; and

- explanations of any material changes in revenue and profitability of a core client over the three-year period.

(iv) Identification of clients whose work might be gained or lost due to the merger, and of new clients that might be secured as a result of the merger (usually existing target clients).

(v) A breakdown of each practice area in the firm, including the names of the existing staff and the types of work done in that practice area. Where possible, provide revenue percentages for each work type.

(vi) The economics for the last three years for the firm in total and for each business unit (be it a department or practice area). Where the firm has multiple offices, an office-by-office breakdown of this information will also be required. (See **Appendix 2** for a pro forma as to how this information can be presented.)

(vii) Identification of parts of the firm that will not/might not be part of the merged firm.

(viii) A summary explanation of the firm's governance and management structure, along with a description of the roles within the structure, and the decision-making process employed (ie who decides what).

(ix) A summary of the partner remuneration system, along with a table indicating the number of partners at each level of income for each of the previous three years.

(x) A summary of the firm's balance sheet highlighting any particular areas (especially in terms of liabilities) that will require discussion.

(xi) An explanation of the capital requirements of partners, plus the firm's policy on retained earnings, distributions and external funding.

(xii) Details of the partnership structure (equity, fixed share, junior, salaried, etc), the difference between each category (with reference to earnings, capital, voting rights, etc), the names of the partners in each category (along with their age and length of time as a partner), and projected changes in the partnership structure at each level over the next three years (ie new entrants, retirements, etc).

(xiii) Summary information about the firm's partnership deed, highlighting areas that might require discussion.

(xiv) Outline details of the firm's technology platform and systems, along with existing upgrade plans.

(xv) A summary of the lease provisions in respect of the firm's existing premises, including annual lease costs, and length of time remaining on the lease and break clauses.

(xvi) Summary of existing negligence claims.

(xvii) Summary of any contingent or unfunded liabilities.

(xviii) Summary of payments to, and/or arrangements with, retired partners and their families.

with the real issues that need to be addressed in bringing them together through a merger.

Other items on the agenda of the first meeting

Two further issues should be addressed before the firms launch into serious merger discussions. One is the use (or not) of outside advisers, which we deal with in **Chapter 5**. The other is the agenda for future meetings, which is dealt with in **Chapter 6**.

Conclusion

There is therefore quite a lot of discussion and planning required in this first meeting (which may, in fact, run over several sessions). We often find that, having decided to enter into serious merger discussions, both sides want to get their teeth stuck into the meaty topics from the outset. Our advice is always to hold back initially, and to spend some time planning the process. In our experience, there is absolutely no doubt that by so doing, the firms will achieve more effective, efficient and productive results further down the line (even if a decision to abort the discussions is taken). Good preparation is a crucial aspect of effective discussions.

CHAPTER 5: IN-DEPTH MERGER DISCUSSIONS – THE USE OF ADVISERS

There are five types of adviser that are commonly used in law firm mergers:

(i) accountants;

(ii) merger search consultants;

(iii) public relations consultants;

(iv) marketing consultants; and

(v) strategic advisers.

In many cases, a single adviser might carry out more than one of these roles. Accountants, whose primary task is the financial due diligence, can play the role of strategic adviser as well at times. For example, the merger partners for TLT Solicitors used a Big Four accountancy firm as their strategic adviser, and used an independent accountant (ie independent to both antecedent firms) for the financial due diligence.

Most mergers involve accountants, given the need for the thorough financial due diligence exercise. Some firms agree that their respective auditors will review the other firm, and will both report to the core negotiating group. Other firms decide to use independent accountants.

Merger search consultants ascertain one firm's merger partner criteria, and then seek out firms which meet that criteria. The role of merger search consultants can also be fulfilled by strategic advisers, who will advise on the overall merger candidate as well as the merger process. Some merger search consultants also act as facilitators during the negotiations. This was the case in the merger between William Sturges & Co and Chethams.

Strategic advisers often play several roles. They are usually involved in the development of strategy in one firm that leads to the consideration of merger. They also assist in finding candidates that meet the merger criteria (provided they have knowledge of the legal market). They can also play a key facilitation and project management role throughout the merger negotiations, not unlike the role of advisers from investment banks in corporate mergers.

In **Chapter 4**, we noted that the use (or not) of advisers should be discussed at the first meeting of the in-depth merger talks. This discussion should cover whether either side will be using advisers and, if so, who. The parties should also consider whether each side should use separate advisers or whether one adviser only should be instructed to effectively advise the potential 'new' firm. Whilst most, if not all, merger participants will instruct accountants at some stage, there is a wide variance of opinion (and practice) about the use of other types of advisers, which we discuss in further detail below.

Use of advisers in the case studies

Table 5.1 below summarises the use made of advisers by the 19 firms in our case studies.

As can be seen, by far the most extensively used advisers by the firms in our case studies were accountants (13 firms used them). Five firms used merger search consultants. As noted in earlier chapters, some firms knew each other quite well already and, when they decided that they should consider a merger, saw the other firm as a logical candidate, so did not appoint merger consultants. Six firms in our case studies used strategic advisers. Two of the firms instructed the same individual to be their strategic adviser and their merger search consultant. Denton Wilde Sapte had a strategic adviser 'on stand-by', but they were never actually consulted. The strategic adviser to Theodore Goddard was also appointed to assist the negotiations on behalf of the potential 'new' firm. PR consultants were used in only one of our case studies (with each firm using its own), although other firms in the case studies may have used them post-merger. One firm used marketing consultants to look at the branding of the 'new' firm.

The implication of this is that, whilst a law firm might be capable of negotiating its own merger, it will generally require outside assistance with regard to financial issues (although even these can be dealt with by the in-house accountants, as was the case with Kidd Rapinet). Advisers, who can bring objectivity to the merger exercise, are not used particularly extensively, unlike in the market for corporate M&A deals.

Christopher Honeyman Brown (chief executive of ASB Law) has a strong view about outside advisers:

5. In-depth merger discussions – the use of advisers

Table 5.1: Use of advisers in the case studies

	Accountants	Merger search consultants	PR consultants	Marketing consultants	Strategic advisers
• Addleshaw Goddard					✔ *
Addleshaw Booth & Co	✔	✔	✔		
Theodore Goddard	✔	✔	✔		✔ **
• ASB Law					
Argles & Court					
Burstows					✔
Stoneham					
• Berwin Leighton Paisner					
Berwin Leighton	✔				
Paisner & Co	✔				
• Blake Lapthorn Linnell					
Blake Lapthorn	✔				
Linnells	✔	✔			
• Brabners Chaffe Street					
Brabners					
Chaffe Street					
• Denton Wilde Sapte					✔
Denton Hall	✔				
Wilde Sapte	✔				
• Kidd Rapinet					
Kidd Rapinet					
Steggles Palmer		✔			
• TLT Solicitors	✔			✔	✔
Trumps	✔				
Lawrence Tucketts	✔				
• William Sturges & Co					
William Sturges & Co	✔				
Chethams	✔	✔			✔ **
	13	5	2	1	6

NB Where a tick is placed next to the name of the merged firm, it means that the adviser was instructed by both sides on behalf of the potential 'new' firm.

* Same strategic adviser as that used by Theodore Goddard.

** Same individual as the firm's merger search consultant.

> 'Consultants are worthless. They have never managed a law firm and, in that regard, bring very little to the process.'

This is not a view supported by other key figures from firms used in the case studies (even those which only instructed accountants). Paddy Grafton Green (previously senior partner of Theodore Goddard) noted:

> 'We had been though merger discussions previously without using strategic advisers, and there is no doubt that their assistance this time added a lot of value to the process. They project-managed the merger, and assisted in unlocking some issues that were quite complex.'

Mark Jones (previously managing partner of Addleshaw Booth & Co) added:

> 'We had used Theodore Goddard's adviser previously, and liked him a lot, so we agreed to use him to assist the overall process.'

Paul Lee (senior partner of Addleshaw Goddard) said:

> 'Lawyers should follow their own advice to clients. An external adviser can play a hugely valuable role because of the objectivity they bring to the process, but they must have plenty of experience in advising law firms, and have real expertise in what they do.'

Although Denton Wilde Sapte did not need to consult its strategic adviser in the end, partner Virginia Glastonbury was of the view that they can be useful: 'Sometimes it can be quite handy to have someone from the outside.'

Neville Eisenberg, managing partner of Berwin Leighton Paisner, said that his firm's decision not to use external advice was not because the firms did not think they had anything to offer, but because the merger was relatively straightforward, and therefore the issues were able to be managed in-house.

Colin Butler (formerly of Steggles Palmer) supports the view that outside advisers can bring a level of objectivity to the discussions: 'The adviser was extremely helpful to us with financial and other advice.' This view was also shared by Michael Franks (formerly of Chethams):

> 'The useful thing about an adviser is that they are someone with whom you can discuss issues without the fear of getting into a negotiating position with the other side from which you can't recover.'

It was also echoed by Ian Gavin-Brown (previously senior partner of William Sturges & Co) and Robert Bourns (previously managing partner of Trumps).

One type of adviser that only one firm in our case studies mentioned is a specialist integration consultant. As we discuss in **Chapter 8**, integration post-merger is one of the less effective areas in law firm mergers. The skills required to achieve integration across a wide range of activities are different to those required to manage effectively, and certainly different to those of a lawyer. Specialist advisers in this area do exist, and firms involved in larger mergers should at least consider using them. Addleshaw Goddard believes it received significant value from the use of an integration specialist, and achieved a very high level of integration within a relatively short period of time.

Use of accountants

There is little dispute amongst most law firms which have been through a merger that accountants are needed in order to carry out the financial due diligence on the other firm, and to provide a letter of comfort with regard to the accounts. Sometimes, the letter of comfort is prepared by the accountants of one firm in respect of the other. Other times, each firm's accountants prepare it with regard to their usual client. Jonathan Lloyd-Jones (partner of Blake Lapthorn Linnell) reiterated this:

> 'Each side used independent financial advisers other than the auditors of both firms. We wanted to make sure there were no black holes in the accounts.'

Whether or not a law firm's existing auditors or a different accounting firm is used depends on the particular transaction. Addleshaw Booth & Co used its own auditors, whereas Theodore Goddard decided to use an independent accounting firm which had more experience of merger situations. Sometimes partners derive greater comfort if the financial report on their potential merger partner is produced by an accountancy firm that is not the auditor of the latter. For others, the existing auditors of the potential merger partner will be acceptable.

If accountants are not used, it is usually because a smaller firm has approached a larger firm with the merger proposal, and the latter believes that it has sufficient in-house resources to assess the financial position of the smaller firm. In this situation, the smaller firm often just relies on the financial accounts given to it by the larger firm rather than instructing an accountant. This was the case with Brabners and Chaffe Street, and with Kidd Rapinet and Steggles Palmer. We are of the view, however, that smaller firms should always obtain an independent financial report on their prospective merger partner.

There is no question that the issue of financial due diligence is one of great importance. Merging with a firm that has financial weaknesses, either in the generation of profit or on its balance sheet (or both), is something to be avoided. Merger integration is difficult enough without having to cope with financial problems as well.

Each party to a merger should receive a detailed financial report on the other firm, preferably covering the previous three years, and containing an analysis of the profit generated over that period, and an analysis of the firm's assets and liabilities. This report should be prepared while the merger negotiations are proceeding and, ideally, be available at least halfway through the process.

Whether a firm should accept a financial report prepared by the other side's in-house accounting team is a difficult one. On the one hand, to refuse might imply a lack of trust (which is the view taken by some firms that have accepted such a report). On the other hand, a decision to merge is (almost) irreversible, and such an important step should only be made based on objective evidence. Whilst the in-house team might be as objective as an external accountant, there is always a risk that the in-house accountant will make certain assumptions that an external accountant would query or even challenge. Given that the financial report is being presented to the partners of the other firm (at least in summary form), it is more prudent to ask an external accountant to prepare it.

Use of merger search consultants

There was not the same level of agreement about the use of merger search consultants amongst the participants in our case studies.

Linnells used one and was happy with the value it brought to the search process. Although it did not instruct one, Blake Lapthorn agreed that merger search consultants could be of use. Steggles Palmer and Chethams both employed a merger search consultant, and expressed satisfaction with them.

Breadth of search for candidates

Whether or not to instruct a merger search consultant depends, to a large extent, on the breadth of the search for a merger candidate. The more narrow the criteria that a firm has identified for its potential merger partner, the more likely it is that only a few candidates will be suitable, in which case there will be less of a need to use a merger search consultant. This would, of course, not be the case if the firm initiating the search was seeking a merger partner in a different region to its own where it had limited market knowledge. In such a case, merger search consultants could prove useful.

Berwin Leighton did not instruct a consultant to assist with the merger search. It had a clear profile of the type of firm it considered to be a suitable merger partner, and wanted that candidate to be situated in London. As Neville Eisenberg, managing partner of Berwin Leighton Paisner, remarked:

> 'We knew all of the firms on our list quite well. We knew Paisner & Co very well as there had been interaction between the two firms previously. I also chatted with Harold Paisner from time to time.'

As we discussed in **Chapter 3**, the merger to form Denton Wilde Sapte arose out of a dinner discussion between James Dallas (then chairman of Denton Hall) and Mark Andrews (then senior partner of Wilde Sapte). Andrews said:

> 'City firms already know a lot about each other. We are often on the same deals, and you meet up with the management of other firms at various activities.'

Steggles Palmer used a consultant to approach Kidd Rapinet, and the merged firm said that, should it decide to seek a new merger partner, it would use a consultant again. Chethams approached William Sturges & Co through a merger search consultant, and both sides found that this added value to the merger process. Trumps and Lawrence Tucketts, however, knew each other already, as did Argles & Court, Stoneham and Burstows, and therefore none of them instructed a consultant to assist in the search.

Chethams, Steggles Palmer and Linnells identified a fairly broad market place within which to find a merger partner. Chethams was looking to merge with a firm from the West End of London, which, whilst geographically narrow, contained a large number of smaller commercial firms. Linnells was looking outside its home territory of Oxford, and lacked detailed knowledge of potential merger partners. Steggles Palmer had a clear idea of the type of firm that would make a suitable merger candidate but, like Linnells, the geographical area it was searching in was wide.

In the event that a firm decides that it wishes to use a consultant to assist with the search for a merger partner, it must be clear as to the type of adviser it is seeking. One choice, as we noted above, is between a merger search consultant who is a 'search specialist' and a strategic adviser who advises on potential merger candidates as a secondary aspect of their role.

Merger search specialists are, in most cases, also involved in recruitment and/or head hunting. Their specialist skill is searching for people, be it individuals, groups or firms. One risk with specialist merger search consultants is that they are not trained in strategy nor in giving strategic advice. Given that a merger must be seen as a strategic implementation step, it is quite important that the consultants have a level of capability in order to be able to interpret the depth of the strategic requirement of a client. There are some merger search consultants who lack the skill and, when asked to find a merger candidate, produce firms with only a superficial match to the criteria required of a merger partner.

This is one reason why many firms turn to strategic advisers, who work extensively in the legal market, when they start searching out merger candidates. In some cases, the merger search follows on from a strategic review, and the strategic advisers to the review are well placed to interpret accurately the requirements of a merger candidate. In other cases, their knowledge of the market is usually as comprehensive as that of the specialist search firms (given that to advise on strategy, an adviser must know and understand the market), and they tend to take a more strategic approach to identifying potential candidates. In addition, the better strategic advisers will also have very strong facilitation skills as these are an essential part of working with a law firm in developing a strategy. These facilitation skills can be invaluable throughout the negotiating process. Strategic advisers also require skills in structures, systems and processes, and their input and facilitation during the due diligence process can also be of high value.

To summarise, if there is likely to be a significant number of potentially suitable firms, and/or the location in which the search firm[1] is looking is other than its home market, the use of a consultant in the merger search can provide value. Addleshaw Goddard is a very good example of both of these points. Both antecedent firms used advisers to assist them in finding a merger partner. Addleshaw Booth & Co had a clear profile of the type of firm it was looking to merge with but, nevertheless, had 68 firms on its initial list, which was then reduced to a shortlist of 17. Given that it was seeking a London merger, this was hardly surprising. Theodore Goddard also had a clear set of characteristics that it was looking for in candidates, but with the additional complexity of considering firms from the US as well as the UK. When it applied its initial set of objective criteria, it came up with a list of 70 firms. This was then reduced, after several further analyses, to a shortlist of nine firms. Where a large number of candidates

---

1 We use the term 'search firm' to denote the firm actively seeking a merger partner (not a consultancy that specialises in search, be it for individuals or firms).

appear to possess the broad set of characteristics of a potential merger partner, a reasonable-sized firm could carry out the initial search process without external help. However, a good consultant will already have accumulated a considerable amount of information about many of the candidates, which the in-house teams might find hard to gather, and this can assist in bringing the list down to a group of candidates which are more likely than others to be 'real' candidates.

Objectivity

Consultants can also bring objectivity to the search for a merger partner. Some firms often have misconceptions about other firms (usually based on a one-off experience or event, or even gossip). In one situation of which we are aware, a potential merger partner was initially rejected because a senior partner at the search firm had failed to get a job as an associate there some 25 years earlier.[2] After considerable thought, merger discussions were eventually initiated between the firms, and a merger was successfully concluded. Other partners have raised objections to potential merger partners based on what they considered to be 'bad behaviour' on the part of the other firm that they witnessed while acting on the other side to it. Completely spurious reasons have also been given, based on no evidence at all. Merger search consultants can often help to counter many of these knee-jerk reactions.

Theodore Goddard, for example, initially wanted to merge with a firm based in London (if the merger was to be with a UK rather than a US firm). When Addleshaw Booth & Co emerged as the most suitable candidate, there was some initial scepticism within Theodore Goddard, primarily because most of Addleshaw Booth & Co's lawyers were based outside London. The adviser was, however, able to demonstrate to Theodore Goddard why this actually helped to make the firm such a good fit. As Paddy Grafton Green (previously senior partner of Theodore Goddard) admitted post-merger, he knew 'absolutely nothing' about Addleshaw Booth & Co, and the firm would not have even made Theodore Goddard's shortlist if a merger search consultant had not been involved.

Identification of essential characteristics

Another way that consultants can add value is by helping the search firm to identify the essential characteristics that a potential merger partner should possess. As we discussed in **Chapter 3**, this part of the process is vital.

---

2 Although this was not the reason given for the rejection at the time, it emerged as the reason at a later date.

Search firms that identify criteria such as good corporate, finance, commercial and real estate capabilities, and being based in London, will end up with a shortlist of 500 firms or more. The profile of the target merger partner needs to be much more precise, especially where the search is to take place in a large and diverse market such as London. What size should the firm be? What type of work is being done in the broad practice areas? Who are their core clients? What is the likely level of profitability? These are the types of issues that need to be addressed if the initial list of candidates is to be reduced to a manageable size. An expert merger search consultant will force a firm's management to be this precise.

Strategic rationality

A consultant can also provide value by ensuring that there is a level of strategic rationality in the process of identifying a merger partner. Following on from the previous point, one way to do this is to make sure that the search firm identifies quite specific characteristics that it would like a merger partner to possess. The second way is to test out whether:

(a) a merger with a firm with those defined characteristics will help the search firm to achieve its strategic goals and to improve competitiveness; and

(b) the firm possessing those characteristics would consider a merger with the search firm as being in its interests.

This is again where the consultant's expertise, experience and knowledge of the legal market is essential. They can assist management to focus on both these points.

It is not uncommon to find that the search firm's specification of a desired merger partner is significantly out of line with its present market position and strategic objectives. An inherent danger in any merger search is the 'marrying-up syndrome'. This is where one firm wishes to merge with a firm that is actually ahead of it in the marketplace, but the other firm thinks that they are both around the same level. It is also not uncommon to hear partners say that they will only agree to merge if it is with Firm X or Firm Y, both of which are stronger than their own firm. To some extent these views are often based on out-of-date knowledge – partners think that their own firm is on a par with others when, in fact, these others have moved ahead significantly in strategic terms.

Conversely, some firms seeking to achieve specific strategic objectives through merger will only merge with a much smaller firm. However, those with market knowledge will understand that no such firm will actually make much difference to the search firm's strategic position. This was the case in the 1990s when many US firms sought mergers with London firms. The common 'formula' required by US firms for a UK merger partner was a 50 fee-earner firm with strong corporate, finance and litigation practices, and which produced high profits per partner. However, the state of the market at the time meant that this was an impossible request. No firm of that size could have had the strength required in the designated practice areas. Nevertheless, some US firms spent a lot of time and money searching for such a firm. A consultant should be sufficiently familiar with the marketplace to be able to test these issues, and to suggest alternatives, where the initial prescription is impossible.

Resistance to using consultants in the search

Resistance to hiring search consultants comes from the experience of some firms with poor-quality consultants. Some merger search consultants will have firms that are looking for merger candidates 'on their books', and they will act as a matchmaker or broker.

A more strategic approach for a search consultant to take is to:

(a) work more closely with the client in order to ensure that the search criteria identified by it is appropriate;

(b) study the defined market and help it identify all the possible candidates on the basis of the broad criteria; and

(c) produce a shortlist of the most likely candidates by applying more specific criteria.

We noted before that people such as Virginia Glastonbury of Denton Wilde Sapte, and Neville Eisenberg, managing partner of Berwin Leighton Paisner, saw potential value in using search consultants but felt that, as the mergers of their firms were relatively straightforward, a merger search consultant was unlikely to add further value over and above what their in-house teams could provide.

Whilst this is clearly a judgement that management is entitled to make in relation to a specific merger proposal, we do not suggest that this approach should be adopted in most cases. For reasons of objectivity indicated above, we always recommend that two firms contemplating merger should, as part of their own due diligence, bring in a consultant capable of conducting a merger search, at least to review the strategic logic behind the merger proposition. This might only take one or two days but, even if the proposal emerges from this review unscathed, management on both sides can then be more confident about putting it to partners. Some might see this as self-serving, but we can truthfully claim to have altered the thinking of a large number of clients about specific merger proposals with only a couple of days' involvement. As we noted before, the decision to merge is not necessarily irrevocable, but it is a major step, and prudence dictates that all caution should be exercised.

Use of PR consultants

Only two firms in our case studies reported the use of PR consultants. We would, however, always advise firms contemplating merger to appoint a PR consultant at the outset. Whether each firm instructs its own or uses one to advise both is a matter of choice, but a good PR consultant is able to play a valuable role in the communication process.

PR consultants with experience of the legal market can advise firms on how to handle the press, particularly in cases where confidentiality is important, and the press gets wind of the merger discussions at an early stage. As we noted in **Chapter 4**, it is important for a firm to be able to answer any enquiries from journalists in a way that does not cause embarrassment later on. Good PR consultants can assist in managing these communications.

They are also valuable in putting together the form of communication to be made to clients and staff. Getting the right message across to these two groups of people is vital. In general, lawyers are not trained to do so, and we have seen many statements that were drafted by lawyers, and failed to generate any excitement about the merger or create the impression that it was a major step forward for the firm.

PR consultants are also able to coach those within the firm who will be making the communication to staff and clients. Ensuring that they all receive consistent messages, both written and oral, is a critical way of communicating the benefits that the merger offers. Furthermore, drafting the final press statement and planning its release requires expert advice, and should not be left to managing partners or marketing directors.

Use of marketing consultants

Whether or not to use marketing consultants will depend on the nature of the merger. Where the aim of the merger is to expand into new practice areas, client sectors or regions, firms could benefit from some high-quality market research carried out by either a strategic adviser or marketing consultant. Furthermore, interviews with clients to test the reaction to a proposed merger are often best carried out by an external consultant, as both parties to the merger will consider their feedback to be more objective. Other mergers might not require the same degree of 'market-testing' or research, or if they do, such research may have already been carried out as part of a firm's strategic development.[3]

Strategic advisers

Strategic advisers with experience of the legal market are able to fulfil a number of roles, including assisting in the merger search, providing marketing advice, conducting client interviews, advising on the merger negotiations themselves and advising on the due diligence process. They can also play a useful role when discussions about a particular issue appear to be at an impasse. A good example is when the two parties are having trouble agreeing on the profit-sharing arrangements for the 'new' firm. Rather than having the negotiating teams from both firms spending a considerable amount of time trying to resolve the issue (particularly if the lawyers involved do not have the necessary expertise in devising profit-sharing systems), it is better to let the strategic adviser devise a scheme that both firms can agree on, and for the negotiators to move on to other items for discussion. Even if the strategic adviser's proposed scheme does not meet all the concerns of both firms, the fact that it is being proposed by an objective third party rather than one of the parties to the merger can make it more acceptable.

In **Chapter 4** we noted the issues that are commonly seen as deal-breakers (or potential deal-breakers). Some of these, such as governance and management and profit-sharing, are quite sensitive, and can also involve quite complex structures. Whilst lawyers are very capable of coming up with acceptable structures and systems, they might not be the best or most appropriate for the 'new' firm. Governance and management and profit-sharing are quite technical in nature, and are areas in which strategic advisers have expertise. Few lawyers at a senior level will have had training on the technical aspects of these areas, and are unlikely to have had exposure to a wide range of structures and systems.

The critical point here is that when the two sides are negotiating the major issues, the aim is not for the two firms to reach agreement on them, but to devise structures

---

3 Where the marketing advice is strategic rather than operational, firms may want to consider using strategic advisers rather than pure marketing consultants. The issues involved are often wider than just marketing, and strategic advisers are able to cover all aspects of strategy, and the relationship with the proposed markets of the merged firm.

and systems that will be the most suitable for the 'new' firm. Too often we have seen firms agreeing to proposals on major issues which were in fact the second-best option for the 'new' firm. It would have been more beneficial to the 'new' firm if some of those issues had been delegated to a strategic adviser who could start from a blank canvas, and devise the most suitable structures and systems for the merged firm.

Advisers versus in-house

This brings us back to the central issue of whether law firms need advisers to assist them in the merger process, or whether the general skills and experience of partners in law firms are enough to enable everything to be done in-house. On balance, the skills and experience of lawyers have very little to do with the strategic and organisational issues that arise when two law firms are deciding whether or not to merge. In other professions and business in general, advisers tend to be instructed when the transaction is important. For example, some of the past investment bank mergers involved a wide range of advisers (including other investment banks and strategic advisers) even though the investment banks themselves had experience of advising on mergers. Similarly, senior management in major corporate businesses are often experts on company mergers, but it is rare for them not to bring advisers in when the company that is merging is their own (if only to ask them to review management's proposals). Very few large corporate merger proposals will be presented to the board without the strategic logic of them having been tested thoroughly by advisers (either from investment banks, strategic consultancies or both). Corporate management views this as part of the due diligence process.

Why then do so many law firms shy away from following the approach taken by their corporate clients? As we saw in **Table 5.1** above, of the 19 firms involved in the case studies, if each firm had hired its own team of advisers, the maximum number of advisers that could have been hired was 95 (ie five types of adviser per firm). The total actually hired was 26 (or 24 if duplicate advisory roles are eliminated). Of these 26, half were accountants. Anecdotal evidence in the legal market would seem to support this statistic.

As was the case with Denton Wilde Sapte and Berwin Leighton Paisner, there will be mergers that do not appear to present any particular problems, and where the issues that need to be addressed can be handled in-house. As noted above, we still believe that, even in these situations, there is value in having the strategic and organisational proposals vetted by an expert. Our guess is that less than one-third of law firm mergers in recent years involved only in-house advisers.

Most firms use accountants, not just for financial due diligence, but also for wider strategic and organisational advice in connection with a merger. Care should, however, be exercised in doing this. Many accountants have no better training in strategic and organisational matters than most lawyers. Furthermore, the fact that the accountant's own firm has been through a merger is no guarantee that the advice they offer with regard to a law firm merger is any better than the advice that a lawyer whose firm has been through a merger previously could give.

There are accountants who have been trained in strategy, organisational matters and management, as well as accounting, and who are knowledgeable about the legal profession. If an accountant is to be used for more than due diligence, their credentials should be tested carefully.

One reason why law firms may not want to use advisers is a lack of appreciation by the partners of the complexity of many of the issues involved in a merger. As we noted earlier, intelligent people are able to resolve many issues outside their particular area of skill simply by applying analytical logic to a problem. However, whether this is the best solution to the problem in that particular situation is an open question.

The legal profession has only relatively recently realised the need for firms in a highly competitive environment to be properly managed. Whilst many law firms now hold training sessions on strategy and management, and partners are being sent on external courses, few would deny that the concepts and principles behind the issues of strategy and management are still a mystery to them.

Take for example an intelligent and successful person who wishes to buy a residential property or to enter into a relatively straightforward contact. Such a person could review the documentation involved themselves, and could probably do a reasonable job of it. However, there will be technical issues which a layman is unlikely to be aware of, and there are a large number of precedent cases where apparently straightforward matters have later gone wrong, which should suggest to the person that a lawyer should at least review the case.

This, in our opinion, is the crux of the matter. Mergers are a big leap in the dark. No matter what due diligence is carried out, only time will tell if the merger has been successful. Mergers can untangle, and, if integration has been carried out post-merger, this is a very messy and costly process. Far better to take all the expert advice available during the merger process. This will, at least, give management the confidence that its merger is likely to be successful or, if it does not, enable management to call off discussions before it goes any further.

Choosing an adviser

The first, and most fundamental characteristic of an adviser, is that they have the training and expertise in the areas on which they are being asked to advise (eg accountants advising on strategy or on structure). One is seeking more than experience here. Furthermore, advisers should have experience of law firm mergers (as an adviser to them rather than a participant). This latter point is crucial. Whilst someone who has been through a merger will have learnt about the things that must be done, and, possibly, things that should not, it is only a one-off experience. As we have stressed already, there is no single correct way to go about addressing many of the issues that need to be covered. Therefore, whilst people with a one-off experience can tell others about what they did, the advice will usually lack a methodological framework constructed around the principles lying behind the issues.

Advisers of good quality will have the training and expertise which provides a suitable methodological framework, and extensive experience of law firm mergers to enable them to advise on the best way to approach an issue in the context of a specific merger transaction. (The best way in one transaction might be quite different to the best way in another.) As Addleshaw Goddard's senior partner Paul Lee commented:

> 'They must have plenty of experience in advising law firms, and have real expertise in what they do.'

Many of the negative comments about the value advisers can or cannot bring come from people who used an adviser who either lacked the experience and knowledge of the legal profession or the training and expertise in the particular area for which they were hired (or both). Choosing an appropriate consultant is therefore vital.

As we noted earlier, whether a firm requires advice on its search for a merger partner will depend on the circumstances. Where a firm decides to make its own choice about the characteristics that it would like potential merger candidates to possess, it would still be advised to test out that brief with a merger search consultant who has the attributes discussed above. We would also advise firms to instruct accountants and a PR consultant. At a minimum, firms should test the final merger proposal with a strategic adviser at the penultimate draft stage before it goes before the partners. Firms may also find it useful to have a strategic adviser 'on stand-by' during the negotiations (as Denton Wilde Sapte did), in case they need help in resolving any issues that require special skills or attention.

By choosing an appropriate team of advisers, and by managing their involvement efficiently, most merger processes will receive enhanced value. As highlighted by the case studies, there will be some situations where no adviser can add any extra value, but from our widespread experience this is the case in less than a quarter of mergers. At the very minimum, the approach in the Denton Wilde Sapte merger should be followed.

In summary, merger negotiations are not just about two firms reaching agreement on difficult issues but, more importantly, reaching agreement as to what structures and systems are best suited to the 'new' firm, and this can require expertise beyond that of lawyers.

Separate advisers for each firm?

If advisers are to be used, should each firm hire its own, or can one adviser assist both parties? The answer will depend on the role of the adviser.

Accountants

Normally each firm will instruct different accountants to carry out financial due diligence. However, there have been occasions when an accountant with no relationship to either party carried out the due diligence on both sides and produced an overall summary of the two firms' positions.

Merger search consultant

If a merger search consultant is used, it would only be by coincidence if both firms used the same one.

PR consultants

It is feasible for one PR consultant to advise both firms, although again, one of the firms may already be using one, and will prefer to use its own. It is probably a good idea for each firm to have its own because if the merger discussions become public knowledge but then break down, each firm's press release might need to be slightly differently slanted. This will be easier if each side has its own PR consultant.

Marketing consultants

The need for marketing consultants will vary case by case. If it is to do with external perceptions of each firm, then one adviser would be capable of carrying this out. Equally, where it is about the brand image of the new firm, only one adviser is required.

Strategic advisers

There is a view amongst lawyers that if one strategic adviser advises both parties there will be a conflict of interest. This view tends to be based on the fact that, in corporate mergers where one side is looking to take over the other, and to extract maximum value in the negotiating process, both sides clearly cannot be advised by the same strategic adviser.

However, law firm mergers are generally different to corporate mergers. A merger of two firms (even where one is significantly larger than the other) means exactly that – a merger. The intention is to combine the two firms, including the partners (or most of them), to produce a 'new' firm. The merger negotiations are not about one firm gaining an advantage over the other, but about the best way for the two parties to create a 'new' firm. There might be difficult issues such as profit-sharing arrangements to resolve (see **Chapter 6**), but the final agreement has to be one that both sides can live with when they form the 'new' entity.

Therefore, having one strategic adviser advising the potential 'new' firm rather than each party having its own can be hugely advantageous in resolving some of the difficult issues. Whilst the strategic adviser will sometimes need to counsel each side separately, this is usually to ensure that the final proposals provide the 'new' firm with the best chance of success. Where each side has its own strategic adviser, the danger is that there is no one advising the 'new' firm on what is best for it.

What if it becomes clear that the merger is not in the best interests of one of the parties? If there is only one strategic adviser, how do they handle this? The answer is simple – the strategic adviser should tell both parties the truth. Their duty is to the 'new' firm, so if the merger proceeds when it is not in one firm's best interests, there will be serious problems for the 'new' firm post-merger. The strategic adviser might be able to assist the firms in overcoming the problems, in which case the merger can proceed, but if not, it might then be in everyone's best interests to discontinue the discussions.

Hence, it is critical that the negotiations are not seen to be an aggressive point-scoring exercise, but a discussion as to how the two parties can create a new firm that furthers both of the parties' strategic objectives better than any other available option.

Addleshaw Booth & Co and Theodore Goddard used one strategic adviser throughout their discussions (and Addleshaw Sons & Latham and Booth & Co used the same strategic adviser in their 1997 merger). As Paul Lee (previously senior partner of Addleshaw Booth & Co) said:

> 'It was not about one firm scoring points over the other. Even though one firm was bigger than the other, we were seeking to create a 'new' firm that was different to either of the antecedent firms. Having one strategic adviser to the deal meant that someone was keeping their eye on what was being created, not what each side felt it was giving up. It was a huge benefit and I'm not sure we would have been as successful [with the merger] without the strategic adviser.'

There are numerous other examples where using one strategic adviser has facilitated what must be seen as a joint exercise rather than a negotiating battle.

Conclusion

Deciding on which advisers will be used, their role and which parties they are advising are important issues to be discussed at the first meeting of the in-depth merger discussions. The subsequent talks will flow more smoothly, and will be more productive, where these issues are out of the way before the serious discussions start. As we noted above, advisers with technical expertise in their area along with considerable experience in both the legal profession and law firm mergers, have the potential to add value. Our experience is that they do so in the majority of mergers. Other professions and businessmen are less shy about taking expert advice when they acquire and merge, and it is our view that lawyers are well advised to behave likewise.

Chapter 6: In-depth merger discussions – strategy and structure for the 'new' firm

In **Chapter 4** we noted that, whilst individual merger discussions might throw up other specific problems, from our experience, and those of the firms involved in the case studies, the most common issues that can become deal-breakers are:

- the business case;

- governance and management;

- capital structure;

- profitability and partner profit-sharing;

- liabilities;

- professional negligence claims;

- potential departing partners;

- premises issues;

- client conflicts;

- substantial merger costs that outweigh the benefits; and

- the name of the 'new' firm.

Apart from those listed above, there are many other issues that will require discussion and agreement before a merger can go ahead. We do not intend to discuss all of these in detail as many are self-explanatory.

We also noted in **Chapter 4** that there are two types of deal-breaking issues:

(i) issues that are non-negotiable; and

(ii) issues that are negotiable, but only up to a certain point, beyond which they then become deal-breakers.

As discussed in **Chapter 5**, when it comes to resolving the difficult issues, strategic advisers can play an important role. As an outsider, they are often better placed to see the impact that one party may be having on the other, and to counsel one side, or both, about the consequences of that behaviour. Furthermore, they can help to facilitate a discussion about a difficult issue so that it is resolved, and does not become an impasse.

In this chapter and in **Chapter 7**, we discuss the critical deal-breaking issues that tend to arise in every merger. We discuss the types of problems that generally occur in relation to them, and the ways to positively resolve them. This is not, and cannot be, an exhaustive list as each merger will throw up issues that are specific to the circumstances of the firms involved. However, by demonstrating the way in which some problems can be resolved, we will hopefully show how firms can address other problems that are not specifically dealt with in this book.

The secret in turning deal-stoppers into manageable issues around which agreement can be reached, lies in three critical principles that need to be at the forefront of the minds of all those involved in the negotiations.

Critical principles for a successful merger

The three critical principles that should underpin the discussions if they are to lead to the conclusion of an effective and successful merger are:[1]

(i) To ensure that the business case supporting the merger is developed rigorously, and incorporates a strategy for the 'new' firm that has a high probability of success given competitive trends in the marketplace, then to conduct all discussions in the context of what is best to achieve the business case.

---

1 Even if a merger turns out not to be the best interests of one or both parties, by adopting these principles, the parties will come to that conclusion much quicker.

(ii) To be generous in negotiations, and to ensure that decisions are made based on what is best for the 'new' firm, rather than degenerating into a 'point-scoring' exercise or adopting a rigid formulaic approach to resolving issues.

(iii) To have a dual attitude throughout discussions – on the one hand, to be very positive about the possibility of merger, and to want to resolve problems, and on the other, to maintain an objective stance, and be able to recognise when it is clear that a merger is not going to go ahead.

An ancillary point that underlies these principles is that if a proposed merger is not beneficial to one party, then it is not going to be beneficial to the 'new' firm, and therefore to neither party, even when one is much smaller than the other. If the merger goes ahead, major problems will develop as individuals realise that the benefits that they expected to receive from the merger do not exist. People will either leave (probably taking work and clients with them) or stay, but be unhappy and perform badly, or a de-merger will at some point occur. Whatever the outcome, a poor merger for one party will be a poor merger for both.

Principle 1: Business case supporting the merger

The first principle, which we have stressed several times already, is that parties need to be clear about the business case supporting the merger – what are the competitive advantages that the 'new' firm will have that neither antecedent firm could have achieved independently (at least not within the same time period)? Whilst the preliminary discussions will have resulted in the business case being developed in sufficient detail to justify a firm embarking on serious merger negotiations, it is rare for the business case to be fully developed until the In-depth Discussion Stage.

This is the single most important element to consider when merging – if the competitive benefits for the two firms are insufficient or do not even exist, the merger should not proceed, regardless of whether every other aspect of the merger appears to be positive. The business case must therefore be the first topic of discussion by the negotiating teams, and this is discussed in greater detail later on in this chapter.

The business case for merger should clarify whether the merger is cost-driven (and how that will be achieved on a sustainable basis) or whether it is market position-driven (and how that will be realised). In both cases, any potential cost savings need to be analysed in relation to the needs of the 'new' firm, and not calculated simply by cutting the overheads of the two antecedent firms. It must also take into account merger costs, and the impact of planned growth over the three years subsequent to merger. Our advice to firms merging to improve their market position is to play down the whole issue of cost savings, and to treat them as incidental to the real purpose of the merger (which they are). See **Chapter 1** for a more detailed discussion of cost-saving issues.

The worst-case scenario is where the business case does not clarify what the primary focus of the merger is, and both sides enter into merger with quite different expectations. At some point in the merger process, one party at least is likely to become disenchanted, which will hinder any attempt to realise the benefits that might exist. In fact, we have seen a number of ineffective and even disastrous mergers which resulted in either a de-merger or significant departures. Whilst it sounds obvious to point out the need to develop the business case in some depth to ensure it meets the needs of both parties, some of these mergers had a business rationale that was so vague that almost any outcome could have been read into them.

We are also aware of mergers where the business case claimed to be seeking to achieve a significant improvement in market position as well as economies of scale for the 'new' firm. If both parties to the merger were managing their overheads tightly prior to the merger, such a statement is likely to be contradictory, as the ability to cut costs is low, and the improved market position will require greater expenditure.

In conclusion, the first principle that should underpin the merger discussions is to ensure that the business case for merger is clear, that it has a primary driver which is agreed and understood by both sides, and which fits with the strategic direction of both firms. See **Appendix 3** for some of the items that should be contained in a business case. During the discussions, it is important that both sides remind themselves periodically of the main dimensions of the business case. It is easy to get caught up in the negotiations themselves, and to start to agree issues without remembering our earlier warning in **Chapter 5** about ensuring that what is agreed is best for the 'new' firm given the business case. This is possible only where the business case is clear.

Principle 2: Be generous in negotiations

The second core principle that should underpin the merger discussions is for each firm to be generous to the other side. There have been situations in the past, for example, where the size ratio between the two firms contemplating a merger was 65:35, and the larger firm wanted all major aspects of the merger to be decided in its favour in the same ratio wherever possible (such as profit share, management roles, voting rights, etc). Whilst the smaller firm in a merger rarely expects equality in everything, there are areas where criteria other than relative size should influence the decision. When a firm seeks to apply such a rigid approach to the negotiations, this could possibly indicate something about the 'culture' of that firm to the other side.

Both sides need to try to agree on what is best for the 'new' firm, and, at the same time, understand that the deal will need to be agreed by both partnerships. The harder the bargain driven by one side, the more difficult it might be for the other side to get its partners to agree to the proposed deal.

In a recent merger, there was a significant difference in size between the two firms. The larger firm was adamant about what profit-sharing arrangements it wanted the 'new' firm to have. The smaller firm had better managers and systems. The net result was that, although the larger firm would not compromise on profit-sharing, the parties agreed that the smaller firm's personnel would hold a disproportionate number of managerial positions, and that more of its systems and processes would be adopted by the 'new' firm. The partners in both firms were prepared to accept the 'balancing' of these key issues. Had the larger firm insisted on dominating everything, it is doubtful that the deal would have gone through.[2]

Principle 3: Adopt a dual attitude throughout negotiations

The third core principle is that both sides need to adopt a dual attitude throughout the merger discussions. Whilst both firms need to be confident that a merger deal can be concluded (unless something emerges to prove otherwise), at this stage, it is not yet a 'done deal', and the discussions need to go into detail, be frank in order for awkward questions to be asked, and probe into areas of concern. From our experience, unless firms enter discussions with a positive attitude, all the trust and rapport that was built up in the preliminary talks can then be undermined. By having a positive attitude, firms will be able to debate tension-ridden issues in an environment that is more conducive to finding a resolution. Firms will also be more inclined to persuade their partnerships of the benefits of the merger, even if compromises need to be made. If firms cannot start with this positive attitude, they should probably not be holding serious merger discussions.

Summary of the three principles

These three principles underpin the in-depth discussion of all issues but, in particular, the deal-breaking issues. These are issues that carry a significant amount of cultural

---

2 As discussed in **Chapter 5**, this is an area where an external adviser can prove useful.

and emotional attachment on both sides, and where some major changes in attitudes might well be required by both firms. The 'new' firm might require some entirely new thinking in these areas, and the negotiating group must be open to this. Our three principles help achieve this.

First discussion topic: the business case

The business case is the biggest deal-breaker of them all, even though most firms do not list it as such. The critical point is that until the business case is developed rigorously and set out in detail, it is not possible for either side to say that it meets its strategic requirements. While the early merger discussions need to test whether a business case appears to exist, rarely is this done to the depth required to be sure. Hence, this must be addressed in the in-depth discussions.

As the business case is so important, it should be the first topic for discussion at the in-depth meetings (and accompanied by further data collection and analyses that may need to be carried out). The development of the business case should be approached like the development of a strategy, and should include consideration about the strategic market position of the 'new' firm post-merger. Too many business cases only deal with what the firm will look like on day one of the merger. However, the real strategic issue to be discussed is what the merger will enable the 'new' firm to achieve over the following three years, taking into account expected market trends. Only then can partners stand back and decide whether the merger will achieve what they want for their firm. As we noted in **Chapter 1**, merger is only a part of the process of implementing a strategy, and there must also be a clear path as to how the rest of the implementation will occur.

Steps involved in the strategic development of the 'new' firm
Step 1 – draw up a profile
The first step is to draw up a profile of the key strategic characteristics that the merging firms see the 'new' firm possessing on day one. The profile should cover:

- size in terms of revenue, fee-earners, partners and total staffing;

- core clients;

- core practice areas and the size of each (revenue, profitability and fee-earners);

- economic structure;

- market sector focus (if any) such as industries or other specific segments; and

- potential direct competitors in the new market position.

Step 2 – review the competition

The second step is to compare the 'new' firm to its potential competitors, and to carry out an overview assessment of the key areas to be addressed if the 'new' firm is to become highly competitive in its new market position over the following three years. As Neville Eisenberg, managing partner of Berwin Leighton Paisner, said:

> 'A merger on its own doesn't change a firm's profile. You have to prove to the market that the merged firm achieves what you said it could. The market is always sceptical, and you need to demonstrate the improvement, whatever that is.'

Step 3 – carry out a health check

The third step is a form of health check. The firms should ask if the proposed position of the 'new' firm in the marketplace is what both firms aspire to, and whether the key action points which need to be addressed in order to achieve that market position are capable of being implemented. This is a critical step, and adequate time needs to be spent exploring, discussing and testing it.

Sometimes this is obvious, and not much time needs to be spent considering it. Certainly, the interviews with Denton Wilde Sapte, Berwin Leighton Paisner and Addleshaw Goddard indicated that each of the firms involved in those mergers very quickly came to the conclusion that their proposed merger 'was the right one'.

However, even if it does seem the 'right one', the negotiating team of each firm must still ensure that all possible evidence to support the business case for merger is prepared. It must never forget that there will be partners in its firm who, whilst not anti-merger, will want to see evidence to support the negotiating team's opinion. Partners will want to see facts, not opinions.

Analysis of strategic trends

A critical issue when putting together the business case for merger is to analyse what the strategic trends in the legal marketplace are, and what this means for the merged firm and for each of the parties to the merger. The key point is that markets change, and what was once a competitive market position might not be so given time.

Furthermore, there might well be a difference in the strategic trends in one segment of the market compared to another. Two firms contemplating merger might both be in a market sector where clients are buying more on price than on value. The merger, however, is aimed at moving them into a market segment where value delivered is the key buying criterion not price. It is likely that the strategic trends in the latter segment, and therefore how the merged firm will need to compete, will be significantly different to those in the existing market segment of both firms.

This market analysis is, in our opinion, fundamental to any merger. If a merger is designed to enhance a firm's competitiveness, either through improved service delivery or by way of economies of scale, it is crucial that the firms understand the trends in the marketplace, and whether, in light of them, the merger can deliver the perceived potential advantages for the firms. Again, this is an area where external advice can be of significant value, as it is always difficult for a firm to interpret clearly the market in which it operates, especially when it also has to deal with the other issues associated with a proposed merger.

Timing

Whilst it is important to start the discussions by developing the business case in some depth, putting it together will take time. This is not a task that the negotiating team should do, but should be delegated to others (either a task force solely of partners or a task force that also includes some of the professional managers from both firms). The task force should then report back to the negotiating team. Assistance from a strategic adviser is also likely to be beneficial.

In an ideal world, nothing further should be discussed until the business case is nearing completion. The more compelling the business case, the more likely it is that people will try to find solutions to difficult issues in other areas. Neville Eisenberg, managing partner of Berwin Leighton Paisner, remarked:

'If partners believe sufficiently in the strategic importance of the new firm, they are prepared to make some compromises in negotiations.'

In addition, given that many of the structural, systems and process issues should be developed to suit the 'new' firm, once the business case is fully developed, what is best for the 'new' firm will become clearer.

In most merger discussions, however, there is not this luxury of time. As we saw in **Chapter 4**, once serious discussions commence, people want to get on with them, and maintain their momentum. Therefore, in reality, other key issues will be discussed whilst the business case is being developed in full. This is easier to do if an outline strategic positioning of the 'new' firm, and the competitive advantages required by the merging firm, have been set out in the preliminary discussions. Indeed, in several recent mergers, partners in the firms were not consulted about the merger discussions until the business case was 75% developed. The business case was treated as something distinct from the other negotiations, and this is the approach that we recommend highly. This then enables the negotiating team to present partners with a prospectus that says, in effect: 'This is what the merger can achieve, this is what we need to do to achieve it, and these are the changes required by each firm to do this.' Partners can then focus on the two questions of 'what is it seeking to achieve?' and 'how will it be achieved?'. Otherwise, they tend to be given a stream of recommendations that are treated as separate issues in their own right, and are not seen in any strategic context.

Other deal-breaking issues
How to go about addressing potential deal-breakers

The discussions in this phase need to focus initially on the deal-breaking (or potentially deal-breaking) issues other than the business case. As we mentioned earlier, there will be a raft of issues that are unlikely to be deal-breakers but will also need to be dealt with such as accounting policies, taxation policies, marketing systems, client relationship management processes, insurance, HR policies, etc.[3] However, there is little point discussing any of these until the serious issues have been bedded down. In larger firm mergers, it is best to delegate these lower priority (although still important) issues to task forces, or to the relevant professional managers. They can then examine what each firm has or does at present, and prepare a report to the negotiating team setting out the current status, and what their recommendation for the 'new' firm is. The worst situation is to have six, seven or eight senior partners sitting around the negotiating table trying to explain how their firm handles these issues (often unclearly), and then both firms trying to reach agreement on them for the 'new' firm.

In respect of the deal-breaking issues, it is also more effective if a couple of representatives (usually from the negotiating team) initially prepare discussion papers

---

3 See **Appendix 3** for a list of these issues.

for each of the relevant issues. For example, if the issue of property leases is to be discussed at the next meeting, two members from the negotiating team should gather together the information on the leases of the two firms, highlight the apparent critical decision issues, and circulate a discussion paper on this ahead of the meeting. The paper might not include any recommendations, but it aids discussion enormously if the participants at the meeting have read a summary of all the relevant 'facts' in advance, rather than having valuable discussion time used up by each party explaining its lease terms to the other. Whilst this might sound an obvious step to take, we have witnessed a surprising number of merger discussions where each of the parties spend considerable time explaining how they do something rather than concentrating on working out how the 'new' firm is going to do it and how they can get there.

Smaller firms have fewer people to whom they can delegate, but we recommend that the same approach is taken. Two members of the negotiating team could take responsibility for gathering information about all of the lower priority issues. Each of the deal-breakers could be allocated two other members of the team, who would then be responsible for gathering the relevant data and presenting a discussion paper to the rest of the negotiating team. Over the course of the discussion, some people might have been responsible for preparing papers on several issues in a smaller firm, but the task is an essential one that should not be avoided because of size.

It is vital that these meetings are businesslike, and that long, rambling descriptions and explanations are avoided. Well-prepared discussion papers, with the necessary background material, focus everyone's mind on what needs to be decided.

Governance and management

Whilst not always a deal-breaker, the issue of governance and management has the potential to be one (depending on the approach taken by either or both parties). We have seen situations where partners have said ahead of the in-depth discussions that they do not have any deal-breaking issues, only then to open a discussion on governance and management with a statement that they must have X or Y. As soon as anyone starts a sentence with 'we must have…', or something similar, the issue being discussed becomes a potential deal-breaker.

In most mergers, the 'new' firm will be significantly larger than either antecedent firm. This immediately makes it highly likely that the governance and management structures of both parties will be inadequate for the 'new' firm. This is something with which many lawyers struggle. There is a considerable body of management theory and practice on organisational theory and structures, and a set of well-developed principles that should always underpin the structure of a firm. One such principle is the need to adapt or change structures as the size of the organisation increases. In almost no merger should the governance and management systems of one firm be adopted by the 'new' firm without change, or at least without a serious discussion on its adequacy for the 'new' firm taking place.

There are two key decisions to be made here. The first is in relation to the proposed top-level structure of governance of the 'new' firm. The second is in relation to the structure of the next level down of operational management, and the 'business unit' structure as part of that. These two levels are explained in some detail below. Smaller firms tend to combine the two levels into one group (single-tier structure), simply because of the number of people involved. Larger firms tend to separate the governance function from that of operational management, and to operate using two groups (dual-tier structure).

A merger that creates a firm of 80 equity partners and 400 fee-earners is likely to need a dual-tier structure. A firm created out of a merger involving 20 equity partners and 60 fee-earners is likely to operate effectively with a single-tier structure. There is no hard and fast rule about when a single or dual-tier structure should be used, but the crossover is usually at the point when a firm has between 20 and 40 equity partners.

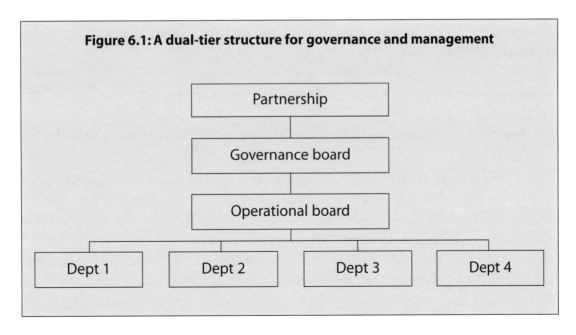

Figure 6.1: A dual-tier structure for governance and management

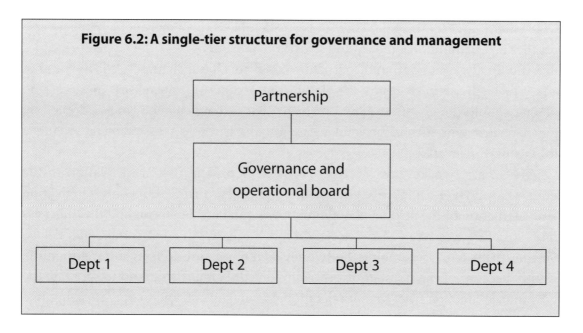

Figure 6.2: A single-tier structure for governance and management

Dual-tier structure

In a dual-tier structure (see **Figure 6.1**), the governance board takes an overview of the firm's strategic development, and acts more as a trustee for the partners, just as a board of directors does for the shareholders of a company. Underneath that, there is an operational business unit structure, the management of which focuses on implementing the strategies, and managing the performance of the business units in line with annual budgets, business plans, etc.

Once a firm has decided upon a dual-tier structure, other issues (which carry strong sensitivities) also need to be considered. These include:

- How many people should be on the governance board?

- How many from each antecedent firm should be on the governance board?

- Should they be drawn from the existing management teams of the two merging firms or should there be new elections?

- Where do the senior partners of the two firms fit in?

- How should the 'new' firm's managing partner be appointed?

- Are the operational business units to be decided based on locations (ie offices), practice groups, departments or something else?

- What decisions are to be made by the partnership, by the governance board and by the management board?

Addleshaw Goddard

Addleshaw Booth & Co had a dual-tier structure in place, whereas Theodore Goddard had a single-tier structure. Theodore Goddard, although smaller than Addleshaw Booth & Co, had more departments in its business unit structure, which were mainly made up of distinct practice areas. Addleshaw Booth & Co's pre-merger size meant that it had already developed four major departments as its business unit structure, with each department incorporating several practice areas. The firm operated out of three offices, and these were also an important part of the structure. The development of governance and management structure for the 'new' firm was therefore critical, as both firms were approaching it from quite different starting points.

The Theodore Goddard team realised that the size of the 'new' firm (800 fee-earners) meant that it was unlikely that one group could be responsible for governance (ie the strategic and ownership issues), as well as for the detailed operational management of the firm.

Addleshaw Booth & Co and Theodore Goddard put considerable resources into devising a new structure for the 'new' firm, and started from scratch so that they could choose what was best for it. Having decided on a dual-tier structure, they also agreed on the need for a split in the role of the chair of the partnership and the chair of the governance board, given that the latter was to be quite active in developing the 'new' firm's strategy. The senior partner of Addleshaw Booth & Co became the senior partner and executive chair of the governance board of Addleshaw Goddard, and Theodore Goddard's senior partner became the partnership chairman (more of a non-executive role which acts as 'the conscience of the partnership').

The 'new' firm's strategy was to pursue specific client types, and to focus on particular practice areas. Therefore, the idea of managing operationally by location was abandoned, and a five-department organisational structure was developed, with each department incorporating a number of practice areas. This was quite a different structure to what either party had before. The issues on which the partnership as a whole could decide also differed from what either firm had pre-merger, in recognition of the fact that a larger-sized firm would need to delegate more issues to management.

The role and responsibilities of the management board were developed and agreed, along with those of the department and practice group heads. Addleshaw Booth & Co's managing partner became the managing partner of Addleshaw Goddard, as Theodore Goddard did not have one (having operated with a senior partner and a non-lawyer chief executive). Of crucial importance was the decision (one that we endorse strongly) to create a management board that included the managing partner as chair and the five heads of department.[4] In a dual-tier structure, it is vital that the department or business unit heads are members of the management board. They are responsible for ensuring that the business units achieve the firm's operational and strategic goals, and must, therefore, be part of the operational decision-making process. This is an important organisational rule that many firms break. Operational management is only effective when those responsible for implementing decisions are also those responsible for making them. Firms that do not include their business unit heads on the management board run a very high risk of disconnecting the making of decisions and the implementation of them. The result is that implementation of decisions is poor.

With Addleshaw Goddard, the management structure was designed to ensure that all areas were covered (both strategic and operational), that all roles were defined in terms of accountabilities, responsibilities and outcomes, and that there was complete integration across the structure. This was a major undertaking that occupied a task force for some weeks. It also required considerable input from the negotiating teams in order to ensure that the final proposal was one that both parties would be prepared to support at their respective partnership meetings.

Berwin Leighton Paisner

Berwin Leighton and Paisner & Co also had to address some crucial governance and management issues. Berwin Leighton, the larger firm, had a dual-tier structure in place with four departments as business units (somewhat similar to Addleshaw Booth & Co). Paisner & Co had a single-tier structure, with 11 practice areas at the business unit level. The negotiations resulted in a dual-tier structure being adopted by the 'new' firm, with four departments at the operational business unit level, made up of 17 practice groups. There was a strong Paisner & Co influence at this level in that the 'new' firm retained a large number of practice groups. The four departments focused on strategic implementation, and the practice groups focused more on day-to-day management and operational issues.

---

4 Some other specific appointments were made as well in order to help bed down the merger.

Denton Wilde Sapte

The merger to form Denton Wide Sapte followed a similar pattern. Both Denton Hall and Wilde Sapte had adopted a dual-tier structure, and there was no question that this would not be retained for the 'new' firm. However, the overall strategic thrust of the two firms had been significantly different. Denton Hall focused strongly on four industry sectors (energy and transport, financial institutions, real estate and retail, and media, technology and telecoms). Wilde Sapte was primarily a finance industry firm with a strong insurance group. The sectors fitted together well, and there was some amalgamation of practice groups.

Single-tier structure

The single-tier structure is the more practical option for a smaller firm. A dual-tier structure requires a minimum of ten to 12 partners at board level, if the two tiers are to operate effectively. It is highly advisable not to have individuals sitting on both boards (other than the managing partner). Hence, if a 20-partner firm adopts a dual-tier structure, half or more of its partners would need to be heavily involved in strategic leadership and management. Even with a 30-partner firm, a third or more of partners would need to be members of management. However, the greater complexity of managing a firm with 40 partners or more makes a dual-tier structure much more desirable (and it also requires a smaller percentage of the partnership's involvement).

The single-tier structure has one major disadvantage compared with the dual-tier structure, and this is the lack of separation of strategic from operational management. For the reasons mentioned above, it is important to have the business unit heads on the management board. However, operational management tends to find it difficult to focus on firm-wide strategic issues. Operational issues are more immediate, with decisions being required then and there, not later. Strategic issues are usually less urgent, and whilst they require analysis, debate and discussion, decisions on them might not need to be taken for some time. The management board in a single-tier structure can, therefore, tend to focus on the more pressing, operational issues, and neglect the bigger picture.

There are, of course, ways to overcome this difficulty, as many firms have found. One approach is to hold a certain number of 'strategic only' meetings a year (we recommend around four), and to ensure that the board sticks to the agenda of strategic issues alone. Another approach, and the most effective in our opinion, is to invite an additional two partners onto the management board for strategy meetings only. These partners should be elected by the partnership. The board should normally include the senior partner as chair when it meets for strategic discussions.

TLT Solicitors

The merger of the two firms that created TLT Solicitors also threw up management issues. Trumps had a managing partner but no formal management board. Lawrence Tucketts had a chief executive, who was a chartered accountant, a senior partner and an operational board (ie a single-tier structure). One had a small number of business groups, whilst the other had a wide range of teams as opposed to business units.

During the merger talks, partners from both firms extensively discussed the options available, resulting in a blending of the two structures. The merged firms adopted a single-tier structure led by a managing partner. The business units were formed by combining a number of practice groups, and reshaping the teams into these practice groups.

Other firms in our case studies

Whilst there was some variation amongst the smaller firms in our case studies as to how their business units were organised, all of them adopted a single-tier structure.

Brabners Chaffe Street, Kidd Rapinet and William Sturges & Co primarily retained practice groups as the business units. ASB Law formed a small number of business units by combining practice groups. Blake Lapthorn Linnell's business units were based more on its offices, with practice groups operating mainly in relation to technical development.

Location

One issue that may impact on the decision as to which structure to adopt, is whether the merger creates a firm with offices in different locations. Addleshaw Goddard, ASB Law and Blake Lapthorn Linnell faced this issue, and took different approaches. Addleshaw Goddard discarded managing by location, as did ASB Law, whereas Blake Lapthorn Linnell retained geographic management.

This highlights the need for the structure chosen to support the firm's strategy. Where a firm's strategy is to develop a client base that requires a multi-office service, then it is essential that the merged firm establishes a structure under which the business units are divided up into practice groups across the firm (not locations). It is essential that a client who uses the firm in more than one location, sees that the firm is adopting a 'one-firm' approach, no matter which office it is dealing with. This structure also requires practice groups to be managed on a firm-wide basis, with consistent documentation, letters, reports, etc. There also needs to be a level of consistency in the approach taken by all practice groups.

The essential point is that if a client initially used the firm in location A, it is only going to want to use the firm in locations B and C if:

(i) it believes that the quality of service it will receive in locations B and C will be the same as it received in location A; and

(ii) in every way, the firm appears to be working as 'one firm', no matter what the location of the office.

Without these two conditions, there is no reason for a client to want to use a firm in more than the one location.

Alternatively, a firm merging to create a practice in several different locations might not be doing so in order to develop a client base that would instruct all of its offices. The firm's aim might instead be to utilise its overall strengths in key practice areas in each separate location. In this situation, the firm may want to have business units based on location, with practice groups taking a secondary role.

The key point is that the 'new' firm's strategy is a major determinant of the type of organisational structure that will be required.

Integration

A critical issue for any newly merged firm is to ensure that integration occurs smoothly and quickly, and that everyone is focused on developing the 'new' firm along the lines envisaged in the merger prospectus.[5] For this to occur, it is absolutely vital that the 'new' firm has a very effective organisational structure from day one. There have been situations where recently merged firms spent the best part of the first year trying to develop a structure that was suitable for the firm in its new state. This resulted in the business not being properly managed, integration not being achieved, and the merger being viewed as a failure, both internally and externally. In some cases, the firms never recovered, and a de-merger or a significant number of departures occurred. In other cases, the firms eventually resolved their structural issues but lost two or three years in the process, and a lot of work was required to restore staff optimism about the merger.

Getting an appropriate structure that ensures effective management of the merged firm the first day of operation is crucial.

---

5 Post-merger integration issues are discussed in more detail in **Chapter 8**.

Chapter 7: In-depth merger discussions – the financials

Introduction

The difference in profitability[1] levels between two firms considering a merger is viewed by those involved to be a major potential deal-breaking issue. In our case studies, it was recognised as one of the most important potential deal-breakers because of the impact it has on profit-sharing.

Paddy Grafton Green, chairman of Addleshaw Goddard, commented: 'The issues are around comparative profitability, and that can always be a problem.' Neville Eisenberg, managing partner of Berwin Leighton Paisner, said: 'The merger was made much easier by the fact that there wasn't a major difference in profitability between the two firms.' The managing partner of TLT Solicitors, David Pester, also remarked: 'Both firms had a comparable level of profitability, so that removed one possible obstacle to the deal.'

It would be naive to think that profitability would not be an important issue. It is, and will remain so as long as law firms are partnerships, and even after that it will still be an issue. When two similar businesses seek to combine, there will always be an issue if the profitability of one is significantly lower than that of the other. The more profitable business will want to be sure that it can generate more profit from the other business in the event of a merger/acquisition. There are, however, two points to note, and which we will continue to underline throughout this chapter:

(i) the importance of having comparable levels of profitability is often overstated; and

(ii) even if profitability is comparable, there might be aspects of how that profit is generated that are potential deal-breakers.

The reason why the issue of profitability is so important in a law firm merger is because it is the sole financial basis on which the two firms come together. Corporate

---

1 Profitability means the average profit per equity partner or PEP.

mergers usually involve the valuation of assets as well as the valuation of the profit-generating capabilities of the two businesses. Furthermore, the price that is paid to the corporate shareholders of the merging business (or to both groups of shareholders where a new entity is being created) reflects the level of profitability, together with the expectations of the new management as to what it can do to improve it. In a partnership merger, however, the tangible assets are relatively immaterial, and the 'shareholders' of the businesses are generally not being bought out. Profitability is therefore the only way in which the relative value of the two law firms can be determined, and so it forms the financial basis of a law firm merger. If the difference in profitability of the two firms is wide, a complex remuneration scheme will need to be put in place in the 'new' firm to reflect this. Otherwise, if all partners are remunerated on the same basis, the existing profits of the partners of the more profitable firm will be diluted. We discuss this in greater detail below.

Whilst examining the issue of profitability in this chapter, we will discuss a number of other related financial issues which include cash flow management, partner compensation systems and funding requirements. All of these issues contain elements that might be considered potential deal-breakers. They also each provide an indication about two other aspects of a firm:

(i)   the nature of its business; and

(ii)   its culture.

Why a difference in profitability levels might be a deal-breaker

The first issue to understand is why a difference in the profitability levels of the two firms might be a deal-breaker.

Consider the following examples:

Example 7.1

Firm A has 30 equity partners and generates £400,000 in PEP, giving it a total profit of £12m.

Firm B has 20 equity partners and generates £200,000 in PEP, giving it a total profit of £4m.

The merged firm will have 50 equity partners and a total profit of £16m. PEP will therefore be £320,000.

Example 7.2

Firm A has 30 equity partners and generates £400,000 in PEP, giving it a total profit of £12m.

Firm B has 10 equity partners and generates £200,000 in PEP, giving it a total profit of £2m.

The merged firm will have 40 equity partners and a total profit of £14m. PEP will therefore be £350,000.

In **Example 7.1**, the profitability of Firm A's partners will be diluted as a result of the merger, and Firm B's profitability will be enhanced.[2] It is unlikely in such a situation that Firm A will want to merge with Firm B. In **Example 7.2**, the profitability of the merged firm will be somewhat nearer to Firm A's existing profitability, and a deal is more likely to be possible.

The point is, depending on the strength of the business case of the merger, and the perceived competitive advantages and benefits a merger would bring, many firms are only willing to merge with another if the dilution in PEP, based on pre-merger figures, is fairly low. As a rough rule of thumb, partners are willing to trade off up to 10% in PEP, provided the business case and supporting analyses demonstrate that this is recoverable quickly, and that the merged firm will be able to generate a sustainable level of profitability above the pre-merger levels.

Comparability is relative, and does not always mean that profitability of one firm has to be within a plus or minus 10% range of that of the other. Unfortunately, we have seen many potentially good mergers fall down at the first hurdle because, based on a superficial analysis of the financials, the difference in profitability between the two firms was thought to be too great. Our view is, if the two firms were attracted to each other enough to consider merger discussions in the first place, they should think twice before walking away simply because of profitability differences. Profitability levels should be considered in conjunction with the perceived business benefits before the possibility of a merger is rejected.

Why profitability might be at different levels

The second point to understand is why profitability might be at different levels. In order to do so, profitability needs to be examined at the 'gross margin' or 'contribution' level and then at the 'net profit' level.

---

2 We will demonstrate below that the deal might not be as dilutive for Firm A as the arithmetic suggests.

Gross margin level

The gross margin level is, effectively, revenue less direct costs, where direct costs include salaries and benefits paid to the revenue generators (ie fee-earners).[3] It is critical that a 'notional salary' for equity partners is included in the direct costs as well. There are three reasons for this:

(i) revenue will include revenue generated by equity partners, so the cost associated with that should be included as a matter of financial logic;

(ii) when making comparisons, if there is no 'salary' component for equity partners, distortions in the gross margin can occur due to differences in gearing[4] between the two firms; and

(iii) given that equity partners are 'working proprietors', the true profit can only be arrived at after deducting the cost of their time as 'workers'. Without this, it is not possible to calculate meaningful ratios for comparison.

Notional salary of equity partners

Notional salary can be calculated in two ways.[5]

The first way is to add a premium to the salary cost of a senior level associate. For example, if senior associates are, on average, paid £90,000 per annum, then the notional salary for an equity partner could be £150,000 (based on adding a premium of £60,000).

The second method is to look at the salary packages paid to in-house lawyers of a comparable standing.

Some firms calculate a notional salary for each level of partner (senior, mid-level and junior), but we generally use an average across the partnership, which is usually sufficient.

The importance of including a notional salary in the direct costs is shown in **Examples 7.3** and **7.4** below.

In **Example 7.3**, the gross margin per fee-earner is almost the same for both Firm A and Firm B.

---

3 Sometimes, direct costs also include the salaries of secretaries and personal assistants.

4 Gearing is the ratio of equity partners to other fee-earners.

5 We usually carry out both calculations.

Example 7.3: Notional salary not included

	Firm A	Firm B
Revenue	£20,000,000	£20,000,000
Direct costs	£8,500,000	£8,600,000
Gross margin	£11,500,000	£11,400,000
Total number of equity partners	33	20
Gross margin per equity partner	£348,500	£570,000
Total number of fee-earners*	116	116
Gearing	1:2.5	1:4.8
Gross margin per fee-earner	£99,100	£98,300
Revenue per equity partner	£606,100	£1,000,000
Revenue per fee-earner	£172,400	£172,400

Example 7.4: Notional salary included

	Firm A	Firm B
Revenue	£20,000,000	£20,000,000
Direct costs**	£13,450,000	£11,600,000
Gross margin	£6,550,000	£8,400,000
Total number of equity partners	33	20
Gross margin per equity partner	£198,500	£420,000
Total number of fee-earners*	116	116
Gearing	1:2.5	1:4.8
Gross margin per fee-earner	£56,500	£72,000
Revenue per equity partner	£606,100	£1,000,000
Revenue per fee-earner	£172,400	£172,400

* Including equity partners
** Including £150,000 per equity partner as notional salary

In **Example 7.4**, when a notional salary of the equity partners is included in the direct costs, it becomes apparent that Firm B is significantly better at generating profitability than Firm A. The gross margin per equity partner for Firm A falls from £348,500 to £198,500. For Firm B, it falls from £570,000 to £420,000. Similarly, the gross margin per fee-earner of Firm B is now much better than that of Firm A.

Example 7.3 could lead people to assume that Firm A and Firm B do not have very different economic structures. **Example 7.4** highlights the fact that they do.

The differences in gearing given in the two examples above also illustrate that Firm A and Firm B have different approaches to carrying out work. Firm A has a much lower gearing than Firm B, so the equity partners of Firm A are likely to be personally generating more revenue than those of Firm B. The fact that Firm B has more associates per equity partner than Firm A suggests the following hypotheses:

(i) equity partners at Firm B prefer to manage more than carry out work compared with equity partners at Firm A; or

(ii) higher level associates at Firm B manage the teams whilst equity partners spend the same amount of time on billable work as equity partners at Firm A; or

(iii) a combination of the two.

Whatever the reason, the inclusion of a notional salary for equity partners in **Example 7.4** highlights a significant difference in the way the two firms operate which follows from the difference in gearing, but which was obscured when notional salaries were not included. A significant difference in profitability at the operational level is an issue that would need to be considered if Firm A and Firm B were to contemplate merger.

Differences in business, working style and culture

Financial information about firms can also highlight other differences in business, working style and culture. Consider **Example 7.5**, which analyses further the statistics of Firm A and Firm B used in **Example 7.3** and **Example 7.4**.

These figures flag up some serious differences between Firm A and Firm B. Whilst each firm might undertake work under similar practice area headings (eg M&A, real estate, commercial litigation, etc), the figures show that the businesses are, in fact, quite different, and so are the working styles (and possibly culture) of the two firms.

	Firm A	Firm B
Example 7.5		
Standard working hours per annum[6]	1,610	1,610
Utilisation rate	102.5%	77.6%
Average billable hours per fee-earner*	1,650	1,250
Average billing rate per hour	£104.50	£137.90
Revenue per fee-earner	£172,400	£172,400
Direct costs per fee-earner**	£115,900	£100,000
Gross margin per fee-earner	£56,500	£72,400
Gearing (+1)[7]	3.5	5.8
Gross margin per equity partner	£198,500	£420,000
Average billable hours per equity partner	1,750	1,000
Average billable hours per other fee-earner	1,610	1,302

*   Including equity partners

** Including £150,000 per equity partner as notional salary

Firm A has a much lower average billing rate per hour than Firm B. Whilst revenue per fee-earner is the same for both firms, this is because Firm A billed more time than Firm B. Furthermore, Firm A's partners billed more hours than its associates did, whilst at Firm B, the associates carried out more of the work. The average billable hours per equity partner of Firm B is 57% below that of Firm A.

These analyses suggest that the work undertaken by Firm A has, on average, a lesser value than Firm B's (this is particularly indicated by Firm A's average billing rate per hour).

---

6 Standard working hours per annum represents the time available if someone works normal hours. The 1,610 hours is based on UK practice which is 46 weeks per annum (ie 52 weeks less six weeks for vacation, bank holidays, etc) multiplied by five days per week multiplied by seven hours a day.

7 Gearing is the ratio of other fee-earners to equity partner. To convert the gross margin per fee-earner to gross margin per equity partner, it is necessary to add one to the gearing ratio because equity partners are also fee-earners. Hence, in Firm A, the gearing ratio is 1:2.5 but as the equity partner is also a fee-earner, there were in fact 3.5 fee-earners producing as average of £56,500 per fee-earner in gross margin.

Based on the average billable hours per equity partner, one should query whether Firm A's partners have time to carry out non-fee-earning activities such as business development, client relationship management, mentoring, training, etc. If they are carrying out these additional activities effectively, then the total time they devote to the business is likely to be well in excess of 2,500 hours per annum. One should also query why, if Firm A's partners put in more billable time than its other fee-earners, the overall average billing rate per hour is low compared to that of Firm B. If the headline billing rates of the two firms are in fact similar, then Firm A must be writing down the partner billing rates by a significant amount. With average billable hours per equity partner of 1,000, Firm B's partners have a considerable amount of time to devote to non fee-earning activities before they would have to work over 2,500 hours per annum. Whilst headline billing rates and write-downs at the time of billing could all be taken into consideration, the conclusion would still be that Firms A and B have quite different businesses and working styles.

If these two firms were considering a merger, the business case would need to demonstrate how the business of each would enhance the other, and also how a dilution of the value in Firm B's business would be avoided. It would also need to address the difference in the two firms' working styles and culture.

The analyses also illustrate that the partners in the two firms operate in a very different way, which could lead to major tensions post-merger. Partners at Firm A might believe that the most important activity is billable work, and that all other partner activities are less important, and, indeed, optional. Hence, post-merger, they are likely to consider that partners from Firm B are not putting in the same effort as them. This will lead to disputes over compensation as well as increased hostility between the partners from the two individual firms. Partners in Firm B might believe that Firm A's partners are doing work that should be left to associates, and that, by not putting time into business development, mentoring, etc, they are not building and developing a business for the longer term.

Furthermore, the merger strategy might be to extend the work carried out by one firm to the clients of the other (ie Firm A's clients would be sold the higher value work being done by Firm B, and vice versa). In this way, the merged firm would cover a wider range of work with each client.

One problem with this, of course, is that Firm A's clients will want all of the work that they give the merged firm to be at the same billing rate that they were charged pre-merger (so Firm B could not charge its pre-merger higher rate for the work it carries out). Firm B's clients might be prepared to give more work to the 'new' firm, but they may be concerned about Firm B's ability to carry out its lower value work, and might not accept that the merged firm could do the work economically. If they do give the lower value work to the 'new' firm, they will also want the billing rate in respect of that work to be at a reduced level.

Integrating two firms with fundamentally different working styles might also prove problematic for clients. Firm A's clients might be concerned about the 'new' partners not undertaking as much work as they were previously used to, and about that work being delegated to more junior lawyers. Firm B's clients might be concerned about the amount of work that the 'new' partners carry out for fear of prices escalating.

The integration of associates will also be difficult. They will need to adapt the way they work depending on whether they are working with their former partners or with their 'new' partners. It might also be difficult to form teams which include partners from both firms. The real danger is that integration at the operational level might never really happen, that hostility between the two partner groups might increase, and that this could result in either a de-merger or a partial one where key individuals and groups depart.

Comparative profitability at the firm-wide level is one thing, but it is crucial that the analysis goes beyond this and examines exactly from where each firm derives its profit. The analyses set out in the examples above would therefore also need to be carried out for each practice group. We have seen situations where the analyses did not demonstrate substantial differences at the firm-wide level, but some of the issues above emerged within practice groups when the analyses were carried out at the practice-group level.

Miscommunication about the type of work and working styles of the two firms can easily occur in merger discussions, particularly where profitability is similar. The negotiating teams are often lulled into a false sense of security that the two businesses are indeed similar. Whilst neither side intends to mislead the other, the discussions assume that the businesses are comparable, and the difficult questions that would test whether or not this is actually the case are never asked. The detailed analyses in **Examples 7.2** and **7.3** above therefore provide the basis for testing business compatibility, as well as deeper issues about working style and culture.

This is a very real concern. There have been quite a number of firms that have struggled with post-merger integration over the last decade or so. A subsequent review of the pre-merger businesses using the analyses set out above then revealed a lack of compatibility from the outset. Having discussed this with management post-merger, it become clear that neither side meant to mislead the other, but the apparent compatibility of the economics at the firm-wide level led the negotiating teams to assume that they were discussing similar businesses when, in fact, they were not.

Net profit level

Another major issue that needs to be discussed in the merger negotiations is that of overhead expenditure. By this we mean expenditure on everything else other than direct costs. It is the deduction of overhead expenditure from the gross margin that results in net profit.

Those negotiating the merger often feel that they need to demonstrate what cost savings will arise from the merger. Whilst the business strategy might be recognised as of primary importance when selling the merger to partners, negotiators believe a key selling point will be showing that the cost per fee-earner of the merged firm will be significantly lower than that of either of the two firms pre-merger.

However, whilst it might be true that the merged firm will have a lower cost per fee-earner in the first year, there is a real danger in projecting these cost reductions for future years. In situations where the strategy for the merger is to achieve an improved market position, it is likely that the cost per fee-earner will increase to a figure similar to that of its 'new' peer group competitors, which in fact could be higher than that of either of the firms pre-merger. The crucial issue for partners to consider in these cases is whether or not the merger will enable the 'new' firm to improve its competitiveness and market position, and therefore raise its revenue per fee-earner faster than any increase in cost per fee-earner.

We discussed reduction in overheads as a reason for a merger in **Chapter 1**, but overheads should also be examined when making profitability comparisons, and on two different levels:

(i) the overall level and the three-year trend in overhead expenditure; and

(ii) expenditure on specific items.[8]

We will touch upon these two levels as we discuss the differences in cost structures of firms contemplating merger.

Cost structures of firms in the same peer group

In practice, firms in the same peer group tend to have similar cost structures in terms of both salary costs and overheads. Property costs are also likely to be comparable (although there are cases, particularly in London, where a firm might have taken on a

---

8 By this we mean an analysis of the major items, not a detailed item-by-item review

lease when the property market was depressed whilst another might have taken one on during a boom period). The salaries of associates and support staff will also be similar, as will the costs of administration, technology, marketing, etc.

However, a difference in the cost structure and cost per fee-earner can occur if the two firms' business models are different (ie the type of resources utilised by one firm and the way they are managed might differ to those of the other). For example, a firm may elect to use a higher gearing than other firms by employing a higher proportion of more junior fee-earners at a lower cost and to manage them differently, but still provide services of a similar quality to that of its competitors. Firms in **Table 7.1** below illustrate this.

Table 7.1: Comparative economic structures – Selected UK firms

Firm	Revenue per fee-earner	Cost per fee-earner	Profit per fee-earner	Gearing	Profit per equity partner
Herbert Smith	£233,000	£158,000	£75,000	1:8.4	£700,000
Lovells	£286,000	£182,000	£104,000	1:4.0	£523,000
Ashurst	£276,000	£187,000	£89,000	1:4.9	£521,000
Simmons & Simmons	£247,000	£190,000	£57,000	1:3.9	£275,000

Source: Legal Business 100, 2004

The firms in **Table 7.1** are all, in effect, full service business law firms, competing in a similar market position. Herbert Smith has a leading reputation in dispute resolution work, although the others also have strong dispute resolution practices. Herbert Smith has, however, adopted a business model that is different to the competitors by employing a higher proportion of more junior fee-earners. This means its gearing is much higher than the other firms in **Table 7.1** (more than double that of Lovells and Simmons & Simmons, and 70% higher than that of Ashurst). Hence, Herbert Smith has a lower cost per fee-earner and revenue per fee-earner than its competitors (as it has a higher proportion of junior people on lower salaries and charge rates than the others). It also has the third lowest profit per fee-earner. However, the combination of its profit per fee-earner and gearing generates a profit per equity partner significantly higher than that of the other firms.

Given the business structures and location of the four firms, it is likely that Herbert Smith's cost per fee-earner would be comparable to that of its competitors if it had a similar gearing to them. However, the adoption of a different business model allows it to operate the same business structure as its competitors in a way that alters the economics but not its profitability.

The key point here is that differences in cost structures within a location where costs are similar can indicate a difference in the business models of two firms contemplating merger. On the other hand, two firms with similar overall cost structures might have different business models, which would be revealed by separating fee-earner salary costs from overheads. Isolating overhead costs and comparing them can be revealing.

More and more firms are realising that the quality of a firm's service delivery is hugely dependent on the quality of its infrastructure. A poor quality infrastructure makes it more difficult to provide services quickly and of a consistently high quality. More things go wrong when the infrastructure is lacking, and clients can tell the difference.

An infrastructure that supports a high level of service delivery is costly – it cannot be done on the cheap. Hence, firms which are competing for a similar type of work, at a similar level of value to clients, need to provide a comparable level of service delivery. Whilst one firm might be able to be more cost-efficient than others in relation to one item of expenditure, it tends to get balanced out when all items are taken into account.

The *Legal Business 100, 2004*, which sets out the economic structure of the largest 100 UK firms by turnover, also illustrates the comparability of the overhead costs between peer group competitors quite clearly. In general, a difference of plus or minus 10% of cost between peer group competitors would be normal at any given time. This is illustrated in **Table 7.2** below.

Within the Magic Circle firms, Clifford Chance is somewhat of an outlier with its cost per fee-earner being nearly 18% above the group average. The others' cost per fee-earner falls almost within the plus or minus 10% norm, although that of Freshfields Bruckhaus Deringer is 11% below the average. Excluding Clifford Chance, whose higher cost base might be a consequence of having more international offices than the others, and a significant presence in New York (a high cost city), the cost per fee-earner group average falls to £195,000. The other four firms are within plus or minus 5% of this.

The next tier of firms, the First Tier, show somewhat more disparity. Norton Rose is a clear outlier in this group, and there is no obvious reason for this. If Norton Rose is excluded, the group average is £178,000, and the other firms all fall within plus or minus 10% of this other than Herbert Smith, which is 11% below the average. (We explained the reasons for Herbert Smith's lower cost base above.)

Table 7.2: Cost structures of selected peer group competitors

	Group	Cost per lawyer £k	% deviation from average
I	**Magic Circle**		
	Allen & Overy	199	<4.8>
	Clifford Chance	246	17.7
	Freshfields Bruckhaus Deringer	185	<11.5>
	Linklaters	205	<1.9>
	Slaughter and May	190	<9.0>
	Group average	**209**	**Nil**
II	**First tier**		
	Ashurst	187	13.3
	Herbert Smith	158	<4.2>
	Lovells	182	10.3
	Norton Rose	119	<27.9>
	Simmons & SImmons	190	15.2
	Group average	**165**	**Nil**
III	**Second tier**		
	Barlow Lyde & Gilbert	151	<6.2>
	CMS Cameron McKenna	167	2.5
	Denton Wilde Sapte	166	1.8
	Macfarlanes	167	2.5
	Richards Butler	158	<3.1>
	Group average	**163**	**Nil**
IV	**UK multi-location**		
	Addleshaw Goddard	131	<6.4>
	DLA	174	24.2
	Eversheds	124	<11.4>
	Hammonds	136	<2.9>
	Osborne Clarke	132	<5.7>
	Group average	**140**	**Nil**

Source: Legal Business 100, 2004

The firms in the Second Tier are all within a range of plus 6% to minus 3% of the group average. All compete in a similar part of the market, and all are London based. Only Denton Wilde Sapte has a spread of international offices.

The UK Multi-location firms show considerable disparity, but again there is an outlier that distorts the average. The cost per fee-earner of DLA Piper Rudnick Gray Cary (as it is now) is 24% above the group average, which is perhaps explained by its extensive network of European offices. The group average falls to £128,000 if DLA is excluded, and the deviation around the average is within a range of plus 6% to minus 3%.

Firms with similar PEP but different levels of overheads

When the two firms contemplating a merger have similar PEP, but very different levels of overhead expenditure on a per fee-earner basis, further issues emerge. This is illustrated in **Example 7.6** below.

Firm A and Firm B have very similar PEP. Hence, on an initial comparison of headline numbers (ie revenue and profitability), they would appear to have comparable financial structures.

Firm B, however, is operating with much higher overheads, even though its revenue is the same as that of Firm A. The difference in overheads is exacerbated when converted to a per partner basis (£181,000 compared with £400,000) and to a per fee-earner basis (£51,700 compared with £69,000). Looking at the total overheads and the overheads per fee-earner levels, Firm B's figures are 33% higher than Firm A's. Whilst the difference on an overheads per equity partner basis is much greater (120%), this is not a valid comparison to make when trying to understand a firm's cost structure as a substantial difference in gearing will skew this. Overheads are incurred on behalf of all fee-earners, hence in examining the overhead component of a firm's cost structure, it is the overheads per fee-earner basis that is the most relevant. Some argue that because partners are the managers of the business, then the overheads per equity partner basis is more appropriate. The fact that partners may agree a budget is a separate issue to deciding what overhead level is required to support a firm with a given number of fee-earners.

Reasons for differences in overheads

Why there is a difference in the levels of overhead expenditure therefore needs to be a subject of discussion between the two firms. Has one firm exercised less control over expenditure than the other? If so, does this suggest a fundamental difference in

Example 7.6: Net profit and PEP

	Firm A	Firm B
Revenue	£20,000,000	£20,000,000
Direct costs	£13,450,000	£11,600,000
Gross margin	£6,550,000	£8,400,000
Total overheads	£6,000,000	£8,000,000
Net profit	£5,550,000	£4,400,000
Notional salaries	£4,950,000	£3,000,000
Distributable profit	£5,500,000	£3,400,000
Total number of equity partners	33	20
Net profit per equity partner	£167,000	£200,000
PEP	£166,700	£170,000
Overheads per equity partner	£181,800	£400,000
Total number of fee-earners*	116	116
Gearing	1:2.5	1:4.8
Overheads per fee-earner	£51,700	£69,000

* Including equity partners

decision-making and accountability between the two firms? Has one firm been under-investing in its overhead expenditure over a number of years so that, whilst it is boosting its PEP, it is creating a problem for the future? Has one firm been 'playing catch-up' (see below) whilst the other has invested regularly and sensibly over a number of years?

We are aware of a number of merger discussions where, whilst the business case looked good, and PEP of the two firms was not substantially different, talks broke down due to the differences in overheads. In some cases, the decision to abandon discussions was right – the difference in overheads reflected a different business model, which in turn reflected a fundamental difference in the type of work being done. General discussions between the two firms had not identified this problem, and it was not until a detailed analysis of the financials had been carried out that the differences came to light. In other cases, we have seen potential merger opportunities disappear because of a lack of understanding as to why there was a difference in overheads between the two firms.

As we touched on above, two reasons why there might be a difference in overheads and why merger discussions are aborted are the 'catch-up' issue and the under-investment issue, which are essentially two sides of the same coin.

'Catch-up'

The 'catch-up' issue is where a firm has fallen behind with its infrastructure investment, but having realised that, then sought to address it, resulting in a big outlay of expenditure over a short period. Whilst the growth in expenditure on an overhead per fee-earner basis should reduce relative to this outlay over the following few years, a prospective merger partner might not take this into account, considering only what the current level of expenditure of that firm is. In general terms, we do not see a 'catch-up' issue as a good reason to abandon a merger that has a strong business case.

Under-investment

The second stumbling block occurs where a firm has been under-investing over a number of years without realising the potential damage it will cause in the long term to the firm's competitiveness. A firm in this position which is in merger discussions with a firm that has a higher (but more realistic) overhead expenditure tends to view the other firm either as profligate or as having poor management (or usually both). Again, we have seen some potentially good mergers not go ahead because an under-investing firm failed to accept the reality of that situation. In such circumstances, a merger might still be possible, but only if the under-invested firm accepts its situation.

Firms with similar business models but different overhead levels and PEP

Difference in overhead spend can also be a reason why one firm has a much higher profitability than another. Two firms can have a similar business model and generate a similar level of gross margin per equity partner. There will, however, be a significant difference in PEP due to the substantive difference in overhead spend between the two firms. In such a situation, assuming the business case for merger is positive, and given the comparability at the gross margin level, we would not recommend that discussions be aborted simply because the overheads are out of line.

Solutions

Three-year timeframe

The first action we would recommend firms to take is to focus in detail on how the merged firm would look three years post-merger, how it would need to perform in order to be competitive in its new market position at that time, and what the infrastructure cost would be to support this. Also include in the calculation other resource costs and revenue that the business case indicates can be achieved over that period.

A successful merger should enable the 'new' firm to increase its profit margin, and to generate a higher PEP than either firm had pre-merger. Even if there is a short-term dilution in PEP in respect of one or both parties in the first year of merger, the overall benefits of the merger will provide a higher PEP over a subsequent number of years than either firm would have been likely to generate in its current market position with its existing strategy.

In considering the financials of a merger, a common major error is that the debate centres on the current financials of the two firms, and the impact of adding them together. Instead, the focus should be on what the financials will look like once the 'new' firm has achieved integration, and is operating competitively in its new market position. This goes back to our comments in **Chapter 1** about whether mergers really do add value.

The first post-merger year should never be considered as a 'value-adding' year. If it turns out to be so, that is a bonus, but the likelihood is that it will not. The real issue is whether the merger will add to 'shareholder' (ie equity partner) value thereafter. Hence, judgements need to be made based on a three-year time frame rather than on what the firm will look like in year one (especially if year one's projections are simply a combination of the two firms' financials in the year prior to merger).

Managing partners often believe this to be fine in theory, but are concerned about how they will be able to convince their fellow partners that the benefits of the merger will overcome any short-term dilution in PEP.

This will be difficult to achieve but it must be done. The argument will depend on the strategic maturity of the partnership, and the quality of the business case being put forward to support the merger.

Minimise dilution of profit of the more profitable firm in year one

The other issue for those negotiating a merger, and who see a difference in profitability as a stumbling block, is to look for solutions that minimise the dilution to one party's profit in the first year, and that allow the benefits of the merger over successive years to come through. How this is done will depend on whether the difference in PEP is due to operational issues or overhead expenditure.

In **Example 7.7**, Firm B has more equity partners than Firm A even though its revenue is 35% less than that of Firm A. The overheads as a percentage of revenues is the same in each case (30%). The difference in PEP arises because of differences in gearing. In the event that the two firms are in a similar market position, and have similar billing and utilisation rates, the real issue is clear – Firm A generates a revenue per equity partner of £1m and a net profit of 27.5% on revenues, whereas Firm B generates a revenue per equity partner of £636,000 and a net profit of 35% on revenues.

Example 7.7: Differences in PEP due to operational issues

	Firm A	Firm B
Revenue	£20,000,000	£14,000,000
Gross margin	£11,500,000	£9,100,000
Overheads	£6,000,000	£4,200,000
Net profit	£5,550,000	£4,900,000
Total number of equity partners	20	22
PEP	£275,000	£222,000
Gearing	1:4	1:2.4
Total number of fee-earners*	100	75

* Including equity partners

Assume that the relativity between these numbers applies for the last three years.

Firm B has achieved a higher net profit percentage because of lower fee-earner costs, a consequence of its lower gearing (1:2.4 compared with Firm A's 1:4), and no equity partner notional salary costs being included in the figures. Hence, it has revenue generated by equity partners but with no associated cost. Firm A has slightly fewer equity partners in total (20 compared with Firm B's 22), but those equity partners represent a significantly smaller percentage of total fee-earners (20%) than those in Firm B (29%). Hence, the proportionate generation of revenue by equity partners is greater in Firm B than in Firm A, as is the impact of not recording a cost of partner time.

In the event that the two firms merge, the PEP of the 'new' firm would be £248,000, a significant reduction for Firm A's partners, and one large enough to scupper the deal. However, the deal could be saved if the merger would result in some major benefit that would wipe out the year-end dilution for Firm A.

One solution is for Firm B to not bring all of its equity partners across to the merged firm. If Firm B converts some of its equity partners to associate or non-equity partner status so that the PEP is then comparable to that of Firm A, the problem is solved.

For example, reducing the partnership of Firm B to 14 partners, and recognising that the gross margin and net profit would reduce by the additional salary costs of eight former partners (say, a cost of £1.1m), the revised PEP for Firm B is £275,000 (ie gross margin of £4.9m less £1.1m in additional salary costs divided by 14).

Of course, it will be difficult to get the partnership of Firm B to vote for a merger in which 36% of the partners will no longer be partners. The expression 'turkeys and Christmas' springs to mind.

Another solution is to agree on minimum performance standards for the 'new' firm, and to allow Firm B's management to identify partners who are performing significantly below that minimum. Some of those partners could be convinced to retire at the time of merger on the grounds that they will find it 'difficult' in the merged firm.[9] Others, who go over to the 'new' firm, could remain equity partners post-merger but on a special profit share arrangement that reflects their lower performance standards. This could be on a permanent basis (although this is not recommended (see below)) or for an agreed period during which time they should be helped to raise their performance to the required level. A combination of special profit shares, retirements and demotions (or de-equitisations as they are often called) could therefore take care of the problem.

We do not recommend maintaining a group of partners on a special profit-sharing arrangement lower than that of their peer group for a long period of time. For one thing, it is tantamount to paying people for performing below the firm's standards. Secondly, when people are placed in a 'second class', under-performance can worsen over time, and there will then be a need to readjust remuneration downwards until those people have to resign or be dismissed. Finally, there is a danger that clients will

---

9 Surprisingly, there are often partners on both sides who support the merger at the 'firm' level but choose to opt out of it, so that may assist with the problem.

consider those partners' performance as typical of the firm, and that misleading signals about the standards of performance required by the firm will be given to the associates.

If a lockstep system, particularly a rigid one, is in place, the issue could be exacerbated. Simply bringing all the partners from both firms into the lockstep will create an immediate dilution of PEP for the partners of Firm A.

A solution in year one is for Firm B's partners to be brought into the lockstep at slightly lower levels than they previously held. One way to achieve this would be for the two firms to agree on the lockstep structure, and to agree to post-merger profits being distributed in the same proportion as the firms' profits in the year prior to merger (or the average profit of each firm over the previous three years).

Using the figures in **Example 7.7** above, if Firm A and Firm B agree to this, Firm A would have 53%[10] of the profit of the merged firm in year one, and Firm B would have 47%. Firm B would then allocate the profit to its partners based on the agreed lockstep. If there are a couple of high-flying partners at Firm B who deserve to be at the top of the lockstep in the merged firm, Firm B might need to compensate for this by placing other partners at a level in the lockstep below the level they were at in Firm B.

If the two firms can reach agreement about the acceptable profit share per partner without Firm B having to reduce partner numbers, it will be crucial that the management of the merged firm seeks to raise the performance of the partners who have been put at a lower level on the lockstep in the first few years. Otherwise, in a rigid lockstep, they would automatically move up to higher profit share levels over time, regardless of any improvement in their performance.

Firms with flexible locksteps (ie where partners can move down as well as up), have a somewhat easier task in reconciling differences in PEP than those on a rigid lockstep. If Firm A and Firm B agreed to a flexible lockstep, partners in Firm B could enter the lockstep at lower levels and, if there was no improvement in their performance, would remain at those levels (provided they still met the minimum standards required of equity partners). If the profit-sharing system is such that all equity partners do need to achieve a minimum standard of performance, there may be the problem of some of the partners in Firm B being below that standard from the outset, and this will need to be dealt with as discussed above.

Firms using merit-based remuneration systems might also find that they can accommodate differences in PEP simply by reflecting this in the performance assessments that lead to the allocation of profit shares. Problems occur, however, where

---

10 53% of £10.4m (£5.5m plus £4.9m).

the performance of some partners results in the difference between the highest and lowest rewarded partners being too wide, as illustrated below.

Assume Firms A and B had merit-based remuneration systems: Firm A's partner rewards ranged from £190,000 to £450,000 which equates to a 'spread' of 2.4 (ie £450,000 is 2.4 times £190,000) and Firm B had a range of profit shares from £150,000 to £400,000 (or a spread of nearly 2.7).

Firm A and Firm B might therefore agree to widen the spread in the 'new' firm to 3, thereby allowing the £150,000 performers in Firm B to be accommodated without increasing the spread to an overly high level. This increase could last for a defined period of time during which the lowest-end performers should be helped to improve their performance (or should resign).

The only problem would be if this resulted in the lowest end of partner remuneration falling below the highest end of remuneration of senior associates. Whilst this could be accommodated by making up the better performing senior associates to partners at profit share levels above the lowest end, it would be better not to do so, and for the spread to be reduced back after an integration period.

There are many firms which believe that it is not healthy for a partnership to have too wide a spread, and a ratio of 3 is often seen as the maximum.[11]

As we have shown above, differences in PEP due to operational issues can be accommodated in a variety of ways. In many cases, firms will use a mixture of all of the above solutions. Some partners (from either firm) might accept a demotion in status, others might accept retirement. Adjustments to the remuneration system of the 'new' firm might be able to accommodate a wider range of profit shares than either firm had before, even if it is just for a short period of time. Overall though, the issue that needs to be addressed is the differing levels of performance of partners. Even if the poorer performing partners can be accommodated into the profit-sharing arrangements of the 'new' firm, it might be better to address their performance issues pre-merger. Where this is not possible (for example, if it will result in the merger failing to get the vote), the under-performing partners must be made aware of the need to raise their standards over the first couple of years in the 'new' firm or face demotion or retirement. The issue must not, however, be avoided, as to do so could result in the merged firm not achieving its projections, and in the better performers becoming disillusioned and resigning.

The solutions are different where the reason for the difference in PEP lies in the differing overheads of the two firms. This is illustrated using **Example 7.8**.

---

[11] The appropriate ratio will depend on each firm – we have seen some firms operate effectively on a spread of 4.

Example 7.8: Differences in PEP due to overhead differences

	Firm A	Firm B
Revenue	£20,000,000	£14,000,000
Gross margin	£11,500,000	£8,000,000
Overheads	£7,100,000	£4,200,000
Net profit	£4,400,000	£3,800,000
Total number of equity partners	20	14
PEP	£220,000	£271,000
Gross margin per partner	£575,000	£571,000
Total number of fee-earners*	100	75
Gearing	1:4	1:4.3
Overheads per fee-earner	£71,000	£56,000

* Including equity partners

Assume that the relativity between these numbers applies for the last three years.

In **Example 8**, Firm A and Firm B perform almost identically – gearing is the same, the revenue per partner and revenue per fee-earner is very close and the gross margin per partner is very close. The difference is purely in the overheads per fee-earner spend.

Assume that Firm A has invested heavily over recent years in premises, technology and general infrastructure, which is only starting to benefit Firm A now, and will benefit Firm B post-merger. Assume also that this improved infrastructure is better than that of Firm B, and Firm B recognises this. The answer here is relatively simple – some form of negotiation on profit shares will take place based on the amount per partner that the negotiators can agree is an appropriate number allowing for the fact that Firm's A overhead expenditure will generate future benefits. Hence, Firm A's partners might well go into the merger on equal terms financially with Firm B's partners.

For example, it might be quite clear that Firm A has invested in new premises that can accommodate the new firm (or a large part of it) and which are both superior to Firm B's, and more appropriate to the image of the merged firm. Assume that this results in a difference in overheads per partner of £20,000. In addition, Firm A has installed 'state of the art' technology throughout all of its operations, and this results in a difference in overheads per partner of £15,000. Furthermore, Firm A has recruited several top-quality professional managers in activities such as HR, marketing, technology and finance. These people are much better qualified and more experienced than Firm B's professional managers, and are also more appropriate to the needs of the merged firm. The difference in overheads per partner in respect of this is £10,000.

Therefore, the total difference in overheads per partner is £45,000, which in fact is about the amount of difference in PEP. In such a situation, there is no magic formula that should be used to come up with the appropriate profit shares for the two firms in the 'new' firm, but carrying out this sort of analysis provides a platform on which negotiations can take place. For example, if Firm A's investment in infrastructure is now complete, its budgets for the next year as an independent firm might prove a better guide to the appropriate profit shares than the past few years. If Firm A's budget indicates that overhead expenditure is declining to, say, 30% compared to nearly 36% in the previous year, then its budgeted PEP could well be closer to (or even above) that of Firm B. Equally, if Firm B had planned to invest in new technology and a general upgrade of its infrastructure in the next three years, then this is a cost that need not be incurred if the merger goes ahead.

What is clear is that Firm A's partners are likely to reject a merger based on a profit-sharing basis using net profit figures of 54:46 if they expect their PEP to rise significantly in the future as financial outlays have already been made. They will feel that Firm B's partners are gaining at their expense. Assume that budgets for the following year indicate that Firm A's PEP will be restored to around £250,000 (or a net profit of £5m) and that Firm B's PEP will remain at the same level. This would then result in a profit share ratio of 57:43 in favour of Firm A.

In this type of situation, the firms would probably reach an agreement on the profit share in a ratio somewhere between 54:46 and 57:43. In our experience, it should be possible for Firm A and Firm B to reach agreement somewhere in that range if there is a strong business case for merger, and if Firm B realises that its overhead costs would need to rise over the next few years in any event.

The difficulty arises when firms lack understanding about why there is a difference in overheads. This is where having peer group data is helpful. As we noted earlier, legal magazines produce financial information on law firms, including statistics on overheads per fee-earner for the top 100 firms. Some accounting firms also provide surveys of key financial statistics of selected groups of firms. Other auditors of law firms make data available on an anonymous basis. There is therefore data available to support the hypothesis (or not) that one firm is under-investing in its infrastructure in comparison with its current peer group. It can also support the hypothesis (or not) that the level of expenditure of one firm would be more appropriate for the merged firm's new peer group. Independent of financial data, it is also possible to demonstrate to a firm with the lower overheads (in **Example 7.8**, Firm B) that having the higher overheads of the other firm (in **Example 7.8**, Firm A) is more appropriate for a firm with the proposed market position of the merged firm.

This is another area where having an adviser who understands the legal market can be of significant value. The adviser should be equipped to help explain to the two firms the infrastructure support that would be required to compete in the market position envisaged in the business case for the 'new' firm. They can also help identify the difference between what both firms have in place pre-merger, and what it will be essential for the 'new' firm to have in order to be competitive post-merger. In the event that the firm with the lower overheads remains unconvinced, and does not consider the business case to be strong enough to overcome the difference in PEP, the proposed merger should probably not proceed. Such an attitude would indicate some fundamental differences in understanding between the two firms about what is required to compete in the future, in particular, as a merged firm. No matter how one attempts to address other issues, any merger between the two firms would only create significant challenges and tensions.

Differences in funding requirements

Another financial issue that bedevils many merger discussions is that of differences in funding requirements. The funding of a firm is made up of capital contributions of partners and borrowing. In some cases, the capital contribution of partners in one firm is double that of partners in the other. A firm that chooses not to borrow is likely to have larger capital requirements from its partners than one that does.

Law firms are not highly capital-intensive businesses. Whilst technology today can be hugely expensive, most of the resources required to provide legal services mainly give rise to operational costs. The use of property can also result in the need for capital contributions and borrowings at certain times in the life of a firm. Moving into a new building requires lease deposits, fit-out costs, new furniture, and costs associated with the move, and can create a need for further funding. Most firms, however, do not move regularly and, whilst some large firms take on new property as they expand, for most, major property costs (other than annual lease costs and maintenance) are incurred infrequently.

A significant determinant of a law firm's funding requirement is the speed at which bills to clients for work carried out are issued and then paid. A high proportion of a firm's costs is paid monthly (salaries, rent and many other operating costs). Some costs that are incurred in one month might also be paid in the following month, but the short-term creditors of most law firms are generally significantly below their short-term assets of debtors and work-in-progress (WIP), particularly where WIP is valued at full recoverable value (see below).

Valuation

Whilst we do not intend to discuss the various means of valuing WIP in great detail, firms do need to agree on a consistent valuation for the purposes of financial due diligence. Changes in UK taxation law affecting partnerships mean that most firms are now required to value WIP at near full selling price (including the time cost of partners) subject to a discount for historical under-recovery. Hence, the value of WIP in the balance sheet includes a profit element as recorded hours are valued at 'selling prices' or standard billing rates which include a profit margin.

The same is true of a firm's debtors and any other major assets and liabilities. It is important that the finance directors of each firm understand the valuation policies in use by both firms and endeavour to agree on a policy for the merged firm. At the same time, they must also convert the valuations in the latest balance sheets, and any projected balance sheets, using that agreed valuation policy.

This is a vital step in forecasting the funding requirements of the merged firm (assuming that merger goes ahead).

The issue of how firms fund their businesses raises all sorts of concerns in merger discussions. The fact that one firm borrows (eg has a bank overdraft) other than for very short-term needs can lead to partners in a firm that almost never borrows categorising that firm as being a high risk-taker, profligate or poorly managed (or all three). The firm that borrows as a part of its funding requirements can view the non-borrowing firm as lacking in commercial good sense.

However, firms need to understand the reasons behind each others' borrowing policies. Firms that do not often borrow think that firms that do are 'borrowing to pay partners' drawings'. In fact, the borrowings are simply a part of the overall funding of the firm's debtors, WIP and other assets, with partner capital making up much of the balance.

There is sometimes an historical and a cultural issue related to the funding policies of firms. We find that many smaller to mid-sized firms who eschew borrowings (other than very short-term) have often experienced a situation in the past that led the partners of the firm to decide not to rely on borrowings. Over time, this has then become part of the cultural beliefs of a firm.

The merger to form Addleshaw Goddard is a good example of this. Theodore Goddard had gone through a difficult period in the early to mid 1990s, and, having survived it, decided it was safer to restrict any borrowings to short-term 'blips' in cashflow (eg when partners' taxation payments were due), and to not have an on-going overdraft.

Addleshaw Booth & Co, on the other hand, had expanded rapidly in Leeds and Manchester, moved into two new buildings in both locations, and invested heavily in upgrading its infrastructure and technology. The firm had borrowed to assist the funding of these developments, but within its agreed ratio of borrowings to partner capital.

During the initial merger discussions, Theodore Goddard's negotiating team was concerned about Addleshaw Booth & Co's borrowings. It felt that Addleshaw Booth & Co was in a somewhat risky position, and had potentially over-exposed itself to debt. Addleshaw Booth & Co's negotiating team was concerned that Theodore Goddard's attitude represented a cultural obstacle that could put an end to the merger discussions. The matter was discussed at some length, including an explanation by each firm of the reasons for its concerns, and the issue was resolved. It was agreed that the merged firm would have a borrowings policy, and Theodore Goddard came to understand that it was not highly risky to do so, given the structure of the 'new' firm. Although the problem was dealt with, it was quite an important issue that could have jeopardised the deal if both sides had not been prepared to discuss it frankly.

The critical step that needs to be taken before the negotiating teams get into a debate about past policies, is to agree on what the funding requirements of the 'new' firm are likely to be. If one side has operated with a significantly higher number of days' revenue tied up in WIP and debtors than the other, some understanding of why it has operated like this will be required in order for both sides to decide on appropriate assumptions to be made for the new firm.[12] As noted above, the finance directors also need to agree on an appropriate value of assets and liabilities that will be transferred into the 'new' firm.

---

12 Debtors and WIP should be converted to the equivalent number of days' revenue in order to compare relative efficiencies in managing these. This is done by dividing the average level of debtors and WIP by the average revenue generated each day (either working days or calendar days) over a year.

In addition, a policy on how profit of the 'new' firm is to be distributed to partners needs to be agreed before considering the funding requirements of the firm.

Some firms distribute a high proportion of the profit on a monthly basis, with only a limited amount carried over to year-end. This means that if the actual profit and/or cash flow fall behind budget to a large extent, the monthly drawings of partners will need to be reduced as the year progresses (or the firm might need to borrow).

Other firms pay a lower amount of profit monthly, and then top it up with quarterly distributions when cash is available. Others distribute low monthly drawings, and then pay out the balance after year-end (or divide the balance up across the monthly drawings of the following year).

Once the finance directors have agreed on these matters, they can then compile a forecast cash flow, profit and loss, and balance sheet for the 'new' firm, and determine the funding requirements for both the whole year and the peaks and troughs during that year.

At that point, the negotiating teams can debate whether the 'new' firm will be funded totally out of partner capital or with a combination of borrowings and capital, and if borrowings are to be used whether they will be on a short-term basis only (eg only using a temporary overdraft to cover tax payments) or on a more permanent basis. The policy on borrowings then needs to be established. Some firms use a percentage of revenue as the benchmark; others define it in relation to the total partner capital; others use both. For example, a firm could operate on a policy of borrowing no more than 15% of revenue, or up to an amount equal to partner capital, whichever is the lowest.

Conclusion

Mergers should not stand or fall on financial matters alone. Nevertheless, it is critical for the negotiating teams to look behind the headline numbers of each firm and understand why they are the way they are. As we have stressed throughout this chapter, headline numbers should not provide the basis for deciding whether or not to merge. A detailed analysis of what constitutes the headline numbers, and the policies and thinking behind that, is a much more important basis of decision-making.

Furthermore, it is important that the financials are translated into forecasts for the 'new' firm (on the assumption that the merger will go ahead). Finance directors might draw up several options for cashflow forecasts based on differing assumptions, and the impact of this on both the balance sheet and the funding requirement of the 'new' firm can then be discussed by the negotiating teams. Only with this detailed analysis is it likely that the negotiating teams will be able to agree on what is appropriate for the 'new' firm, and, if the policies vary significantly from a firm's existing approach, how they will win the vote of partners who will be sensitive to the financial issues. Whilst the partners are the owners of the business, and should therefore make key strategic decisions (such as whether or not to merge) with a long-term perspective in mind, they are also working proprietors and depend on the firm for their income. Hence, when analysing the financials, firms must consider both the short and longer-term impact for the 'new' firm.

CHAPTER 8: INTEGRATION

Introduction

Merger negotiations take up a lot of time and effort. Once the negotiating teams have agreed on a deal, they have to present it to and discuss it with the partnership. Not only are these latter stages of the process labour-intensive and tiring, members of the negotiating team also have the pressure of having to carry out their day-to-day work at the same time. Most team members put in long hours at this stage in the merger process, and still fall behind on their 'normal' work.

When this happens, lawyers often feel that the negotiating process has taken over their lives. Even corporate lawyers who are used to being involved in company merger discussions find it totally absorbing and stressful because it is their own firm that they are dealing with, rather than the business of a client. This makes a significant difference. A corporate lawyer who participated in the merger discussions of his firm remarked: 'Now I know how my clients feel. It's different when it's your own business.'

As a consequence, many mergers are completed without very much thought being given to the process of integration. Furthermore, no one is in the mood to deal with it immediately post-merger either. Members of management, in particular the managing partner, are the logical people to take charge of integration, but they are in the same position as everyone else – areas of their work will have been neglected, especially in the closing stages of the merger negotiations, and they will also feel pressured into getting back on top of their 'normal' job as soon as possible. Equally, given the intensity of the final stages, they will also want to take a step back from the whole issue of merger for a short period of time.

This is the danger point in any merger situation. Having developed a business case that appealed to the partners, having addressed all of the various organisational, financial and client issues, and (hopefully) having drummed up excitement amongst the staff, nothing happens (or at least nothing of significance appears to happen) in the immediate post-merger phase. Eventually, task forces will be appointed, practice groups will gradually start to work together (although this is often driven by individuals personally rather than as part of a planned process) and the infrastructure of the two firms will be gradually brought together.

Usually, progress will occur in areas such as finance, HR, technology and marketing (the infrastructure departments) because there is an obvious need for these to be combined.[1] However, if integration does not occur in the legal practice areas as well, the promised competitive benefits of the merger will never be achieved.

One firm with which we worked some years ago was the product of a merger eight years previously. People in the merged firm, however, still referred to 'us' and 'them'. Whilst members of each practice group sat near each other, there was no integration of the antecedent firms' client teams, no fusion of documentation, precedents and standard forms, and no attempt to develop consistent approaches to working. The firm was, in fact, still two firms which just shared space and resources (apart from the infrastructure departments which had all been integrated). Clients still instructed the lawyers from whichever firm they had used pre-merger. They were not aware of the size of the merged firm, nor the added depth in key practice areas it now had. They had, no doubt, read promotional material at the time of the merger, but, as they had not seen any evidence of the merger in practice, soon forgot what they had read. Consequently, the firm did not present a cohesive, 'one firm' image to the market, and did not demonstrate any enhancement in its competitive capabilities. The business had grown since the merger but not in any strategic sense, and certainly not in a way that achieved any of the key strategic objectives set out in the business case for merger. There have been many similar mergers over the last decade. It is therefore not surprising that post-merger integration is generally considered the most difficult part of the overall merger process to achieve.

The (incorrect) argument that 'most mergers fail' (that we introduced in **Chapter 1**) should therefore be restated as 'most mergers that fail do so because of poor integration'. Executing an integration plan is a fundamental requirement of making a merger work, no matter how well devised the merger was, and no matter how strategic.

Post-merger, management has a huge amount to do in the first three to six months in the life of a merged firm. There will be two areas of management that will need to be co-ordinated. First, management will need to focus on the day-to-day operations of the business, and ensure that people do not lose sight of the fact that they need to grow and develop a profitable business. Alongside this, is the need for management to ensure that each business unit (department, office, practice group) from the two firms

---

1 In the merger proposal, it is often these areas where cost savings are promised.

is combined to form a cohesive group of people, is focused on the merged firm's strategic objectives, and works in a consistent way. Implementing work processes, documentation and knowledge management processes so that the 'new' firm has a consistent process for preparing correspondence and opinions is all part of achieving a 'one firm' approach.

Getting to know people and understanding how the 'other side' of the business works are also important. However, these things should not take precedence over the two key issues:

(i) maintaining a focus on business operations so that the firm still makes the required profit; and

(ii) implementing the changes that are a necessary part of achieving the business case for merger, and the strategic objectives for the 'new' firm.

This chapter sets out the vital elements of the process that need to be carried out in order to ensure successful integration. Some firms might have found other processes that work, but all of them will have contained the elements set out below.

No matter how strong the business case for merger is, and no matter how enthusiastic people are on day one of merger, things can go horribly wrong if the integration process is not extremely well managed. Whilst many of the points made in this chapter about achieving an effective integration process are directed more at medium-to-large sized firms, the principles can still be applied in a smaller firm, albeit in a modified way.

What must not be lost sight of is the fact that successful integration will transform the firm and its business. To achieve its strategic objectives, the firm needs to be fundamentally different in five years time than it is on day one of the merger. If it is not, the firm needs to question why it merged in the first place.

If a firm carries out the tasks set out in this chapter, and does so well, integration will be achieved within a three-to-four-year period (or even quicker). Clients, partners and staff will be able to see the firm change, enhance its competitiveness, and operate in the way that it should in order to be successful in its new market position. Enthusiasm will be maintained across the firm, it will attract new staff and clients, and important clients will be retained and will give it better-value work. Furthermore, if management is doing its job, levels of profitability will move towards the desired targets.

Integrating a merged firm is more difficult than negotiating the merger deal, and will generally take place over a much longer period of time than the in-depth talks did. There is therefore little point in merging if firms are not prepared to devote the resources necessary for a successful integration, and to exercise the discipline that pursuing an effective integration plan will require.

Five principles to support an effective merger integration process

There are five principles that support an effective merger integration process:

(i)   recognise that the integration process should start before closure of the merger deal;

(ii)   communication can never be overdone;

(iii) plan the integration process rigorously;

(iv) manage and monitor the integration process; and

(v)   execution must be across two main activities, operations and integration, with both competing for the same resources.

Integration starts before closure

The first principle is that the integration process should be started before the merger deal is closed. If integration is postponed until after the merger, it might never get off the ground. As discussed above, the actual merger negotiations are exhausting and result in those involved lacking the time and energy required to launch straight into devising the integration plan. However, if a gap is allowed to open up between closure and integration, there is a very high risk that any integration that does occur will only be partially effective.

Due diligence

In **Chapter 4**, we explained that there comes a point in every merger negotiation when it becomes almost certain whether or not an agreement between the two firms can be reached. Once this point is reached, the due diligence exercise should be undertaken and, as part of this, firms should start to draw up an integration plan.

Heads of the infrastructure departments of each firm should meet to discuss what their policies currently are and how they operate, and also how the two departments can be integrated. They should then report back to the negotiating team, not just saying whether or not they foresee any problems with the integration process and what those problems are, but also how integration will take place. A problem which is often raised is that only one of the heads of department at the antecedent firms will be head of department at the merged firm. However, this should not prevent the two heads working together on an implementation plan. In fact, if one person proves difficult, that should help management decide who to select as head of the department in the 'new' firm.

The same is true for each practice group and office (if the merged firm is to have multiple offices). The due diligence exercise is not just about working out the degree of compatibility of each practice group, but also about how the two practice groups can be integrated. Even if they are compatible in terms of the way they work, they could be extremely difficult to integrate, particularly if every partner has their own documentation, precedents, knowledge base and style. If neither antecedent firm had any cohesive and consistent processes across its partnership previously, the integration process will be even more difficult.

Hence, by the time the prospectus for the proposed merger goes before the partners, the negotiating team should have put together a reasonably comprehensive integration plan (which includes a plan for its implementation within the first six months). However, given what we have already noted about the intensive nature of the closing stages of merger negotiations, it is rare for the negotiating teams to focus on the integration plan at this stage.

Integration task force

The solution is to put together a small interim integration task force (ITF) made up of individuals from both sides who are practical, commercial and 'doers' rather than 'conceptual pontificators'. This task force could include more professional managers than partners, although in such a case, the managers would be reliant on partners in the practice groups to provide them with the relevant material. The group should elect one member as chair, who should also be approved by the negotiating teams. The interim ITF should be appointed as soon as it is clear that a deal between the firms can be reached.

Its role, at this stage, is to provide the framework for the integration plan, and to monitor the various discussion groups (as suggested in **Chapter 4**) to ensure that the individual integration plans are being developed at the same time that compatibility is being discussed. They need not contain every action step, but do need to be in sufficient detail so that people are fully aware as to what has to happen in order for the merger to be effective.

The interim ITF should report to the negotiating groups jointly, and keep them informed of progress. It should not, therefore, include any member of the negotiating teams. Ideally, it should also not include anyone in a key management role, as they will be busy ensuring that the ongoing business is being managed effectively, overseeing the drawing up of integration plans, and possibly being involved in the merger negotiations at the firm-wide level. We appreciate, however, that this will be difficult in a merger of small firms.

As soon as the merger has been agreed, the interim ITF should be made permanent, and its membership should be reviewed. Again, people in key management roles in the 'new' firm should not be members of the task force. Other changes in the structure of the merging firms might also require changes in the ITF's composition when it becomes permanent. Ideally, the chairman of the interim ITF should be retained (something to be kept in mind when making the initial appointment).

The permanent ITF should be appointed initially for one year, with the option of being re-appointed. It should report to the managing partner and the management board (at operational level) of the merged firm.

Many firms which are involved in a merger only get the 'outer edge' of integration right at the outset. Many launch the 'new' firm on day one with new nameplates on buildings, new letterheads, brochures and other publicity material, and some even manage to get a new website (often a temporary one) up and running. However, when dealing with the lawyers they used to instruct pre-merger, clients see little real change, and, if they then start to deal with lawyers from the other firm involved in the merger as well, they see a stark difference in their work processes and style of communication.

As noted earlier, many firms tend to only integrate the infrastructure departments, and just assume that the lawyers in each practice group and department will somehow form a cohesive unit by themselves. However, this rarely happens without an effective process that guides, drives and pushes for integration.

The heads of practice groups and departments are usually too busy in the months following a merger to focus on integration. Instead, they tend to be preoccupied with trying to keep the enlarged business on track financially, and with answering a myriad of enquiries that people have about day-to-day issues.

The same applies in respect of the managing partners of merged firms. A major task for them in the months following the merger is to get to know people from the other firm, and to come to grips with managing a business significantly larger than they had before. Another huge task is to ensure that the budgeted revenue and profitability targets are met. When this is achieved, it results in a huge psychological boost for those in the merged firm. A failure to do so, however, can lead to people focusing on the problems of the first year (and there will be difficulties and disruption), and becoming gloomy and pessimistic about the future of the merged firm. If it becomes apparent that the firm might not hit its targets in the first year, then the management team will need to work hard to explain the issues behind the shortfall, and to maintain motivation and morale.

In the first merger year, the managing partner has the twin responsibilities of ensuring the firm achieves:

(i) its operational targets; and

(ii) the required level of integration.

To achieve the first, the managing partner needs to work with the department and practice group heads of the firm. To achieve the second, it is vital that an ITF is formed to implement the activities required for integration throughout the firm. The managing partner cannot afford to be too deeply involved in one activity. To do so will mean that attention given to the other will be reduced, and will result in a significant increase in the risk that the firm will not achieve what is required.

The role of the ITF must be clarified, and a set of targets should be agreed for it. This requires the heads of practice groups and departments to work closely with the ITF to devise an integration plan and timetable that complements the plan and timetable for them meeting their responsibilities in regard to operational performance.

In larger firms, it is important that the structure of each group mirrors the top-level structure, and that someone is appointed to be in charge of integration, to report to the head of the group, and to be the key liaison with the ITF. It is at this level that most integration problems occur. The operational groups are already busy dealing with clients and overseeing the associates' work, as well as handling marketing, billing and other 'normal' activities. The integration process therefore imposes an additional burden on them. However, the tasks required to attain integration need to be carried out within each business unit, and by those in the unit. The ITF's job therefore is to assist in planning what has to be done in each group, agreeing a realistic timetable (taking into account the need to maintain business operations), obtaining any support the group requires to assist with the integration tasks, monitoring progress with the timetable in mind, and reporting back to the management board. Without a group focused on the integration process, business units will always focus more on day-to-day operational issues and client work, and will tend to push the integration activities down the agenda (and off it).

Members of the ITF

Many law firms should take a leaf out of their clients' books. Successful mergers of mid-to-large-sized companies are almost always supported by a task force dedicated to achieving a quick integration. As noted earlier, the reasons many mergers do not add the value expected tend to be more due to poor integration than anything else. Corporate management realises the importance of integration activities, and recognises that they cannot simply be added to the work of people who are running operations without something going awry. The actual skills required to carry out the integration process are different to the skills required to carry out day-to-day management, and very different from those needed to be a lawyer. Firms which leave integration to the management team (some members of which will also have client responsibilities) are imposing a huge burden on the individuals involved.

Firms are increasingly becoming aware that integration requires a different set of skills, and that it needs to be a separate activity, and will structure the process accordingly. In some cases, people from within the business have been 'seconded' to the integration team for a certain period of time. In others, the assistance of specialist consultants has been enlisted. Firms which adopt the second approach recognise the need to use people with a different skill set.

Addleshaw Goddard followed the second approach, and employed consultants who specialised in post-merger integration. The consultants advised management on the integration plan and timetable, and interacted with each business unit to ensure that progress on integration was being made at the same time as they carried out normal business activities. Having been through a merger previously that had taken some time to bed down, the partners from Addleshaw Booth & Co saw the benefit in bringing in experienced people to drive the integration process.

Berwin Leighton Paisner, however, adopted the secondment approach, and put in place an integration team made up of individuals from within the firm. A timetable was established, and the integration team ensured that each department spent as much time monitoring integration as it did business activities. Denton Wilde Sapte left the task to the central management team. Whilst that approach worked for it, Denton Wilde Sapte also had a significant number of people in key roles who could drive the process. A small firm will not have that resource available.

Clearly, a smaller firm will find it more difficult to 'second' people to work on integration full time, and may also find external consultants too expensive. Nevertheless, the process of integration is so important to the success of the merger that it is very risky to leave it in the hands of management.

The low-risk approach that a small firm can take is to appoint one person to oversee the integration process, and to report to the managing partner on progress. If progress occurs quickly, the managing partner might be able to take over the role after three to six months. It is high risk, however, not to have someone in place at the outset, and to assume that the managing partner can focus on both the business and integration activities. To reiterate, when people are busy it is always the latter activity that suffers.

Communication can never be overdone

Successful integration requires consistent communication between management, partners and others within the firm. The business case for merger will contain the key strategic objectives of the 'new' firm, and the market position that it is seeking to achieve. Whilst a lot of activity might occur in the aftermath of the merger, some of the issues that underpin the strategic objectives justifying the merger may never get addressed. For example, whilst many merger prospectuses stress the need for the merged firm to operate in a consistent manner and to present a unified approach to the market, two years on, little may have been done to integrate the work processes within the practice groups. It is the integration of these work processes that will send a clear message to the market about a 'one firm' consistency.

As discussed in previous chapters, a clear and unambiguous strategic vision for the 'new' firm should form part of the business case for merger. Once the merger is completed and integration is under way, management needs to develop a statement that embodies the vision of the 'new' firm, its key strategic objectives and the activities and processes required to achieve them. This must be stated and restated at every opportunity. The process for communicating this vision is set out in **Table 8.1** below.

Early on in the post-merger phase, a statement that reflects steps 1 and 2 needs to be repeatedly made internally.

	Table 8.1: Process for communicating a shared vision
1.	Review the vision for the 'new' firm set out in the business case.
2.	Develop the strategic objectives that emanate from this vision.
3.	Develop some clear goals for each objective which are measurable and understandable.
4.	Define the activities and processes required for each objective.
5.	Develop a work plan for integrating each activity and process throughout the firm.

For example, a simple and clear statement that reflects the merged firm's vision might be: 'To be recognised by the market as one of the three or four leading firms in the region.'

This goal is measurable. Interviews with buyers of legal services over a two-to-three-year period will show if the firm is recognised as one of the three or four leading firms in the region. Furthermore, people from the 'new' firm will know from the outset which other firms will be competing for this position, as some assessment of them will have been done pre-merger in order to identify the strategic objectives necessary for a firm in that market position. (Of course, some of these objectives might need to be amended to reflect changes in the marketplace.)

The initial communication for this firm should therefore be:

'We intend to be one of the few leading firms in our region. To achieve this, we need to increase our market penetration within our largest 50 clients, to build greater critical mass in practice areas A, B and C, and to have highly consistent ways of working so that clients receive a quality of service that they identify with us.'

Another way of communicating the same message is:

'There are four objectives that will achieve our merger aims:

(i) we need to attract more large clients from our region;

(ii) we need to receive more work from our biggest clients spread across more practice areas;

(iii) we need to "bulk up" some practice areas; and

(iv) we need to work in a consistent way so that clients view us as a firm, not a "loose" group of individuals.'

In practice, there might be a couple more areas of change required to achieve the vision, but the above provides an example. Note that the statements above are all action-focused. Statements which denote action include the phrases 'intend to be', 'need to develop', 'need to increase', and 'need to build'.

At the same time as this message is being communicated, management also needs to communicate the goals of the firm. For example:

'There are 450 large corporates based in our region, many of which we do not provide services to at present. Thirty of them see us as one of their main legal providers, another 15 use us in specific areas regularly, and some of the others are aware of us. Sixty-five companies view one of our competitors as their main legal provider. We therefore need to grow our market share to at least that over the next three years, and treble the number of corporates which use us regularly.'

A statement like that made time and time again soon communicates the challenge to the firm.

The message also needs to be strongly communicated by the marketing department as it develops plans and works with partners to define the marketing activities to be put in place to achieve the objectives of the firm.

The same statement can be made in various ways. Another way to make the statement above is:

'If we are to be one of a few leading firms in the region within three years, we need to take on another 35 large locally-based corporates as clients which see us as their main legal provider.'

Key messages also need to be communicated in a purposeful manner. There should be no qualification or hesitation. This is what will make the merger successful, and management must not equivocate about this.

Once these messages start to have an impact, the other steps in **Table 8.1** need to be introduced (ie steps 3 to 5). For example, the marketing plans for each practice group should focus on the type of client that the 'new' firm is targeting as part of its strategy. Both firms might have had quite different marketing priorities pre-merger to those required post-merger. Hence, whilst articulating the vision, objectives and goals, management also needs to articulate the areas of change. The fact that each group needs to adjust its marketing focus to address the needs of the 'new' firm should be articulated clearly.

Communication must be external as well as internal. Whilst firms must avoid building up expectations in the marketplace which cannot be met (as yet), it is important that communication is made to existing clients, potential clients and other important market intermediaries. These messages need to stress the key aspects of the 'new' firm consistently, and to ensure that people's expectations are being appropriately built up.

Central management will have an important role to play here, particularly in communicating with the 'new' firm's core clients. Partners in charge of key accounts will also be major communication channels. It is vital that they send out a consistent set of messages about the 'new' firm, and that these messages reflect the firm's ability to deliver what they say they are going to.

Whilst all of this sounds like common sense, it is true, as the old saying goes, that 'common sense is not all that common'. We have worked with a large number of firms on post-merger integration, often some time after the merger took place. In areas such as targeting the clients that formed part of the strategic focus of the merger, we found that very little had happened. Marketing plans for the merged firm often did not exist, partners were still just marketing to the targets of their antecedent firm and, most commonly, very little marketing had been done at the practice group level. The firms were in a state of limbo, waiting for clarification.

Client relationship management is another area where nothing often happens unless a very conscious effort to focus on this activity is made during the integration process. Despite statements (such as in the example above) about increasing the merged firm's market share of the legal spend of major clients, partners are slow to make changes to client teams and client contacts, and to introduce clients to people from the other side of the merger. In fact, this and the development of consistent work processes, documentation and reporting style are two of the most resisted areas following a merger. Whilst they are both key to the success of many mergers, they are also the areas which require the greatest change of behaviour by partners. Even when the need for change in both of these areas is articulated prior to the merger, a significant amount of resistance can be encountered post-merger, even from partners who were enthusiasts for the merger.

All sorts of excuses, rationalisations and avoidance tactics are used. For example, partners will often say that they cannot introduce new people to clients until 'we get to know them better themselves', or they will say that 'it isn't the right time to bring in new faces'.

Integration of work processes also meets the same level of resistance. Comments such as 'who says their way of doing things is better than ours?', 'we have enough to do at the moment without tackling that', and 'let's wait until we get to know each other better' are often made.

There must be a constant communication that reminds people of the strategic vision that drove the merger, the objectives that support that vision, and the key targets for each objective. This has to come as a consistent message from everyone in a management role. Partners and others who are busy with their 'day job', need to be reminded regularly that their 'day job' post-merger must include carrying out new activities focused on integration, and that these will require partners to change the way they have worked in the past.

Of course, the firm has to also back up its statements of vision, objectives and targets by providing the resources and the means to effect change.

Plan the integration process rigorously

We discussed earlier in this chapter that significant issues affecting integration should be developed during the pre-merger due diligence process, and that an outline integration plan should be in place at the time of merger under the guidance and direction of the interim ITF.

We also noted that once the merger has been agreed, the permanent ITF should immediately be appointed. Firms should not wait until the date on which the merger actually takes place to do so. It is quite common to have a gap of three or four months (or even more) between the agreement to merge and the 'official' start date of the merged firm. This time should be used to kick-start the integration process.

Develop a work plan

The first task for the ITF is to develop a work plan for integrating each activity and process (see step 5 in **Table 8.1** above). There are five key areas of activity that should be included in the integration plan. These are set out in **Table 8.2** below.

Whilst many of these activities will have been addressed and decisions about them made during the merger process, the ITF's responsibility is to ensure that each activity is actually integrated. For example, the structure of the partnership will have been decided as part of the merger agreement (ie whether the merged firm will be made up of equity partners only). Nevertheless, a considerable amount of work will be

Table 8.2: Key activity areas				
Ownership	Strategy	Top management	Management processes	Administrative processes
• Partnership structure • Capital/funding • Compensation/ profit sharing • Profit distribution processes • Decision-making structure and voting • Appointments/ retirements	• Strategic objectives: – Client-type focus – Practice area focus • Competitive capabilities • Practice area processes/ documentation • Knowledge management • Geographical issues – Merging offices	• Organisation structure • Management information • Technology • Core client development/ management • Key policy areas • Performance standards • Personnel compensation policies	• Business planning • Budget • Performance management • Marketing • Client management • Personnel: – Recruitment – Remuneration – Training/ development • Technology • Communication	• Finance/ accounting • Personnel • Databases • Technology • Support staff • Property and facilities

required to document the roles and responsibilities of each level of partner, at the same time as setting out the financial and other requirements of the partnership. It is not the ITF's role to do all of these things, but it should ensure that they are done within an agreed and necessary timeframe.

As such, the role of the ITF will be a complex one. Managing an integration process across so many areas of activity, particularly where many of them are, at least partially, dependant on each other, is bound to be difficult.

Take for example, the key activity of strategy and the sub-category of client-type focus. The strategic vision of the 'new' firm and the related objectives might identify target client types for the merged firm which differ from the targets of both antecedent firms. The ITF's role is to ensure that all groups in the firm which carry out marketing activities make sure that their business/marketing plans are geared towards the merged firm's target clients, not those of the previous firms. However, prior to the plans being drawn up, the marketing department will need to be involved in order to help with research into the prospective targets, and to explain industry issues. In this way, the plans developed by the practice groups will be more effective.

This illustrates a very good reason why firms should focus on integrating the infrastructure of the firms first. The biggest turn-off for busy lawyers is to be pushed into integrating their work group when the marketing department is still in considerable disarray, and is therefore unable to help them develop the necessary detail for marketing plans. Such a situation will result in lawyers putting the integration plan to one side, and it will be difficult for them to go back to it a later date. Focusing on infrastructure integration first will ensure that the work groups obtain all of the support and assistance they require when they start to develop their plans. (However, the problem is that integration for many firms stops at the infrastructure level.)

Ideally, each work group should have business and marketing plans on day one of the merger. Some firms will be able to achieve that. For others, the period between the agreement to merge and the merger date is insufficient to allow the infrastructure to be integrated enough to enable them to provide support to the integration processes at the practice group level. In our experience, it is preferable to accept that certain integration activities within the work groups (eg the development of business plans) will occur after the merger date, than to rush everything through and to only do things by halves. This will just lead to disillusionment and frustration during the post-merger period, the time at which there needs to be a high level of motivation and excitement about moving the 'new' firm forward. If people start off highly motivated, they will want to progress the integration activities. A key way to sustain motivation is to ensure that all aspects of the infrastructure support have been integrated, the roles and responsibilities of the people in those departments have been defined, and that those people have the skills and resources necessary to assist others.

Be aware of 'change overload'

It is also important that the ITF is conscious of the 'volume of change' that its organisation is able to absorb over a given time. We have seen integration plans that set out what had to be done and had established priorities, but had tried to cover too much, too soon. The organisation must be able to keep operating effectively and efficiently at the same time as it absorbs major changes to its activities, systems, processes and methods of operation. When people are subjected to too much change, this can result in a state of 'change overload'.

Resistance to change during the early period of a merger is, more often than not, due to this phenomenon. When someone starts to resist change activities, before making any assumptions about their attitude towards the merger, management should review what the person has been involved in over recent months.

For example, a senior partner of a firm which was eight months into merger became increasingly obstructive to the integration process, even though for the first five or six months, he had been actively supportive. An examination of his role over the first six months of the merger revealed:

- he was the prime contact for four major clients which were all actively using the firm for large, high-value engagements;

- as well as handling the work for these clients, he was also managing a team of five associates;

- he had conducted performance reviews for all associates on the team and for three junior partners;

- he had billed 75% of his annual fee income target;

- he had been a member of a task force charged with developing a client relationship management process for the firm;

- he had been a member of a task force charged with reviewing the management information to be given to partners; and

- he was on the strategy board of the firm, and had helped draft its vision and objectives communications paper.

A discussion with this partner made it very clear that his reaction was due to a case of 'change overload'. There were a number of other partners from the firm in the same position.

Not only is it easy to try and do too much, too early on in the integration process, it is also easy to give key individuals too much of the work. Given that there will always be some aspects of the organisation that will not be working effectively in the early days of merger, the more people are asked to do, the more they will encounter problems. This, coupled with 'change overload', can lead to them resisting any further change until the workload lessens, and the issues causing the frustrations are resolved. The old adage of giving tasks to busy people might sometimes work, but it is a dangerous one during a merger integration process.

Part of the role of the ITF is to ensure that key individuals are not overloaded, and that they are given appropriate levels of support. In a medium-to-large sized firm, the use of task forces to develop new systems, processes and reports is extremely valuable. However, whilst the ITF is there to manage the process, it is not there to do everything.

Be clear as to the type of merger

When planning the process, another important issue for the ITF is to be clear as to the type of merger it is dealing with, and the impact that will have on the integration process. Whilst it might appear obvious what type of merger it is, this needs to be confirmed to the ITF by the negotiating teams.

Where two firms are broadly similar in size and market position, and the merger is primarily based on achieving greater critical mass and depth of expertise in order to improve its market position, the merger is likely to be a merger of equals or a 'real' merger. For this type of merger, there will be a need to develop processes and systems that are appropriate to the 'new' firm and its target market position.

Whilst it might be agreed to adopt processes from one of the antecedent firms, it must be because they are right for the 'new' firm. Firms must not adopt a 'horse trading' approach (eg 'we'll agree to your management information system if you accept our process for managing clients').

Where one firm is much larger than the other, and further advanced in the market, the merger is likely to be a 'take-over' or 'absorption' merger. The smaller firm will be absorbed into the larger one, and will take on its systems and processes. This should not, however, be automatic. The ITF should review the due diligence reports and identify whether there are areas in which the smaller firm might have the better approach.

In one merger situation, it was assumed that all of the larger firm's processes would apply in the merged firm, and so the negotiating teams did not bother to check whether certain systems would in fact work. Post-merger, the partners originally from the smaller firm complained about the merged firm's management information system. Management initially dismissed their complaints, believing them to be down to 'resistance to change'. On further investigation, it was found that the management information system of the smaller firm had been in fact infinitely better than that of the larger firm. The change was therefore made, and the smaller firm's system was adopted.

Merging firms should therefore never assume that the larger of them has the better systems and processes. Part of the ITF's role is to ensure that this assumption is tested, at least in key areas. A merger provides an opportunity to stand back and question whether either firm has the systems and processes appropriate for the merged firm. It might well be that the larger firm's systems and processes are not even appropriate by today's standards, let alone for the next three to five years.

We appreciate, however, that where a small firm is absorbed into a larger firm, the actual increase in size might not be that significant in terms of the impact on systems and processes, and the strategy behind the merger might be more about strengthening an existing market position than developing into a new one. It might not therefore be appropriate to look to see which new systems and processes are best for the 'new' firm.

However, in the majority of cases, it is vital that there be a real attempt to develop systems and processes that are suitable to the 'new' firm and its target position. Whilst this might seem obvious, some firms query how one can tell what systems will be required in the new market position, and believe it better to start with the systems of one firm (and with which partners from that firm are comfortable), than to develop a whole range of systems and processes that are new to everyone.

This is an area where the use of experts may be required, and the ITF should take this into account in the planning process. There will be outside consultants who will be able to advise on the systems and processes in use by firms in the merged firm's target position. There will also be HR experts, finance experts, etc who can advise on what processes will be required to ensure that the merged firm operates effectively and efficiently and at a competitive level, regardless of what potential competitors are doing. Some of these experts might already be in the firm, whilst others might be employed in an advisory capacity for a certain period of time.

This also reinforces the need for an ITF. Where one group is carrying out negotiations and trying to plan integration, the time constraints and work overload can result in one firm's system being adopted purely because it seemed better than the other side's. An ITF will have the time to stand back and ask what is best for the 'new' firm. A crucial role for the ITF in planning integration is therefore to ensure that time is available to develop competitive systems and processes, and to not fall victim to expediency.

Plan in detail

The ITF must also ensure that the integration plans are in sufficient detail to make things happen. Too often, plans are merely broad statements of intent.

For example, integrating the client relationship management (CRM) processes of two firms post-merger is a complex task and requires a detailed plan. An example of what a detailed plan for the integration of CRM processes might look like is set out in **Table 8.3** below.

Each of these steps will be made up of a series of sub-steps. For example, Step 5 would include the following sub-steps:

1. Determine the parameters for core clients in the firm and agree them with central management.

2. Analyse client lists for the last three years of each antecedent firm and identify a 'first cut' list of core clients.

3. Seek out clients on those lists that do not meet the core client criteria, but could, and add them to the 'first cut' list.

4. Analyse the 'first cut' list and establish priority groups.

5. Select the initial core client list (say, 50 clients) and agree it with central management.

It is only when plans get down to this level of detail that they are likely to be carried out. If plans remain conceptual statements of intent, busy people will not find the time or motivation to sit down and work out what has to be done. They will put it off because they have other, very clearly determined, priorities. Time and time again, firms complain about not being able to implement integration plans. However, as soon as the plan is set out in detailed steps, and once the required support to carry out the steps is provided by the firm, action almost always follows. A major responsibility of the ITF is to ensure that every plan is developed in such rigorous detail, to monitor it, to provide encouragement, to ensure that the firm provides the required level of

Table 8.3: Detailed plan for integrating CRM processes

Step 1 — Specify the main components of the CRM process of each antecedent firm. Assess their apparent effectiveness in each firm.

Step 2 — Design a competitive CRM process for the merged firm in its target market position as at the end of the first post-merger year taking into account Step 1.

Step 3 — Assess the support required from the firm's infrastructure:

(i)   to get the new CRM up and running; and
(ii)   to maintain it at the level required.

Step 4 — Discuss requirements with infrastructure groups. Determine timetable based on their ability to support the CRM process.

Step 5 — Identify the core clients of the 'new' firm and any priorities in light of the strategic vision. Obtain central management agreement to the identified list.

Step 6 — Select five clients from the core client list as the initial targets for implementation of the CRM process. Consult with the existing core client partner or equivalent on the current status of the CRM process in place.

Step 7 — Develop a plan and timetable for each client to move from the current status to that envisaged in Step 2.

Step 8 — Develop training workshops, etc necessary to bring participants up to the skill level required by Step 2.

Step 9 — Select the initial client teams for the five initial targets. Hold workshops with each and take time to describe the desired CRM process, and obtain their input into how to move to that.

Step 10 — Work with each team to develop a plan directed at achieving an effective CRM process within an agreed period of time. Institute a monitoring feedback process.

Step 11 — Select the next five core clients and repeat Steps 6 to 10.

support, and to help overcome any difficulties that occur along the way. It is not an easy task, but one that is helped enormously by having an effective planning process in place.

Execution must be across two main activities, operations and integration, with both competing for the same resources

We touched on this fifth principle earlier in this chapter, but its importance requires reinforcement. The least risky approach to post-merger management is to have central management positioned so that it manages the two main activities of operational performance and integration simultaneously. This structure is set out in **Table 8.4** below.

The pressure point in the integration process is business unit management, which is the primary channel through which operational results will be achieved. In the first two years of a law firm merger, staff and clients need to be reassured that the merger

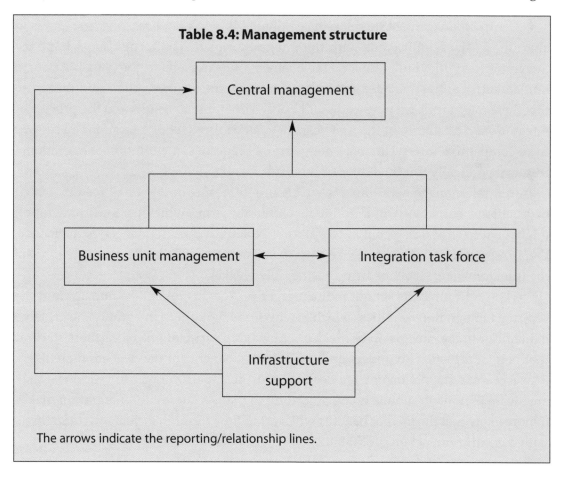

Table 8.4: Management structure

Central management

Business unit management ↔ Integration task force

Infrastructure support

The arrows indicate the reporting/relationship lines.

is working. A firm can do this by producing a set of financial results that match expectations, by retaining core clients and by attracting major new clients. Retaining good staff and attracting more are other signs that a merger is working, although they tend to flow from the previous factors. Therefore, the heads of the business units need to focus on achieving the targets set out in the business plan. A failure to achieve business plan targets can undermine the success of a merger.

However, there is also a need to integrate the business units, develop a consistent CRM process, and implement a new set of working practices that will reinforce the firm's unified approach. This is done by the ITF, which will be seeking to achieve full integration within a relatively short timeframe (one to two years at most given that it will take another year or so for it to be evident in the market).

Business unit heads will be more familiar (and comfortable) with carrying out what they need to in order to achieve budgetary targets than they will with implementing integration plans. Left to their own devices, they will therefore focus on short-term operational results, not integration.

Central management therefore has a pivotal role to play here. The first aim is to align the business unit plans with the integration plan. The former must have the integration activities built into it (ie the business units must have one plan, not two, to implement). Central management must sign off on the business plans and recognise that there might well be some trade-off between operational results and the process of integration, particularly in the first year. To achieve the level of integration necessary to be competitive three years post-merger might require some dilution of operational results (specifically financial) in year one and possibly two.

Central management must also ensure that the operational results match expectations, particularly of individuals within the firm. Achieving a fast integration might be seen as a success, but if it results in a serious decline in financial performance, the subsequent resignations of key partners might nullify any advantages in the medium term, and leave the firm considerably weaker.

The profit forecasts set out in the merger prospectus must take into account the proposed integration activities (which is why some thought to integration needs to be made prior to the conclusion of the deal). Managing expectations of partners starts at that point. Partners who understand the potential benefits of the deal are more likely to accept some stagnation or even decline in financial performance in year one if they are aware that integration is going according to plan. A successful integration makes it more likely that the merger benefits will start to flow through in years two and three, with a positive impact on profitability.

Hence, central management has a complex balancing act to play in the first few years of merger. It needs to ensure that the firm produces a set of financial and other operational results in line with expectations, and retains motivation. It also needs to ensure that integration proceeds at a pace that ensures the firm can achieve the required level of competitiveness over the three years post-merger.

The integration process will, by and large, require the involvement of many of the same people who are responsible for delivering the operational results. The ITF will therefore need to liaise with the business unit heads. Initially, they need to confer about development of the business plans to ensure that both operational results and integration are dealt with. Secondly, they need to liaise about the time commitments of key personnel and the use of infrastructure support. There is the potential for conflict in all these areas, so the objective should be to avoid it via discussion between the ITF and the heads of the business units. When they cannot agree on an issue, it should be referred to central management which should have the final say.

As we noted earlier, central management will have a significant number of priorities in the first post-merger year. Reconciling the needs of the business unit heads and the ITF is an important one, but not the only one. Coping with issues raised by a new structure, new roles and responsibilities, and getting to know people are other major tasks. It also needs to ensure that the new management team starts to work effectively in a short period of time.

In addition, ensuring the internal and external communication flows are at an appropriate level and are consistent is vital. Maintaining a link with key clients of the 'new' firm is imperative as well, particularly where a new CRM process is being implemented. Similarly, maintaining contact with key people inside the firm is important in order to quickly eliminate any frustrations or disillusionment.

Hence, central management also needs to plan how it will spend its time in the first year of merger, and how it will resolve conflicting demands on it as a resource. As in many other areas, this may require some 'front end' work that is not directly related to the key objectives. However, if that work is carried out effectively, it will facilitate the achievement of those key objectives. One such 'front end' activity is to carry out some intensive development work with the new central management team in order to ensure that everyone is clear about the vision, strategy, goals and key objectives of the 'new' firm, and that the group is able to work effectively together. The latter point might require issues of group dynamics and individual behaviour to be addressed.

At a strategic board meeting of a newly merged firm, the chairman's opening remark was:

'While as a group we seem to get on very well, and have had some valuable discussions, there are two areas where we haven't performed well, and these have reduced our effectiveness. The first is the attendance and time keeping of members, and the second is the constant flow of members in and out of the meeting once they have arrived. Both of these issues are reducing our ability to make clear decisions that everyone should be signing up to, and to ensure that everyone here understands why decisions have been made. We intend to address both of these behavioural issues over the next few months.'

This is one example of a behavioural issue that can reduce the effectiveness of a management group and can impact negatively on many of the integration issues. A second type of difficulty can be tensions between specific individuals that result in problems in decision-making. A third is the behaviour of one or more individuals who then disrupt the group processes (eg the person who always labours the point and wastes time, the person who always has to find another angle to an issue even though it is irrelevant, the person who is always negative about proposals unless they are their own, etc). In some cases, an effective chairman or senior partner will be able to address these issues. In others, expert help might be required. Whatever the case, it is crucial that attention is given to the effective working of central management within the first year.

One firm commissioned a survey of its staff at differing levels at the end of the first post-merger year to test their perceptions of management over that period. The results were somewhat frightening and shocking. Seventy-five per cent said that they thought management had performed either below expectations or badly (with only 25% believing management to have met or exceeded expectations). This led the management team to re-examine what it was doing. It realised that its meetings had become a 'talking shop' rather than a forum for discussions and actions. They therefore addressed this.

A similar result emerged out of an interview survey at another firm. Having examined the achievements of management against the interview responses, it was clear that, whilst a lot had been done, it was not obvious to 'the front line'. The firm therefore improved its communications to ensure people knew what management was doing.

It is therefore vital that whilst central management monitors all of the various operational and integration activities, it also needs to monitor its own progress in managing conflicting priorities. Like everyone else in the firm in the early years of a merger, management must have a clear plan as to where it should be allocating its scarce resources of time, and it must also ensure that what it is doing is effective and perceived to be so. No matter what else happens in the early post-merger years, maintaining the direction of a firm is dependant on partners witnessing that progress is being made in line with the merger prospectus, and that problems and difficulties are being addressed. Partners also need to see that their management team is capable, effective and efficient and is prepared to deal with difficult issues whilst still remaining focused on the vision and the strategy of the 'new' firm.

Integration is about people

This could well be a sixth principle in the integration process, but it is also a fundamental issue that underpins all of the above five principles.

The reason some firms have problems with integration is that they de-personalise many of the systems and processes, and fail to understand that, unless the 'people' issues are addressed, then systems and processes will never be truly integrated.

We noted earlier in this chapter that one of the impediments to integrating systems and processes is the 'let's wait until we know them better' approach. Whilst this can be used as an argument to obstruct integration by those who are unsupportive of the merger, it does have a degree of truth to it. The issue behind it is one of behavioural trust, particularly when it occurs in areas of client relationships, working practices, documentation, etc. When it comes to resistance to integration in these areas, there is a very fine line between people resisting because they are refusing to change, and people resisting because they are genuinely concerned that the work style and approach of the other firm will be detrimental to a client's relationship with the 'new' firm. Sometimes, partners are purely being protective of their own position. Given that this lack of a team approach can occur amongst partners in a firm that is not involved in a merger, the problem is obviously compounded if a firm with these attitudes then goes through a merger.

The integration process should therefore seek to create as much interaction between people as quickly as possible. This should initially be at partner level, because until partners get to know each other, there is likely to be an ongoing lack of behavioural trust that will impede the integration process.

The use of small task forces with representation from both sides of the merger is one way to do this. This also has the advantage of ensuring that recommendations about changes are seen to be coming from the partnership itself rather than from management or external consultants. The composition of the task forces needs to be thought through carefully, as does the identity of the leader of each. An effort should be made to ensure that each task force works effectively. The ITF should play a key role in monitoring the task forces and make sure they produce recommendations.

There are partners who will resist the formation of a multitude of task forces on the grounds that they distract from the real business of serving clients and earning profits. To some extent, of course, they are right, but it is management's responsibility to ensure that operational results are achieved along with progress on integration. Given the enormous amount of work required to achieve effective integration, delegating it to numerous task forces spreads the burden. The ITF must, however, manage the process, and the number of task forces at any one time will be determined by the ITF's capability.

The crucial aspect of the task force approach, however, is that it gets people working together, sharing ideas, debating issues, and having to agree on recommendations to be made to the partnership (or management directly). Whilst there will always be people in a group who will never get along well, by putting most people together to work on issues will help to overcome any behavioural mistrust. During the process it will become apparent that, whilst there will be some differences of opinion, people do have good ideas, are committed to making the merger work, have client interests at heart, and are prepared to compromise. A level of cohesion will then start to form.

The task force approach needs to be managed in order for it to be effective. The members need to be carefully selected, their tasks must be clear, and a desired output and work process agreed. Once this has been done, the task force approach to building cohesion and breaking down resistance is far superior to any other. Social activities are useful, but should take more of a supportive role. Partner meetings about issues tend to have a slow impact. Business unit meetings are helpful, but take time to achieve a team spirit. Task forces, however, bring people together to discuss an issue, and mirror much more closely what organisational coherence is about.

CRM is another area where people from different sides of a merger can be brought together. There can, however, be strong initial reactions against this because of a misunderstanding of what is required. The existing client relationship partner needs to be reassured that the initial phase of an integrated CRM process is to devise an appropriate system for a client, and then to ensure that everyone on the team understands how a client wants people to work. It is not about 'licensing' each member of the team to go off and individually sell into a client.

Generally, we find that initial resistance to opening up the CRM process to integration can be overcome by:

(i)   reminding partners that the basis for the merger was to generate more work from existing clients, and that this requires a consistent team approach; and

(ii) making the initial task for each client team the development of a process for managing the client relationship that all members of the team agree with and will follow.

It is the client partner's role to ensure that such a process is in place and being followed. Similarly, marketing and other non-fee-earning activities involving the client should be co-ordinated by the team with the client partner managing the process.

Resistance to opening up a client relationship might be due to an individual trying to protect their position and their client base. More often, however, it is down to a lack of understanding of the process. Once partners understand the CRM process, they realise that opening up the relationship is likely to result in a greater volume of revenue and profit being generated, and interaction between the firm and the client being managed better. Establishing a new CRM process in a merged firm quickly can produce excellent results when trying to build organisational coherence.

Conclusion

As a general rule, it is better to over-structure the integration process in the first year than under-structure it. This means putting in place a structure that can manage the integration process on day one, be it one person in a smaller firm or an ITF in a larger one. If integration moves ahead quickly, it can be brought more directly under the control of central management. However, by starting with an expectation that central management can manage everything in year one will almost always lead to problems. Operational results will be below expectations, the integration process will move too slowly, infrastructure support departments will not operate effectively, and difficulties that arise in the first year will not be adequately addressed.

All of this will reduce motivation and enthusiasm amongst staff and will increase frustration and disappointment. Clients will fail to see the promised benefits and, instead, will see disgruntled people and a falling of standards. Some key players may also 'jump ship'. Trying to resurrect a process where integration has gone off the rails, or when it is being put into place at the expense of other processes, is a very difficult task. It can be done, but it is decidedly more costly and disruptive than if an effective process had been put in place at the start.

One of our fundamental beliefs is to never underestimate the amount of work that an effective integration will take, and never overestimate the ability of management to manage it. Year one of any merger, no matter how large or small the firms involved, is a very difficult time for anyone in management. They will have many competing priorities, many new issues to address and many out of the ordinary questions to answer. Management needs to demonstrate a conviction about and commitment to the strategic vision of the firm. It needs to reassure and provide guidance about what is (and is not) appropriate behaviour. It needs to address problems that might derail success in any major area, and to get to know and work with new people in a cohesive manner.

As we stated earlier, reaching agreement to merge can be, in relative terms, easy. A successful integration, however, requires a planned, disciplined and rigorous approach, whilst simultaneously being aware of the need to be empathetic and understanding to many of the 'people' issues that will inevitably arise. The complexities that this creates demonstrate why execution of an integration process is the single most important reason why many mergers do not deliver the promised benefits.

CHAPTER 9: UNDERSTANDING THE CONTEXT – USING DUE DILIGENCE TO THE FULL

Introduction

There is no one way to go about deciding to merge. That is the consistent message in this book. Nevertheless, some approaches carry more risk of a merger failing to produce the promised benefits than others. An example of this was given in **Chapter 8** in regard to integration – leaving central management to organise and implement the integration process, whilst it tries to manage everything else, carries with it a higher risk of failure than if integration is implemented by a team specifically created for that purpose. Denton Wilde Sapte took the higher-risk approach of having management do everything, and made it work. Probably the context in which that merger was undertaken reduced the potential risk in that the two antecedent firms knew each well, and were clear about what they required from a merger. It is, however, still a higher-risk approach. Addleshaw Goddard, mainly because it had had previous merger experience, used the lower-risk approach and employed external consultants to carry out the process, and that was effective for it.

Therefore, when deciding on the actual level of risk in any approach, context is important. In this book, we can only generalise, and leave it to firms to try and understand the context of their particular merger, and to select an approach that will be the most effective for them.

In this chapter, we probe more deeply into 'understanding the context' through the process of due diligence. We touched on some of the due diligence issues in **Chapter 4** in relation to in-depth merger discussions. In this chapter, we use the due diligence process to understand more about the internal workings of the two organisations that are contemplating merger.

In our experience, the process of due diligence is too often little more than a 'tick the box' exercise. Merger prospectuses contain statements such as 'we examined the property leases of the two firms (see details below), but found nothing that could prove detrimental to either party in the event of merger'. That is a 'tick the box' statement. Whilst these are necessary, they are not a sufficient use of the due diligence data. What would have been more useful was to look at the context of the firm's property and leases. Did one party take shorter leases than the other? Is the fact that the two firms chose different locations in the same city of relevance? Did one firm appear to have negotiated better lease terms than its competitors which are based in a similar location? Did one firm have better 'let out' provisions than the other?

Questions such as these will provide clues about the contextual differences between the two firms, and might result in a different approach to integration being taken. Equally importantly, they might give clues about the differences in management and operational style, and indeed about culture (see **Chapter 10**), of the two firms, which might result in a need to reassess the feasibility of the merger.

What these questions also raise are issues about the negotiating process (see **Chapter 4**), in particular the extent to which the negotiations should be kept to a small, tight-knit group or widened out to involve a greater number of people. In this chapter, we argue that it is more risky to keep negotiations to a tight-knit group. However, we will also discuss the circumstances where other considerations might outweigh this risk. How to reduce the risk of widening out the negotiations to involve a number of people will also be discussed.

Henry Mintzberg[1] described 'management' as part craft (ie experience), part art (ie insight or intuition) and part science (ie rational analysis). His point is that effective managers are able to combine the three elements equally over time, even though there are situations where there is a need to put more stress on one element than the others. We contend that the same three elements are required in the process of deciding whether or not two firms should merge. This chapter takes one aspect of the merger process, due diligence, which is normally a rational and analytical process or 'science', and explains how it can be used to gain insights into firms. Put these insights together with someone who has experience in dealing with law firms,[2] and quite interesting results can emerge. As we argued in **Chapter 5**, a skilled strategic adviser, who knows law firms and the legal profession, can be particularly valuable through the whole merger negotiating process.

Although we have assisted in many successful mergers, we have advised more firms against merging than for it. Interestingly enough, the reasons for our advice

---

1 Henry Mintzberg, *Managers Not MBAs: A Hard Look at the Soft Practice of Managing and Management Development* (San Francisco: Bennett Koehler, 2004).

2 This is another reason why we contend that a low-risk approach in a merger is to involve an outsider who has significant amounts of experience in working with law firms at the strategic and organisational level.

against merger are usually based less on business case issues, and more on other, less tangible, criteria. These criteria mostly emerge from the due diligence process, although the people who carried out the due diligence did not necessarily identify these as issues at the time. Our experience with law firms enables us to look across a number of areas of activity within a firm, and to develop a series of hypotheses about the 'context' of a firm (ie what it is that makes a firm work as an organisation). These hypotheses can then be explored with people from that firm to test whether they reflect reality or not. Most of the time they do. Sometimes the issues that the hypotheses throw up are serious enough to call a merger into question, no matter how strong the business case for it is.

For example, we discussed in **Chapter 7** the different approaches taken to financial policies (specifically borrowings) by the two sides to the Addleshaw Goddard merger. Theodore Goddard thought that Addleshaw Booth & Co had a high-risk financial profile, whereas Addleshaw Booth & Co thought that Theodore Goddard was overly conservative about finance, which could prove to be difficult when it came to investing in future growth. Whilst not a deal-breaker, the difference in approaches had the potential to become one. The two sides discussed why they had adopted a particular policy, and it emerged that the reason for the difference lay in the historical context of each firm. Once this was understood, it was relatively easy to come up with a financial policy for the 'new' firm which both parties could agree on.

A similar issue arises with partner remuneration systems. This is one area that is worth exploring in some depth when the two firms have different approaches. (In fact, the use of a particular type of partner remuneration system is often given as one of the criteria for a potential merger partner.) A firm that has operated for a long period with an exclusively performance-based system is likely to have some cultural differences to a firm that has operated with a strict lockstep.

When a firm uses a performance-based system, it is likely to place greater importance on individual performance, and to see the need to reward high performers. When a firm uses a strict lockstep, it will place greater emphasis on partnership cohesion and team/group-based performance. The underlying thinking is that individuals perform highly more to boost performance of the firm (thereby benefiting everyone), and not to obtain a higher income for themselves.

In fact, however, the differences in partner remuneration systems might not be as great as initially thought. The performance-based firm might have defined performance so that it also includes a significant number of team-based activities, and such that it recognises passing clients and work onto others. On the other hand, the gap in what the two firms believe might be huge.

The same perception difficulties can arise when the two firms have different lockstep systems of partner remuneration. One has a strict lockstep, which allows partners to move one level a year until they reach the plateau, but with no individual incentives. The spread from top to bottom of the lockstep is 2:1. The other firm has a flexible lockstep (people can go down as well as up), which allows high performers to jump two levels at a time, and also has a bonus system in operation and the top-bottom ratio is 4:1. Although both firms have a lockstep system, their views regarding performance and remuneration might be fundamentally different.

Using the examples above, it is critical that the due diligence process not only describes the two remuneration systems, but also explains why they exist. What are the assumptions and beliefs behind each one? In the first example, the lockstep firm might believe that performance-based systems indicate selfishness and greed, whereas that might not be the case at all. Individuals in the performance-based firm might be just as committed to their firm's success as the partners in the lockstep firm are, but they also believe that it is only equitable to give further reward to those who contribute more. The two positions might or might not be reconcilable, but no one will ever know unless the due diligence goes beyond a mere statement of describing the system used. Coming up with a composite scheme that blends two different systems into one for the merged firm is unlikely to satisfy anyone if the pre-merger systems were based on deeply held beliefs, and the thinking underlying the two systems needs to be understood.

In many merger negotiations, it was found that the different approaches taken in relation to important policies by the two firms involved were driven more by historical context than any deeply held beliefs. Sometimes, the differences could be reconciled once the context for a certain policy was known. In other situations, it could not. In other cases, differences can occur because of the current context of the two firms – one firm might be under different pressures to the other, and dissimilarities in policies and approaches emerge because of this. However, understanding why firms have different policies is at least a first step to trying to reconcile those differences, even if that is not always achieved.

Understanding why there are differences is vital if the merger is to proceed and succeed. In most cases, there is no right or wrong answer. The issue is whether or not the merged firm will face the same market pressures as either of the antecedent firms did, and what is the best approach for reconciling those issues in the 'new' firm's context. Once this is understood, it is far easier to obtain agreement on issues (although this might involve both firms having to shift their ground in respect to policy).

The due diligence process
Areas requiring due diligence

In **Chapter 6**, we discussed the need to identify issues that could be potential deal-breakers, and to address them at the outset. We also listed the common areas which can give rise to deal-breaking issues. When addressing these, a form of due diligence must be carried out to identify where the problem is, and how it might be resolved. In this chapter, we list all the areas where due diligence is required. Depending on the transaction, some items might also need to be dealt with as potential deal-breakers, but all of them are items that should be covered under the normal due diligence process.

In the tables below, we list the areas requiring due diligence under group headings (ie partnership issues, financial issues, etc). The areas that are usually of major importance in any transaction are marked with an asterisk. Those that are not, whilst important, are generally secondary level issues.

Table 9.1: Partnership issues

* • Structure of partnership:
  * equity/non-equity categories
  * roles, responsibilities and rights of each category
  * the selection process for each category
  * movement between categories
* • Partner remuneration system:
  * basis of partners' compensation by category
  * profit-sharing policy
  * drawings policy
  * period over which profits are paid out
  * bonuses or equivalent policy
  * determination of changes in remuneration relativities
  * approval of partner remuneration
  * partner benefits policy

Table 9.1: Partnership issues (continued)

*   •   Partnership agreement:

    •   date of last revision

    •   decisions reserved for partners

    •   special versus ordinary resolutions

    •   policy in relation to retirement, expulsion or early retirement

    •   policy in relation to election

    •   other identified key areas

*   •   Partner performance management:

    •   formal or informal system and process

    •   structure of system

    •   method of carrying out the system

    •   implications flowing from the system

*   •   Composition of partnership:

    •   list each existing partner by name, giving status (equity or non-equity), age/birth date, length of time as partner, length of time with firm, previous firm and final status there (if applicable), entry status to firm (if recruited above trainee), and short CV

    •   list any consultants, of counsel or equivalent, providing same data as above

    •   list any person designated for partnership in the current year or the following year, providing same data as above, and also give current status in relation to approval and notification

    •   list retirements from the partnership in the last three years and the current year, giving reasons for retirement

    •   identify any partner who might choose to resign in the event of merger

    •   rate importance to the 'new' firm of such a resignation

•   Communication:

    •   how is communication managed within the partnership?

    •   what regular channels are used?

    •   what is communicated?

    •   how is communication of major decision issues managed in the period leading up to a decision?

Table 9.2: Financial issues

* Financial issues:
  * Accounting period and any recent change
  * Capital structure and borrowings policy
  * Tax reserves and tax position
  * Treatment and valuation of work in progress (WIP)
  * Policy in relation to provision for bad debts and bad debt write-off
  * Assets and liabilities to be assumed:
    * current net asset history
    * long-term liabilities
    * fixed assets and valuation policy
  * Three-year performance in relation to billing of WIP and collection of debts
  * Identify cost allocations by main expense headings
  * Key variables analysis in economic performance over previous three years (by firm and by business unit):
    * variables to include utilisation, average billing rate per fee-earner and realisation, cost multiple, revenue per fee-earner and profit per fee-earner, revenue per partner and profit per partner, leverage, overhead percentage of revenue
  * Non-operating costs past and ongoing:
    * eg annuities
  * Future liabilities incurred:
    * lease contract details
    * others
  * Any other balance sheet issues
  * Budgeting process and approval mechanism

The information in the tables is not exhaustive of all the areas that will require due diligence. The structure and work of different firms might raise other issues. Furthermore, the information given about the areas set out above can give rise to further issues.

Table 9.3: Quality control

- Process for controlling quality:
  - extent to which system is audited
- * Outstanding claims for professional negligence:
  - separate those covered under professional indemnity (PI) policy, and those not covered
- * Three-year claims record on claims settled
- * Policy on treatment of claims
- * Current policy on PI insurance
- * Existing PI insurers

Table 9.4: Organisation and management

- * Organisation and management structure:
  - identify primary business units (where more than one) eg practice group, offices, etc
  - set out relationship between different types of business unit (ie how practice groups interact with offices where more than one office exists)
  - what is the main responsibility line for profitability, and what is the line of authority from the centre in regard to this?
  - roles, responsibilities and authorities of all management positions and reporting line
  - examine the various points of intersection for overlap/gap
- Method of appointment for each position and term of office:
  - current incumbents in each position and length of time in role (if re-appointed, total time in office)
  - where any incumbent has been in office for 12 months or less, role of previous incumbent, length of time in office and reason for change
- Method of assessing performance of those in management roles:
  - note amount of time each incumbent is expected to spend in management role, and any special adjustments to other aspects of performance (eg reduced billable hour targets)

Table 9.4: Organisation and management (continued)

- Integration of other structural aspects:
  - eg client relationship teams, special projects
* - Process by which the primary business units are managed:
  - note whether a consistent approach exists and, if not, what is done in each business unit
* - Business planning process:
  - methodology and level of consistency
  - marketing process
  - review process
  - review business plans over last three years and actual outcome compared to plan
  - current business plans and forecast results at year end
  - approval mechanism
- Decision-making process:
  - review minutes of partner meetings over the last three years and identify the key decisions taken
  - review minutes of board/management meetings over the last three years and identify key decisions taken
  - for both of the above, review nature of issues covered by the minutes and rank in terms of strategic, operational or administrative areas
  - identify a number of key decisions taken in the last 12 months, trace through the actual process by which the decision came to be made (particularly who was involved, at what level and at what stage), and identify where the initiative came from that led to the decision
- Management information:
  - review information given out and who gets what
  - assess in terms of its effectiveness
  - identify how it is used by different groups

Managing the due diligence process

The tables above contain a large list of issues, and firms will need to devote a considerable amount of time to clarifying each one. Many of the categories also contain

---

Table 9.5: Infrastructure

* • Set out infrastructure departments and management structure within each:

- incumbent in each key management role, length of time in role and CV:

  - roles, responsibilities and authorities for each key management role and reporting line

  - method of appointment to key roles and appointments within departments

- Detail management information systems:

  - who receives what

  - period of reporting

- Set out interaction line between infrastructure departments and business units

- Method of assessing performance of people in key roles:

  - performance management within department

- Set out reasons for any major changes in infrastructure in the current year and previous three years.

Table 9.6: Client issues

- Provide a definition of 'core client' as used in the firm

- Review and describe the client relationship process (if any)

- Analyse history of each of last three years with the top 50[3] core clients:

  - revenue per client in total and by practice area/work type

  - amount and percentage of total revenue generated by the top 50 clients, built up from top 5, top 10, top 20, top 25, top 50

  - identify any industry or other market sector focus in the top 50:

    - is there any particular focus further down the client list?

  - identify within the top 50, the number of clients which required services from one practice area, two practice areas or three practice areas or more in each year

  - identify within the top 50, the number of clients which required services on a significant scale in each year (for 'significant', establish a benchmark such as the average revenue of the top 50 or 100 clients in each year)

---

3 We use the top 50 clients as an example only. Depending on the number of clients a firm has, firms may wish to substitute 50 for another appropriate number.

Table 9.6: Client issues (continued)

- Identify any potential core clients outside of the top 50:
  - ascertain reasons why clients are not seen as 'core', and any plans to convert them to a 'core client'
- Client gains (major) over last three years:
  - process by which client was gained
- Client losses (major) over last three years:
  - reasons for loss
  - identify clients who were 'core' at one point but are now consistently outside that group
- Identify potential client conflicts due to merger:
  - specify (with reasons) client and practice areas affected and estimate revenue at risk
- Identify other areas of revenue loss due to merger:
  - specify reasons, client, practice areas, estimated amount
- Identify clients where merger could generate an increase in work:
  - specify client, practice area and estimated revenue enhancement
- Identify other areas of revenue enhancement due to merger:
  - specify reasons, client, practice areas, estimated amount
- Identify potential clients that neither firm serves at present but are seen as likely to be attracted by merger:
  - specify practice areas, estimated revenues, current supplier
- Client relationship management process:
  - set out in detail

---

some technical issues, and these are unlikely to be addressed adequately by a 'lay person'.

This is a major reason why it is difficult, in our view, to contain merger discussions within a tight-knit group. The negotiating teams will be over-burdened if they try to take on the role of putting together all the due diligence data as well as carrying out the merger negotiations. It might be possible in a merger of two small firms to have the negotiating teams do everything, as the smaller scale might mean that some of the technical issues in areas such as marketing, technology and personnel are not as complex as in mid-to-larger-sized firm mergers. Nevertheless, if one team does everything, there

Table 9.7: Personnel issues

* • Staff grades, remuneration and benefits policies (for business units and infrastructure departments):

*   • promotion policies for each group

• Performance management process and what is recognised as success in the firm

• Recruitment and induction processes by group and grade (where necessary)

• Training and development policy:

    • current programmes by grades

• Mentoring or other development process

• Career planning processes:

    • link with performance management

• Policies on secondments

• Staff dismissal policies

• Incentive or reward schemes not included in normal remuneration scheme

* • Growth of personnel over the last three years:

    • by grade and category

* • Current staffing by name, grade, category

• Policies with regard to trainees

Table 9.8: Technology issues

* • Detail of systems and specifications

• List major investments over last three years and in current year:

    • type and cost

* • Planned upgrades already approved or not yet approved

• Major suppliers of software, hardware

is still the risk that it will not have the time to go into the depth required on major issues, and this in turn might result in a few nasty surprises post-merger.

Denton Wilde Sapte and Addleshaw Goddard both followed a procedure that we believe works very well, and which was discussed in a different context in **Chapter 4**.

Table 9.9: Property issues

* • List property leases – current rentals, length of lease, period remaining, rent review details, potential liabilities

* • List properties owned – when purchased, amount paid, current value, annual maintenance expenditure, income generated

• Note any major changes in property in last three years and in current year

• Detail any planned changes in property not yet actioned

• Note any difficulties in relation to property caused by merger

Table 9.10: Marketing issues

• Current policies in regard to marketing

• Main categories of expenditure in each of last three years and current year to date

• Costs of department split between personnel, marketing activities, outside support and other (in detail, if major)

• Breakdown of marketing costs between firm-wide activities and practice area, industry sector or other sector

• Policy in regard to directions and other forms of marketing communication

• State focus of marketing over last three years, and note any planned change for the next year

• Extent to which outside consultants are used – specify areas and cost of major engagements over last three years and in current year

• Process by which marketing campaigns are initiated and managed, and interaction between departments, practice areas/offices, etc and individuals

• State whether marketing expenditure and activities are all managed or monitored by the marketing department or whether practice groups and/or individuals have own plans and budgets outside marketing department control

• State the primary marketing messages that are being communicated in all media formats:

  • are there any secondary messages?

Table 9.11: Business units

* Business units:
  * Detail work types carried out in each practice area:
    * total revenue for practice area and percentage by work type for each of last three years plus current year to date
  * If departments, list the practice areas that come under each
  * If there is more than one office location, and they are managed separately, list the practice areas that operate in each office:
    * provide office revenue for each of last three years and current year to date, broken down by practice area
  * List personnel, by grade, in relation to location by:
    * department and practice area
    * office and practice area
  * List infrastructure staff attached to:
    * department and practice area
    * office and practice area
  * For each practice area, list the average billable hours for equity partners in each of the last three years and current year, and the same for other client service personnel by grade
  * Identify the extent to which there is a consistent approach to documents, precedents, letters and other correspondence, and work processes within practice areas:
    * is there any variation by office?
    * growth of personnel, by grade and category for each practice area (and office, if applicable)

The initial discussions around the business case for merger, the strategic implications, the major organisational issues, and the potential deal-breakers were all handled by a small negotiating team from both sides. Once it was clear from the discussions that a merger was both achievable and beneficial, the group was widened out to include a range of people who were capable of addressing the various due diligence issues.

In the case of Denton Wilde Sapte, this was done late in the process, and on a somewhat limited brief to devise what was required for the 'new' firm.

In the case of Addleshaw Goddard, task forces were elected for each due diligence issue at an early stage. Once the negotiating teams agreed that a deal was possible, the task forces were given the go-ahead and a timetable to follow. They were required to report to the negotiating teams on progress at least fortnightly (and more frequently if they felt it important to do so). Members of the negotiating teams were responsible for ensuring that the specific task forces kept to the timetable. Some negotiating team members were also on a task force, but only in a chair or co-ordinator capacity. Every task force reported on time.

In the case of William Sturges & Co, a different approach was taken. A small group on each side hammered out the deal including many of the due diligence issues. However, this approach must be seen in the context of this particular merger. William Sturges & Co had been through several small mergers previously, and had experience in addressing issues of due diligence. Both antecedent firms were small, and the managing partner of each was on top of most of the issues. Hence, they could easily access information (without major questions being asked), and they were very familiar with the content behind each issue.

Therefore, the size of the firms in a merger is a major determinant of whether the due diligence process is contained within the negotiating team or 'outsourced'.

Another situation where it can be contained within the negotiating team is where a larger firm is absorbing a much smaller firm. Whilst there will be a need for the smaller firm to carry out some due diligence on the larger firm, it will be a less complex process than where the two firms merging are medium-to-large in size. In one 'absorption' merger, the managing partner and finance director were able to deal with all of the due diligence issues requested by the smaller firm in one, four-hour meeting. In an 'absorption' merger, the main areas the smaller firm will wish to understand about the larger firm are:

(i)   partnership issues;

(ii)   business unit issues (in part);

(iii)   client issues (primarily conflicts);

(iv)   personnel issues (at least in part); and

(v)   potential liability issues.

In an absorption merger, the smaller partner must be fully informed on some matters (such as the partnership agreement) but might not need to delve deeply into other areas such as every aspect of how a business unit operates.

Whilst the smaller firm may also want to know how some other issues will affect it (eg the workings of the infrastructure departments), as it will be absorbed by the framework of the larger firm, it will be more concerned about where and how it will fit in, and whether it will be comfortable with the style and approach of the larger firm.

For medium-to-larger-sized firms, there is another advantage in widening out the due diligence process to others (which we touched upon in **Chapter 4**). It enables others, especially partners, to be involved in the process, and, assuming all goes well, means that an understanding of the potential benefits of merger will develop amongst a group of people well ahead of the merger proposal being put before partners. In our experience, most task force members tend to become strong supporters of the deal, and will act as facilitators when the proposal goes out to the wider partnership for discussion.

In addition, establishing task forces initiates the process of integration. Task forces are composed of people from both parties to the merger. Given that the primary role of the task forces is to analyse the issues, compare the approaches of both firms, and develop solutions to any problems or concerns where differences exist, they must work together. The task force meetings are not point-scoring sessions, nor are they 'we are right, you are wrong' situations. The brief of the task forces is to identify whether there are issues that will cause problems, and how these can be overcome. Furthermore, in our experience, task force members generally develop a favourable impression of their peer group on the other side (with the odd exception), which helps enormously when it comes to dispelling the views that the inevitable doomsayers in the firm have about the other side not being worthy of merging with their firm.

There are occasions, however, when those negotiating a mid-to-larger-sized firm merger will want the discussions to remain highly confidential, and, rightly, feel that the wider the group involved, the more chance there will be of a leak (intentional or not). They face a dilemma when it comes to managing the due diligence process. They can either widen out the group, and run the risk of the negotiations becoming public knowledge, or cut back on the due diligence exercise, and complete it in two stages – stage one before the deal is announced and stage two afterwards. In stage one, only the areas that are identified as potential deal-breakers, along with issues that partners would require reassurance on before voting, should be examined. In the list of due diligence issues set out in the tables above, these sort of areas are marked with an asterisk. Other issues might also be included if a general discussion about them indicates that they might give rise to a significant problem. Stage two would deal with all the other issues in the table above.

Even addressing the high-priority issues will require some widening out of the negotiating team to certain individuals in the firm (unless these people are already members of the team). Usually, the finance directors of both firms will be on the negotiating team, and so the financial information should be available without bringing others into the confidence (although, in some cases, there might be a need to inform the finance director's deputy). Client information is also usually accessible by the finance director and the managing partner, and so again, this could be accessed in many firms without involving anyone else.

A problem does, however, exist in respect of the business units. It will be difficult to address those issues without involvement of the business unit heads. The compromise is to decide which are the most important business units to the deal, and to only address the issues in respect of them at stage one. (Firms may want to put the heads of these business units on the negotiating team from the outset for this reason.) The managing partners of the two firms should have enough general knowledge about the other business units to recognise if they are likely to throw up any serious problems. They may need to ask a few questions to be certain, but this can probably be done without raising any suspicions.

Therefore, the due diligence process can be reduced down to a level that does not require the involvement of significantly more people than the negotiating team, and a deal can be put to partners on that basis. This approach does, however, run the risk that an issue could arise later on which causes a problem. The selection of issues for the stage one due diligence should be designed to ensure that if a problem does arise, it will not sabotage the deal. In any event, if something major does come 'out of the woodwork' later on, there will probably be a large enough incentive to resolve it.

In our opinion, there are, however, two further major problems with this approach.

The first is that it complicates the integration process. We noted in **Chapter 8** that the integration process should get under way as soon as firms can tell whether a deal is able to be concluded. Where the deal is being contained within a small group up until announcement of the proposed merger, it will not be possible to start the integration process. Furthermore, the period between agreement and the effective start date of the merged firm is likely to be taken up with completing the due diligence exercise, and so the integration process is unlikely to commence until after the firm has merged. This runs the risk of the integration process being slow to get off the ground, which can lead to a sense of disillusionment about the transaction setting in which is hard to reverse.

The second, and equally important, problem is that there is no one who can stand back from the deal, and take an overview of the various pieces of information being collected as part of the due diligence process. The negotiating teams will be looking at each item of due diligence and asking whether or not there are any issues that will cause a problem for the merger. However, there is a second, almost more important, task to perform, and that is to ask questions about the other side's 'type' of organisation (ie its internal context or operational style). This will be revealed, at least in part, by examining the due diligence data as a whole. This requires a more reflective approach to studying the data than is normally taken, and it requires someone who is slightly detached from the actual negotiating process to do it. The tighter the negotiating group, the less likely it is that this function will be carried out (or carried out adequately).

We noted earlier that when considering a merger, there is the need for a combination of art, craft and science. Usually, the carrying out of the due diligence process primarily involves science or rational analysis. The process we shall discuss in the rest of this chapter overlays the science with art (intuition or insight) and craft (experience). This will then lead to a discussion of culture, and its role in the merger process in **Chapter 10**.

Building a contextual perspective

There are seven hypotheses that can be tested to varying degrees of completeness throughout the due diligence process which will help firms understand the internal context of the other side. Bearing these hypotheses in mind from the beginning will enable the due diligence teams to probe further into the data than they might ordinarily have done if the only issues they were looking for were immediate impediments to merger. By examining the due diligence data as a whole, these hypotheses can be tested, and some tentative conclusions reached. These conclusions will then need to be examined with individuals from the respective firms, and discussed with the negotiating team.

Seven hypotheses

The seven hypotheses that help to understand the internal context of each firm are as follows:

(i) the firm is highly structured internally (ie there is a significant degree of centralised decision-making);

(ii) the firm's environment encourages team/group initiative over individual initiative;

(iii) this is a firm that encourages and supports those who take business risks (within reason);

(iv) senior people devote significant time to firm-wide development activities (such as coaching and mentoring, new client development and succession planning around clients) rather than personal billings;

(v) people identify first with 'the firm', and secondly with their particular unit;

(vi) communication is transparent, widespread and two-way; and

(vii) performance across a range of activities defines success (rather than high personal billings, etc).

If the primary exercise is to conduct a complete organisational review, a number of other issues would also need to be explored. However, our experience is that testing these seven hypotheses provides a good summation of the internal workings of a firm within the time available during a merger negotiation process.

Before we examine each hypothesis in turn, and the means for testing it, two further points require attention.

The first is that just because two firms rank very differently against an hypothesis does not necessarily mean that there is a serious problem. In the discussions between the two firms, it might be made clear that there is a process in both firms that would lead to convergence over a couple of years. The merger is a way to speed this up.

One merger demonstrated this very clearly. One of the two firms had a highly centralised decision-making structure, with the managing partner and a small board having the power to take a significant number of major decisions. The other firm had a much less centralised decision-making structure in that the partnership as a whole had the power to make most of the decisions, and the business units tended to operate semi-autonomously. Central management played much more of a co-ordination/administration role. In terms of the first hypothesis (the firm is highly structured internally), the two firms were almost at opposite ends of the spectrum, and the due diligence team highlighted this as a major problem. However, in reviewing other data, it became apparent that neither firm operated quite the way defined. In the so-called highly centralised firm, it became apparent that the managing partner actually did a considerable amount of consultation before major decisions were taken. In looking at the business planning and budgetary process, the board simply set a few parameters for the business units, and then asked each unit to prepare its own plan and budget in line with them. In theory, whilst the board established the operational targets for each business unit, the activity was delegated to the business unit heads.

The same was true across a range of other due diligence issues. A new property lease had been taken out at a significant cost, and the board had the power to sign the lease without partnership approval. The managing partner had, however, issued a memorandum about the new lease prior to signing it, and had held several discussion groups about it.

What transpired was an organisation that had well-defined, high-level powers at the centre, but where central management used consultation and delegation quite widely before coming to a major decision. In discussions with people in the firm about this, it emerged that the existing structure of decision-making had been put in place some years before when the firm had been through a major crisis, and when tight central control was required to pull it out of that. Over the following years, the degree of central control had been relaxed significantly, but no change had been made to the defined powers on the formal structure as described.

The second firm was moving the other way. Although the managing partner appeared to have little defined power in deciding any major issues, the present incumbent had been able to informally take a greater degree of management control than was defined in the formal organisational structure.

It was clear from reviewing minutes of partner meetings and board meetings (as well as from exploring the process by which decisions were made) that most major initiatives came from the managing partner, who was highly trusted by partners, and who had built up high levels of consensus from the partnership for those initiatives. Hence, whilst the records showed that the partnership held widespread powers, the managing partner had informally built up a power base, and was the force behind major decisions.

The interesting thing was that when this emerged, both sides realised that, in terms of actual operating style, they were not too different. An organisation structure with roles and responsibilities that reflected the middle ground between them was therefore drawn up, and this was approved by both sides without any debate.

Some people might think that, in the case of the above example, as soon as the due diligence report 'hit the table', both sides of the negotiating group would have known that it did not reflect reality. In this particular case, however, no one reacted like that. Both sides accepted that the report was correct, because technically it was – the defined powers of both firms were in fact quite different. Although both managing partners stated that their firms worked differently in practice, each side of the negotiating group reacted with 'well they would say that wouldn't they', and the difference in the defined organisational structure almost became a deal-breaker. It was only when a significant amount of evidence emerged that demonstrated that the actual decision-making processes were different to the way that they had been defined, that the negotiating groups were able to move on to deal with other issues. (It also helped that a strategic adviser carried out the work that demonstrated the firms were not too far apart. People found it easier to accept this as objective evidence.)

The second point is that the assessment against each hypothesis needs to be done in respect of both firms, and the issue is not whether they are both above or below average relative to similar firms but how close they are to each other. The issue is about where each firm ranks in terms of its general principles about structure, communication, risk-taking, etc, and how close or divergent the firms are on this scale. (This is another reason why using an external consultant who is familiar with law firms is useful when carrying out this exercise – people inside a firm often lack any external perspective or knowledge of general organisational principles.)

Hypothesis 1: The firm is highly structured internally

The example above provides some explanation of the first hypothesis. A large part of the evidence to test the hypothesis that the firm is highly structured internally will be found in the organisation and management section of the due diligence process (see **Table 9.4**). Further evidence will also be contained in the section on management information (how much is given out) (see **Table 9.4**). To see the extent to which issues are centrally managed or more widely delegated, look at the information on partner remuneration, partner performance management and partner retirement/expulsion (see **Table 9.1**). Data coming out of the infrastructure section will also provide evidence, especially in relation to the decision-making authorities of each role in those departments (see **Table 9.5**). Finally, the operations of the business units will provide further evidence with which to test this hypothesis (see **Table 9.11**).

Hypothesis 2: The environment encourages team/group initiative over individual initiative

The second hypothesis can be tested across a number of areas. A crucial one will be the client relationship management process in each firm, and the extent to which this is truly team-driven or to which clients are still the 'property' of individuals (see **Table 9.6**). Business unit analysis will also assist – do partners generally engage in the management of their unit or do they see that as the job of the unit head (see **Table 9.11**)? The extent to which partners play an active role in people management issues is another piece of evidence (with team-driven firms generally scoring much higher here than individually-driven firms – see **Table 9.7**). The partner performance management process will also be instructive in this regard (if one exists) – the extent to which performance is judged individually as opposed to by reference to a team (see **Table 9.1**). The marketing section will also be a useful indicator of the extent to which marketing is a team or individual activity (see **Table 9.10**).

Hypothesis 3: This is a firm that encourages and supports those who take business risks within reason

The testing of the third hypothesis, whether or not people are encouraged to take business risks within reason, is not quite as straightforward as the testing of the first two. However, it can be done. The first thing to point out here is that we are not referring to unnecessary risks or high levels of risk. The issue is more to do with the premise that in developing and building a business, people will need to take some risks, and will, at times, fail. The extent to which the initiative is recognised positively (even if it results in failure), is an important consideration, and the extent to which failure is 'penalised' is another.

The evidence with which to test this hypothesis will be dotted throughout the due diligence process, and will require more insight into the workings of the organisations than the first two. One important piece of data is under personnel issues (see **Table 9.7**) – how each firm defines success from a personal viewpoint, and who the individuals are who appear to be more successful. Are they people who have 'put themselves on the line' in terms of marketing, people development and other, similar issues, or are they of a more conservative ilk? Asking questions about failed initiatives, and the impact on those who led them, is also useful.

Evidence will also come through other sources. Is there a perception that the firm is conservative in its approach to recruitment and promotion? Has it promoted risk-takers ahead of more conservative people? Does its business strategy have a robust sense of boldness and bravery? Does its marketing strategy take risks on new and innovative approaches?

Hypothesis 4: Senior people devote significant time to firm-wide development activities

The fourth hypothesis is the extent to which senior partners devote significant time to the firm's development and succession planning. What this is seeking to identify is the extent to which the firm focuses on short-term activities at the expense of long-term investments.

Evidence with which to test this hypothesis will be found in the sections on personnel issues (particularly in performance management and in the mentoring section – see **Table 9.7**), client relationship issues (see **Table 9.6**) and marketing (see **Table 9.10**). There should also be evidence in the partner performance management section and when looking at billable hours of senior partners relative to mid-level and junior partners (see **Table 9.2**).

Hypothesis 5: People identify first with 'the firm' and secondly with their particular unit

People identifying primarily with the firm is the fifth hypothesis. This is relatively difficult to assess through the due diligence process, but one piece of evidence can be found in the client analysis (see **Table 9.6**). The extent to which clients buy from more than one practice group on a regular basis indicates some widening out of the relationship to the firm as a whole. Marketing issues should also reveal some data – the extent to which people participate in marketing initiatives that are at the firm level (see **Table 9.10**). Partner performance data will also provide some evidence (see **Table 9.2**).

Another sign lies in how well any regularly held partners' meetings are attended. The composition of firm-wide task forces, committees, etc is another sign – are the members of these people from across the whole partnership or are they just the 'same old faces'?

Hypothesis 6: Communication is transparent, widespread and two-way

The sixth hypothesis can be tested in a number of areas. The management information system (see **Table 9.4**) provides an important piece of evidence – do partners get the information in a clear, understandable and actionable format, or is it a mish-mash of data or very limited? Are major issues communicated clearly throughout the partnership? Are key discussion issues at board level 'floated' around the partnership? Does management seek to engage partners in key issues through communication? Do people know who the firm's core clients are? Are people informed about major engagements for which the firm is instructed? Is performance management circulated in a clear, understandable and actionable way? How widespread is financial information disseminated, and do people know if the firm is performing to budget? Do they know how their own unit is performing? Are roles and responsibilities of key management positions disseminated widely? At what point are people informed that they are in line for partnership? Is everyone in a unit aware of its business plan? Are all client team members fully informed about the needs of the client as well as the way in which services need to be delivered?

The issue of communication runs through many areas of the due diligence process, and it is something that all involved in the process need to explore as a part of their 'fact-finding' mission.

Hypothesis 7: Performance across a range of activities defines success

The final hypothesis concerns performance and the extent to which it is widely or narrowly defined. The performance management processes (see **Tables 9.1**, **9.4** and **9.7**) are a key piece of evidence here, but it is not enough to simply review the criteria. The outcome also needs to be examined. Are the top performers rated highly across a number of key criteria? Where remuneration is linked to rewards, are the highly remunerated partners strong performers across a range of criteria?

In relation to this second issue, it is not enough to review the highest remunerated people or note that they are the highest billing partners, and to then conclude that billing is all that matters. (Believe it or not, people actually do that.) There is also a need to review the performance of these people against the other criteria. It is not unusual to find that high-billing partners also out-perform others on a number of criteria. Hence, the superficial observation that billing is the only criterion that matters could well be wrong.

The performance management system should be reviewed in order to assess how performance is defined and used. The system might appear to have a wide view of what constitutes performance, but if on examination one criterion has 50% or more of the weighting, then it is actually a very narrowly defined process.

Where a firm has a lockstep as the basis of its partner remuneration, it is, of course, not possible to use remuneration as a measure of how performance is evaluated. More and more firms with lockstep remuneration are introducing either a flexible lockstep, where partners can move down as well as up (and sometimes fast track upwards), or some type of bonus or incentive system alongside the lockstep. In either case, the actual results of the performance evaluation can be tested by reviewing the placement of partners within these systems.

Where a firm only has a lockstep system with no remuneration element or promotion/demotion linked to performance element, the testing of performance evaluations is more difficult. Furthermore, many firms do not have well-developed performance management systems, which makes the assessment even more difficult. In order to overcome this problem, each side could produce a list of partners ranked by management in terms of performance. Comparisons can then be made between partners who have been ranked by their respective firm at a similar level. For a large firm, this can be by a sample list of partners at each level, whilst in a smaller firm merger, all partners could be compared. (As we noted in **Chapter 6**, this is sometimes necessary where there is a profitability difference – an appropriate performance ranking will be required in order to know where partners 'fit' within the remuneration system.)

The outcome

In our view, the outcome of this exercise is highly valuable for testing many of the 'softer', organisational issues of the two firms – issues that can get lost in the detailed analyses of business cases and financial data, devising organisational structures, and carrying out the 'hard edge' due diligence.

Despite the value we place on it, there are many who feel that it is an additional burden to what is already a time-consuming process. The argument we hear most often is: 'Well, we can discuss these issues amongst ourselves, and see how comfortable we are.'

The first point we make in support of this process is that it is not particularly time-consuming provided that the due diligence includes questions that relate to the seven hypotheses set out above. Collecting the required data during the due diligence process itself adds very little time to the basic task.

The second point is that, of course it is possible to discuss these hypotheses, and to gain some assurance from the answers given. However, two problems, quite common to law firms, can distort the answers given (quite unintentionally).

The first problem is one which we come across time and time again in organisational reviews, and this is the difference between what management believe is happening and what is really happening in practice. We call this the 'perception/reality gap'.

The second problem is one of relativity. Both firms agree that they are 'reasonably good' at communication, and produce evidence to back this up. It emerges subsequently, however, that there is a major difference between what both meant and understood by 'reasonably good'. We elaborate on these two problems below.

The 'perception/reality gap'

The 'perception/reality gap' is very common in law firms (in fact in most organisations). What management believes it is doing is not translated into reality at ground level. Management genuinely believes that its firm's high performers are very good at bringing in fees, marketing, client management, management of WIP and debtors, etc. An examination of the hard data, however, often reveals a more inconsistent pattern or, in some cases, that the 'good performance' of an individual is actually a result of other people's actions. We have seen many situations where an individual partner is credited with considerable success, for example, in marketing pitches. Investigation of a number of such pitches indicates, however, that the success was very much due to a team effort. What happens is a partner builds a reputation for winning marketing pitches on the basis of a couple of major wins. People then start to assume that the partner is the main person responsible for other wins with which they are associated, when this might not be true at all. There is evidence in psychology as to how this works. Once people are convinced about the way a certain event occurs, they look at future events with that assumption in mind, and sub-consciously seek evidence to support it rather than refute it. Using the example above, the mind can start with an assumption, based on a limited number of facts, such as:

- 'Partner X won two major clients through pitches. Hence, Partner X is clearly very good at winning pitches.'

This is then followed sub-consciously as:

- 'We have won six major pitches this year. Partner X was involved in all of them. Partner X is very effective in pitches. Hence, Partner X was the major factor in these wins.'

When set out like this, people initially deny that there would be such a slide in their logic. However, the fact is, people do it all the time, especially busy people who do not always have the time to examine all of the evidence. Using the example above, this can be reinforced in a partnership if Partner X is also a fairly charismatic person and highly visible in the partnership. In the absence of hard evidence, people such as Partner X are often attributed a greater role in events than they actually had. Unintentionally, management can become blinded by a few facts, and does not see the evidence that contradicts its beliefs.

Relativity

The second problem of relativity is also common in law firms. Whilst partner mobility has increased in recent years, there are still many partners who have only ever worked at partner level at one firm. In addition, some firms' management teams will not have been deeply involved in management for a long period of time, and generally lack benchmarks against which to assess themselves when it comes testing the hypotheses set out above. Hence, without intending to do so, management's answers to how well its firm performs against others in these areas is given in a contextual vacuum. 'We are pretty good at communicating' might simply mean 'we are better than we were' (ie moving from a level of 'very poor' to 'well below average' might seem 'pretty good' to them). Hence, how firms rate themselves on these 'soft issues' is often relative to their own historical development rather than to any general market benchmark.

Another point that is relevant here is the composition of most negotiating groups. The members selected are usually heavily weighted towards people in management roles together with some strong opinion-formers in the firm. It is not uncommon to find that their review of these issues will produce different responses to those that the 'average partner on the ground' would give. For example, they are unlikely to see management as over-centralised, as they are a part of it. Furthermore, communication is usually good between members of this group, they are usually seen as high performers, and will interpret the firm's approach through their own eyes. Whether this reflects reality is a different matter.

Organisational dysfunction

We have noted several times that more mergers go wrong (or fail to achieve their potential) due to poor integration than to the business case and strategy being wrong. We noted in **Chapter 8** a number of ways in which firms can achieve a better integration process. What we did not mention, because it is a theme in this chapter, is the impact of organisational incompatibility or organisational dysfunction between the two firms that was not identified in the negotiation and due diligence process.

There have been a number of mergers in the UK where the business case supported the merger, the two firms were able to sort out organisation structures, remuneration systems, etc, and the due diligence process produced no major problems. Nevertheless, the merged firm struggled to move forward on integration, and there was a constant tension between the two sides from day one. In some cases, there was a subsequent de-merger or, over time, there were a significant number of departures from one side of the merger, including the departure of large teams.

In one case, Firm A (of 20 partners) merged with Firm B (of 35 partners). At the end of three years, the merged firm consisted of 65 partners, 30 of which were from the original 35 of Firm B, but, from Firm A, only eight remained, and only five of the initial Firm A partners reached retirement age in that period.

In this example, a subsequent review demonstrated a very high level of organisational dysfunction between the two antecedent firms. This was despite premerger discussions touching on a number of relevant issues, including the degree of centralised management, the evaluation of performance, the degree of risk taking and the communication process. One partner from Firm A who was involved in the negotiations stated later:

> 'It sounded so plausible in the discussions, and I'm sure they were not misleading us. We were the smaller firm, and expected some change, but the actual difference in Firm B from day one compared to what we thought it was made the difference almost irreconcilable.'

It transpired that Firm B was highly centralised in management even though the formal structure appeared to contain a significant amount of delegation. In actual fact, the managing partner and two other members of management had a high degree of power and influence, and there was little challenge to them by other partners. When partners from Firm A tried to object, they were initially told that this was how large firms were run, and that they should get used to it. When some continued to object because they knew that some other, similar sized firms were not so centralised, they were labelled as trouble-makers by Firm B's partners. Whilst pre-merger partners from Firm A had generally felt that they required more centralisation, they found Firm B's centralisation too extreme.

The same was true in respect of performance evaluation. Despite what had been said in the merger discussions, it was clear that personal billing was the overriding success factor in Firm B, and so lip service was paid to other criteria. Firm A had a broader view of performance, and some of their better-performing partners suffered in the first round of evaluation (and rewards) because performance was only based on billings.

Firm B proved to be very conservative. Despite the merger and several other initiatives that had been mentioned in negotiations, it was very averse to taking risks. Whilst merging was used as an example of its risk-taking, it was very clear that Firm B minimised that risk by taking control of the merged firm very quickly, and by effectively ignoring efforts by partners from Firm A to exercise influence. Whilst Firm A's managing partner had become deputy managing partner of the merged firm, it was not a role that held any influence. He resigned from the firm two years post-merger.

Firm A's partners stressed that they did not believe that Firm B had deceived them. It was simply that when many of the 'soft' issues were discussed, very different definitions were used, but, at the time, there was no testing whether the two firms meant the same thing by 'delegated management', 'broad-based performance', etc. This goes back to the main theme of this chapter, which is that firms must probe below the surface on key areas during both the negotiating process and the due diligence exercise. People might state honestly what they believe about their structures, systems and styles. However, these statements must undergo further testing, first to ensure everyone means the same thing, and secondly to see if whatever is under discussion actually operates in the way it is described. This requires both sides to go beyond receiving word-of-mouth explanations, and simply reading written policies. It is how these policies operate in practice that will indicate whether there is a dysfunctional aspect to a firm, and whether the way it operates will prove dysfunctional in the merged firm.

Even in some, eventually, very successful mergers, the first year of the merged firm proved to be somewhat tension driven whilst both sides tried to come to terms with aspects of organisational behaviour by the other side that they had not expected. Whilst these cases were not as bad as the example above, they did mean that the first year of their mergers was more about trying to resolve issues of a potentially dysfunctional organisational nature than quickly integrating.

Organisational behaviour

Organisational behaviour (ie the way an organisation operates, the way it manages, and the way it deals with issues) is related to culture, but it is not the same thing. As we noted in **Chapter 4**, when people speak of a similar culture in merger negotiations, in most cases, they are really saying 'we seem to get along pretty well'. In a few cases, firms go further (more in line with the approach set out in this chapter) and probe below the surface. In these situations, people mean: 'We seem to get on pretty well and the other organisation seems to operate in a similar way to ours.' However, as we will demonstrate in **Chapter 10**, neither of these statements tell us very much about culture.

What is true, however, is that no two organisations behave in exactly the same way. Two organisations can have similar strategies, and be targeted at the same part of the market, recruit people with an apparently similar background and appear to be equally successful over time. The organisational behaviour, however, can be vastly different. There is no single correct way for an organisation to 'behave' for it to be successful. Whilst there are some behaviours or approaches that are likely to prevent success, there are a number of ways an organisation can behave and be successful.

Organisational behaviour is a product of many things, including the historical development of a firm, the level of trust that has built up for key people, the associations that people make between the firm's success and certain organisational constructs, and the degree of movement in and out of the firm by its staff. There are other issues as well, but the above examples sufficiently illustrate the complexity of organisational behaviour.

Three firms demonstrate this very clearly and they are a part of the UK's Magic Circle: Clifford Chance, Freshfields Bruckhaus Deringer and Slaughter and May. All have very different paths in their historical development. Clifford Chance was the product of a merger in 1987, and then launched into re-inventing itself as a leading international firm. Freshfields Bruckhaus Deringer, for a long period of time, was one of the UK's blue blood firms, but it transformed itself into a corporate and finance powerhouse and developed into a leading international firm (mainly through merger). Slaughter and May, possibly with the bluest blood of them all, has also gone through significant change (although less than Clifford Chance and Freshfields Bruckhaus Deringer). It had a strong corporate focus well before the other two did, but it has not grown internationally through merger. It has also had much less movement of people in and out of the firm, especially at partner level, than Clifford Chance and Freshfields Bruckhaus Deringer.

Despite some apparent similarities between these firms in a strategic sense, people report major differences in organisational behaviour between them. Whilst Slaughter and May is seen as very different to the other two, people from Freshfields Bruckhaus Deringer view their firm as a different organisation in the way it goes about things to that of Clifford Chance, and vice versa. From the outside, it would appear that there are very different management styles and decision-making processes at work at these firms, but the approach taken within each firm seems to work for it.

As we said before, there is no necessarily right or wrong way to behave. The critical issue is that the organisational behaviour matches the needs of the firm and its people. Some people are perfectly happy in a relatively highly centralised management structure. Others 'chafe at the bit' and are very dissatisfied with that approach. Some people want to receive a constant flow of communication about everything whilst others are happy to have limited amounts of very meaningful communication.

It is this combination of many strands that makes organisational behaviour such a complex thing to get to grips with. This is illustrated by the fact that some people, who do not perform well in one organisation, can become stars when they move to another. A change in organisational context can release a much higher level of motivation and energy which, in turn, results in significant performance improvements.

Hence, the 'standard' way of negotiating a merger, even when done very well, is unlikely to even 'grab the tail' of deeper issues about organisational behaviour, let alone 'capture the body'. Yet, without a reasonable grasp of what actually goes on inside one firm when compared to another, serious mistakes in assumptions about merger compatibility can be made. The superficial methods often employed to understand behaviour in each firm are rarely enough, and the assumption that behaviour will not be an issue because 'we have similar cultures' is simply erroneous.

The hypotheses set out in this chapter are essential in developing a strong business case for merger. Two firms with a strong business case will fail if they create a dysfunctional organisation. Similarly, two firms with compatible organisations will fail if the business case is weak. Whilst there are a number of important issues to address when seeking to test whether a merger will be effective, the business case and organisational behaviour are the two most fundamental ones in the whole process.

In **Chapter 10**, we examine the whole issue of cultural compatibility, explain our scepticism about the approach taken in many merger discussions, set out a process that will be helpful in identifying particular cultural indicators, and link it back to organisational behaviour.

CHAPTER 10: CULTURE – THE ELUSIVE ASPECT OF MERGERS

Introduction

In a merger, a cultural mismatch is just as dangerous as a strategic mis-match. Interestingly, however, although culture is recognised as a major issue in most mergers, it is rarely analysed in sufficient depth to enable one firm to understand the culture of the other, and never in the same depth as many of the more tangible aspects of a merger. Most assessments of cultural compatibility in mergers are superficial. Often aided and abetted by consultants (unfortunately), management sometimes carries out a few so-called 'tests', and concludes from them that the two firms' cultures are compatible. The results are, however, largely facile and meaningless in terms of judging the true compatibility of the two cultures. In fact, more effort goes into the post-merger rhetoric about developing a so-called new or joint culture for the merged firm than ever goes into attempting to understand the cultures pre-merger. However, if the cultures of the two antecedent firms have not been understood, then any talk about developing a new or joint culture, or picking out the best of each culture, is no more than hyperbole. Most people in merged firms outside of management are cynical about the cultural rhetoric post-merger, and they are quite right to be so.

When dealing with the management of a merged firm which is having trouble integrating the antecedent businesses, one question we always ask is: 'What was done to assess the culture of the two organisations pre-merger?' The most common answer is: 'The negotiating teams hit it off from the start, and when we brought partners from each practice group together, they also got on well. Of course there were a few exceptions, but most people liked each other. No, the problem can't be cultural.'

The second most common answer is: 'We knew each other very well. We were often on different sides of deals and litigation matters. Many partners knew and respected those in the other firm generally, and we always got on well in meetings.'

Believe it or not, that is what a high proportion of law firms call a test of cultural compatibility. (Even worse, there are consultants who actually recommend this as a valid process.) You might as well bring together a Frenchman, an Irishman, a Mexican, a German, an Englishman and an American, serve drinks to them for an hour, and assume that because no one shouted at or threw their drink over the others, their cultures are compatible. Would two law firms merge on the basis that the profits of the two firms looked about the same, and the accounts were prepared in a similar style, without carrying out in-depth due diligence? Unlikely, so why take a different approach to culture?

The need for compatibility

At the heart of the success of any law firm merger are people. No matter how good the strategy, no matter how well designed the organisational structure, and no matter how few problems the due diligence process throws up, if people are not motivated to perform in the way that the post-merger strategy requires, the merger will fail (and could even be a disaster). The fundamental concept of a successful law firm merger is ensuring that people from the two firms come together in a way that creates a highly motivated group which is committed to ensuring the success of the merged firm. This is never going to happen if the two cultures are not sufficiently compatible.

The critical point here is that culture in an organisation is much more than people 'getting on with each other', or being socially compatible. This problem can be seen clearly when individuals move firms. There are numerous examples of a firm recruiting a highly talented individual who was regarded as an excellent performer in their previous firm but does not perform as well in the new one. They seem somewhat unhappy, are not highly motivated, and their performance is barely average. One could blame the individual, and assume that they were over-rated by their previous firm. The other, more likely, reason is that the individual has not changed, but does not fit comfortably into the culture of the new firm, and so, over time, their performance is adversely affected.

Organisational culture has a very powerful influence over the motivation and performance of people. Put a high-performing person or group of people into a culture which they do not feel suits them, and their performance will always worsen over time. Whilst the content or quality of their work may not decline, other aspects of their performance will – they will become unhappy, frustrated and increasingly disagreeable. They might appear to be quite friendly with others, but they will express dissatisfaction with the organisation, its management and the way it operates. At some point they will leave, or their overall performance will decline to such an extent that they will probably be forced out. However, put the same person or group in a more compatible culture, and they will thrive. Culture is a very potent tool, and is ignored at great peril.

As we noted above, the need for cultural compatibility is recognised in most law firm mergers, but the process that firms use to identify the culture of the other is woeful. At best, meetings are arranged with various groups of people to ensure 'they get on'. Meanwhile, the negotiating teams reach agreement about structures, remuneration systems, performance management systems, and all the other more tangible issues dealt with in earlier chapters of this book. Then the firms vote in favour of the proposal, and the merger takes place. This is followed by a huge amount of rhetoric about building a common culture, and the announcement of a new set of 'values' for the merged firm. These 'values' are either an adaptation of those of one of the antecedent firms, or a blend of the supposed values of both. Terms such as 'respect each other', 'committed to clients', 'teamwork', 'integrity', 'innovation' and 'adding value' are often reeled off as the new values. Everyone agrees that these are appropriate, and nod approvingly. Sometimes a 'culture consultant' is called in to conduct workshops so that everyone understands what is meant by 'integrity', 'teamwork', 'innovation', 'respect', etc, and these 'values' are then assumed to be embedded in the organisation. At one level, there might not be any harm in carrying out such workshops, and, indeed, some good might come out of them. For example, if a 45-year-old partner does not understand terms such as 'respect for others', 'integrity', 'teamwork', etc, there is some value in the process. However, to assume that such a process creates a new culture and set of values for a merged firm is pure delusion.

The danger is that nothing is actually done to address the real cultural issues, and there will then be a cultural clash in the merged firm (in which case one side's culture will win), or there will be a long period of time when the two cultures are working side by side or a long period of cultural confusion. Any of these situations is likely to result in some damage to the motivation and performance of people in the firm, and the ability of the firm to meet its business goals and required level of competitiveness. It can also harm the firm's efforts to get the integration process started.

Our fundamental point is that if post-merger management is going to make statements about culture and values, it needs to carry out the due diligence necessary to identify aspects of these (as a minimum) in the two antecedent firms. Relying on 'people getting on' and anecdotal comments about their culture is grossly insufficient. We were involved in a case where the pre-merger management teams rejected the argument for a cultural audit of both firms on the grounds of cost, even though the cost would have been one quarter of what was paid to external accountants for a financial due diligence exercise. (It transpired that serious cultural conflicts emerged post-merger which damaged the merged firm for some time.)

Culture is not something that management finds easy to address, and this goes a long way to explaining why it is a neglected issue in the pre-merger negotiations. However, once the merger is completed, management feels more able to describe a new culture and a set of values for the merged firm – it is far easier to describe the culture it wants than to grasp and understand the one it had!

A problem, of course, is that if the new culture of the merged firm enunciated by management is too different from the culture of one or both of the antecedent firms, there will be a significant level of cultural incompatibility. Furthermore, if all management does is talk about a new culture (and even explains what it means by that), it is highly unlikely that the culture will become embedded in the merged firm.

We are of the view that the main area of failure when it comes to a merger is integration, but that is due to the failure of management to address the issue of cultural compatibility in both the pre and post-merger phases. This also affects the integration processes set out in **Chapter 8** adversely, and can also reduce performance below the level required for the merger to be perceived as successful.

Behavioural norms

What management actually means when it talks about 'culture' and 'values' are behavioural norms.

For example, when management announces 'we shall be client-focused', what it wants is for its partners (and others) to spend more time with clients.[1] That is about behaviour (what people do and where they spend their time), not culture. There is unlikely to be a deep-seated cultural belief about 'spending time with clients' or even 'not spending time with clients'.

If the aim is to spend more time with clients, the starting point should be to find out why people do not do that already, rather than to make a culture change announcement. One obvious reason why people do not spend more time with clients is because each person thinks that they are spending enough time with them already, and, if there is a problem, it lies elsewhere. Another reason might be that people are already expected to work very long chargeable hours, and that the firm's strategy is focused on bringing in new clients. Therefore, carrying out those two tasks as well as other day-to-day activities takes up all of people's time. Another reason might be that the firm's systems operate 'against' people spending more time with clients. For

---

1 We use the example of spending time with clients for illustrative purposes only. The same point applies to many of the other so-called 'culture change' statements.

example, if the reward system of a firm is focused on billing, people will want to spend their time doing that before they 'waste' time with clients.

There is a myriad of behavioural reasons why people do not respond to the urgings of management. However, to call these reasons 'values' and to use a 'culture change' to implement them is a travesty. It also explains why many implementation programmes fail. If organisational constraints are causing people to fail to adapt their behaviour, the solution is simple – start by changing what is causing the problem, and do not confuse it with 'culture change'. We discuss this in further detail below.

In the rest of this chapter, we discuss the issue of culture in a law firm, what it is, how it comes about, and some of its points of recognition. We then describe a process by which cultural compatibility can be assessed by the two firms contemplating merger. This also relates back to **Chapter 9**, where we discussed aspects of organisational behaviour, and how to identify some of the underlying patterns behind specific behavioural norms in a firm.

In our view, **Chapter 9** and this chapter are the two most important chapters in this book. This is not to downplay the importance of the other chapters, but to reinforce the comments that culture is greatly misunderstood in law firm mergers, even though it is recognised conceptually as very important.

Recommended reading

Whilst the thoughts and processes set out in this chapter are drawn from our own consulting work and research, we have developed a strong admiration over the years for the work of four others – Henry Mintzberg, Edgar Schein, Ralph H Kilman and Chris Argyris.

Whilst we like to believe that our interest in these writers is due to the commonality in thinking between us, it is undoubtedly true that their writings over the years have influenced our thinking and work processes in this area. Furthermore, whilst none of them are particularly concerned with law firms, or even professional service firms, their thinking on organisational culture is entirely appropriate (with slight adjustment) to the professional services environment. If the reader would like to explore the issue of organisational culture in more depth, we suggest the following books.

By far the most relevant book is Edgar Schein, *Organisational Culture and Leadership*.[2] Alongside this is Schein's later and shorter book, *The Corporate Culture Survival Guide*.[3]

---

2 (San Francisco: Jossey-Bass, 1995).

3 (San Francisco: Jossey-Bass, 1999).

Henry Mintzberg, *Mintzberg on Management: Inside Our Strange World of Organizations*[4] contains some very powerful observations, especially in Chapter 12, as does his *The Structuring of Organizations: A Synthesis of the Research.*[5]

Ralph H Kilman, *Beyond the Quick Fix: Managing Five Tracks to Organisational Success*[6] is also recommended, especially Chapter 4.

Chris Argyris is a prolific writer on subjects related closely to cultural issues. See his *On Organizational Learning,*[7] particularly the sections on defensive reasoning and defensive routines. The same author's *Reasoning, Learning and Action: Individual and Organization*[8] and *Knowledge for Action: A Guide to Overcoming Barriers to Organizational Change*[9] are also valuable in this context.

What is culture?

In **Chapter 9**, we explored ways of understanding differences in organisational processes and systems. For example, why one firm may have a performance-based remuneration system for partners, and why another may have a lockstep or seniority-based system. As we noted there, it is one thing to decide on a remuneration system for the 'new' firm that blends together aspects of the systems of the two antecedent firms, but it is another, more critically important, issue to understand why each firm had the system it had. Understanding the reason why will not tell a firm about the culture of the other, but it can help to show the potential differences in organisational behaviour that may or may not converge if a blended process is installed in the 'new' firm. Such an approach might provide some clues as to the culture of the two firms. Note that we say 'might'. There are a number of processes that can help to understand the culture of an organisation, and we will discuss some of these below. The true nature of an organisation's culture might be able to be sensed, and people might even be able to articulate certain aspects of it. However, whether it can really be understood in full, or merely some aspects of it understood, is a moot point that will become clearer as we proceed.

The starting point to understanding culture is to know what we are trying to understand. As we touched upon above, the problem with many law firms is that they

---

4 (New York: Free Press, 1989).

5 (Englewood Cliffs NJ: Prentice Hall, 1979).

6 (San Francisco: Jossey-Bass, 1984).

7 2nd ed (Oxford: Blackwell Business, 1999).

8 (San Francisco: Jossey-Bass, 1982).

9 (San Francisco: Jossey-Bass, 1983).

confuse behaviour with culture. Whilst the two are indirectly related, the way people behave in an organisation is influenced by many things as well as culture. Hence, the saying 'culture is the way we do things around here' is a mis-statement. Instead, it should be 'our culture is reflected in the way we do things around here', which is somewhat different. Another incorrect statement is that culture is 'our internal environment' or 'our firm's climate'. Again, there will be a relationship between the two, but they are not necessarily (and rarely) the same.

Behaviour, internal environment and climate, the systems and processes in the firm, the way a firm operates, and even its strategy and goals, are all manifestations of an organisation's culture, but they are not 'the culture'. Not every act of every person can be attributed to culture. Over time, and across a firm, some behavioural patterns will be followed by a large majority of people, and whilst these patterns are reflections of the culture, they are not 'the culture'. The reasons behind why these behavioural patterns occur, why some systems are used and others not, why some people are comfortable with the organisation and others not, provide a set of hypotheses about culture that can then be tested.[10]

Definition of culture

There is no single definition of culture that satisfies everybody, but a definition that appears to meet widespread agreement is the following:

At its deepest level, it is a set of beliefs, values and assumptions that are shared within a group (ie an organisation).

Organisational cultures are strongest where a high percentage of people hold that set of beliefs, values and assumptions in high esteem, even though they are not issues that people consciously share or discuss or, in many cases, are even near the surface. Take for example someone who has a profound belief in God. That belief shapes much of their behaviour, and they will justify everything they do on the basis of that belief. If asked why they did a certain thing, they would probably say 'because it seemed right' or 'it was appropriate'. If pushed a bit further, they might say 'it was fair to others' or 'it seemed the action that would cause the least offence'. If pushed even further, they might start to talk about how they believe people should treat others, and, if pushed really far, they might articulate a belief in God. In other words, respecting fellow human beings is a consequent value of their belief in God.

---

10 This is why we suggested in **Chapter 9** that exploring the reasons why firms use certain systems and processes is important.

Much of our behaviour is driven in this way. Each of us holds a deep-set view of how the world works, about human nature, and how we believe we should interact with those around us. We develop these views as children from our parents, siblings and school, and through growing up. By the time we reach adulthood, most of us have a set of beliefs and assumptions about what drives and motivates people, and how the world works (ie how we need to interact in the world in order to achieve what we want). We rarely articulate this, and mostly take our beliefs for granted. However, the following are statements that illustrate people's views about human nature and how the world works:

'At the end of the day, people are motivated by money and nothing else.'

'People basically want to co-exist in a harmonious way, and we should be seeking to ensure this happens.'

'At the end of it all, people will take all they can get so you have to protect what is yours.'

Just as each of us has a view about human nature and the workings of the world around us, the same is true of organisations. The founders of an organisation inject many of the beliefs, values and assumptions into the structures, systems and processes of their organisation. Over time, other strong leaders adapt these, reshape them, and a culture therefore evolves. In some organisations, the culture is very strong. In others, it can be much weaker. Some people may find their organisation an 'uncomfortable' place to work and complain 'it is very formal', 'they are always checking up on you', 'it is run by systems and procedures', 'there is no freedom', etc. Others may find that their organisation operates the way they think it should.

Deep down in every organisation there is a set of beliefs and assumptions about human nature and the world. A set of values flow from this, and it is the combination of these (ie the beliefs, assumptions and values) that is the culture of the organisation. This culture shapes the structures, systems, processes and behaviour in an organisation. The culture can provide direction, motivation and purpose to people, or it can be wasted by leaders and managers who, in failing to understand their organisation's culture, start to reshape the structures, systems and processes in ways that are contradictory to the underlying culture. This is what can happen post-merger when the new leadership announces a 'new' culture for the merged firm, without being aware of the underlying cultures of the two antecedent organisations.

Organisational beliefs and assumptions are learned over time

The beliefs and assumptions of an organisation are 'learned' over time. New people join, and, if they become absorbed into the culture, adopt many of these assumptions and beliefs (often tacitly). The deeper meaning behind many of these beliefs is not always explained to those people, but by accepting the implications in behavioural terms, they are tacitly endorsing those beliefs. Two real-life mergers illustrate this.

Example 10.1

Firm A had been through a 'near death' experience some 15 years previously. Most (but not all) of the partners at that time retired or moved to other firms. Firm A, however, survived and the belief/assumption was that its survival was primarily due to the appointment of a strong, autocratic leader. Power was centralised in the hands of that leader and two others (one being the finance director), partner drawings were cut severely, a number of partners were forced out, and overheads were slashed.[11] Partners worked individually, and the belief was to 'keep one's numbers up'. Anyone who suggested a change to any of this was soon put in their place, and either had to accept the status quo or leave. This is an example of a culture at work. Deep down people believed that their firm's success and survival came from a combination of autocratic leadership, tough decision-making, frugality and a focus on individualism. However, a subsequent investigation revealed that there were other more likely reasons why the firm survived the 'near death' experience, one being a significant increase in market demand in the areas it had a high reputation in. Nevertheless, people still believed in the autocratic leader/tough decision formula.

Although it was never articulated, a deeper belief emerged when we worked with groups of people from the firm to find out why they held to this strong leader theory.[12] This belief was linked to how partners saw human behaviour and the world, which was a deep-seated belief in 'heroic leaders'.[13]

The problem with Firm A was that the leadership at the time stuck to the formula that individuals needed to perform (and performance was defined individually) or were out. It also kept costs under tight control. Furthermore, there was no clear strategy, and the firm was losing ground to rivals. Looking back at the crisis, it became

---

[11] Even today the firm operates with a similar structure, low overheads and low monthly drawings.

[12] Note that culture is often shared amongst a group.

[13] In one exercise, we asked partners who they saw as inspirations (from present or past history), and a high proportion named tough and heroic leaders.

clear that the leader at that time recognised the shift in the market towards a higher demand for specific services, and steered the firm in that direction. So whilst the 'strong leader' was a key person in the firm's revival, this was reinterpreted as him being an 'effective leader' who recognised the need for a strategic shift. The folklore in the firm had defined it as 'strong' rather than 'effective', and had failed to recognise the strategic content of that leader's contribution.

Further probing into the history of Firm A revealed a particularly interesting event. The firm had been formed 30 years previously as a result of a merger between a successful 'founder firm' (relatively new then) and a smaller, much older firm that was not doing very well at the time. Whilst no one from that time still worked at Firm A, some of the older partners recalled what they had heard. The founder firm had a very strong and autocratic leader who focused on costs. The merger was actually a takeover by the 'founder firm' which quickly (and ruthlessly) sorted out the problems. Firm A prospered. The leader retired ten years after the merger (five years before the crisis). In the years leading up to the crisis, Firm A become more democratic, with devolved responsibility for management and decision-making. The firm's performance also steadily declined, with profits per partner falling by over 50% at a time when profitability in other firms was rising. Costs rose uncontrollably, and partner performance slipped. Then the crisis hit, and Firm A almost became insolvent. In stepped another strong leader who acted ruthlessly and 'saved' the firm. A simple lesson emerged which then became deeply embedded in the firm's culture – autocratic leadership, tight cost control, individual performance and ruthless decision-making is the secret to a law firm's success.

A firm's culture is therefore a combination of the experiences learned over time – 'this is the way we do things around here'. In truth, however, people will only accept 'the way we do things' if there is also an underpinning belief that supports that way of doing things. Firm A's culture was based on both the history of the firm, and the deep belief of its partners. They generally subscribed to the heroic leader theory of how the world works ('things only happen when there is a strong leader'), and also believed in a dependency role for others ('we must support the leader'). They valued security, and the strong leader gave them that, provided they maintained their personal financial performance.

The trouble was that, 15 years on, this approach to operating a law firm had become more of a problem than an advantage. New people wanted more involvement in decision-making than their predecessors had, and they also wanted more of a strategic approach at the firm-wide level than simply each partner pursuing their own agenda. However, the culture of Firm A (ie the beliefs and assumptions of the 'old-timers') was very resistant to these pressures. The learned experiences aspect of its culture emerged as people remembered the last time the firm had 'gone democratic', and which had proved disastrous. Newer partners argued that plenty of successful firms took a more democratic approach, and that other issues were probably a cause of some of the past problems.

What was happening here was a major cultural clash. The longer-term partners believed that they should simply carry out the legal work, and that a strong leader should manage everything. Newer partners wanted to be involved in decision-making, and believed that, with some training and support, management could and should be more widespread in the firm. When examining the thinking of the 'newcomers', it emerged that they were sceptical of the heroic theory of leadership, and believed much more in broad-based team efforts as the path to success.

Therefore, a new set of beliefs and assumptions had 'crept in' to the firm which sought to challenge the established culture. This was much more than a debate about how to manage the firm (the management issue was superficial). The real issue was the clash of the two cultures – the one ingrained on the longer-serving partners was being challenged by a different set of beliefs held by the partners of a later generation. Tensions surrounding the management issue ran quite high, and it was not until we helped people articulate why they supported one approach over the other that they realised the issue was more to do with culture. Once this was understood, it became possible to work on the real issue, ie seeking to adapt the old culture to a newer way of thinking without it resulting in longer-term partners resigning or 'going to ground' and lowering their performance levels. Cultural change or cultural adaptation? We shall return to this below.

Example 10.2

Cultures by themselves are neither good nor bad. The issue is whether the culture is appropriate to the needs of an organisation within a changing external environment. Take, for example, Firm B which was a very long-established firm (with the founding partners having been dead for over 100 years). It had long had a strong reputation for high-value work within its market position, and the firm took huge pride in both its reputation and 'pedigree'. It competed regularly for high-value work against firms that were larger than it, and more than held its ground.

Firm B had always been a strong M&A firm, and the transactions practice group dominated its management board. As far as anyone was aware, the managing partner had always been from this practice group. (In fact, the firm's founders had also been transactional lawyers.) Other departments tended to play a supporting role to the transactions practice. Whilst they were expected to grow their own client base, whenever a major transaction was up and running, everyone from those departments was expected to drop everything if required (or told), and to support the transaction. Partner remuneration was based on a lockstep system, and this seemed to match the firm's ethos and approach to work.

Over a five-year period it became apparent to those outside the firm that the size difference between Firm B and its peer group of competitors was growing, and that Firm B was now half the size of the firms in its peer group (the difference for a long time had only been between 20% and 25%). Its competitors had become much more aggressive, and were increasing their market share of Firm B's core work. For the first two or three years of that five-year period, Firm B held a sufficient market share to keep itself busy and to sustain profitability over the third and fourth years. However, it faced declining profitability and, whilst it was busy, was doing much more lower-value work than before.

At first, partners dismissed the decline as only a temporary one. They argued, using evidence to back them up, that the firm's reputation was greater than that of a number of its larger rivals, and this was all that mattered. By the end of year five, there was a complete state of denial within the firm. Some partners said the whole market was down (evidence indicated this was not the case). Others argued that competitors were doing much worse than their publicity indicated (ie that they were lying). Others pointed out that the firm was still doing work for its core clients (but ignored the fact that 25% of the core clients had not given the firm any major mandates for two years).

Internal tensions broke out which had never happened before. Partners attacked management for allowing costs to get out of control, and blamed this for the falling margins. Some of the traditional high-profit departments deflected criticism of their falling margins by attacking other departments where margins were even lower. The firm's lockstep remuneration system came under attack as individual partners claimed that, whilst they were performing well, others at the top level of the lockstep were not 'earning their keep'.

Defections commenced, especially by the younger partners and senior associates who had become disillusioned with the infighting. Firm B's performance continued to decline over the sixth year, and open warfare broke out between departments. The previous big-profit departments still dominated the management of the firm, and focused on the underperforming partners and groups. A later analysis showed that many of these partners and groups were doing no worse than they had before, and were in practices where the margins were not as high as in the core practice areas.

We were called in initially to review the firm's cost structure, and to look at the economics of each department. We identified reasonably quickly that the firm's cost structure was below that of its major competitors, it did not have the leverage of its competitors, and its average hourly rate had been decreasing for the last seven or eight years. Profits had actually been sustained in the early part of the cycle by speeding up the billing of the work in progress, but there had been an underlying decline in the quality of work being carried out for at least seven or eight years.

This caused a huge debate amongst the partnership. We were accused initially of 'getting our arithmetic wrong', and then management was attacked for not foreseeing the problem. In one very tense meeting, a partner said: 'Why do we need a consultant to come in and tell us what should have been blindingly obvious to management?'[14]

We convinced partners that we should interview some of Firm B's clients in order to understand the pricing issue, and how the firm was viewed in the market against its competitors. The feedback was devastating, and partners attacked the evidence and accused us of asking leading questions. In essence the feedback was:

(i)   Firm B was too small to handle the size of transactions being given out at the top end of the market. Transaction size had grown but the firm had not.

(ii)   Firm B lacked the internal infrastructure to provide a quality service delivery. The lawyers and their technical advice were great but that advice was delivered badly.

(iii)   Firm B's pricing was out of line with that of its competitors for the type of work it was now perceived to be capable of doing (ie no longer large, premium deals). Part of the reason was that partners undertook too much of the work, and clients were unable to carry their charge-out rate.

Some solutions were obvious. Firm B needed to grow its transactional practice significantly, and to invest heavily in new technology and more support staff in order to improve service delivery. Partners also needed to delegate more. All of this was hotly resisted in meeting after meeting.

---

14 A slight memory lapse given that, until two years previously, he had been on the board for more than ten years.

We therefore used small group discussions to try and help partners understand what was going on. They wanted to compete at the top end of the market, which they saw as 'their right'. Secondly, over a number of months, they accepted the client feedback (but only in part). They, however, refused to accept that size was an issue on the basis that no single deal would require all of their lawyers. They were also blind to clients' concerns about the firm not being able to handle more than four or five deals at once, which resulted in those clients giving the bigger deals to the larger competitors. Clients also noted no particular technical advantage in Firm B. They also believed that the service delivery problems stemmed from the firm being too small, and not being able to invest as much as larger firms.

Firm B also only accepted in part the delegation issue. Despite the clients' feedback, senior transaction partners passionately argued that their greater use of partners gave clients better advice and added value. Whilst clients had refuted this view, partners responded: 'But how would they know the quality they are getting? How can they judge?'

The more we probed, the more it became apparent that the issue was cultural. A strong belief in the firm was that 'small is beautiful' – a 1970s concept that many of the senior partners subscribed to. Discussing the way the firm was 20 or 30 years earlier with senior partners, it transpired that it had always 'punched above its weight'. Furthermore, a second belief emerged within the firm that 'quality will always win out against size'. A third belief also surfaced in the discussions that, whilst teamwork was essential, there were always going to be a few stars who should be nurtured and supported by everyone else. We were given example after example as to how this was reflected in 'real life' – no team ever had more than a few stars, and if everyone tried to be the star then infighting would result. (In Firm B, the transactional lawyers had always been the stars.)

The amazing thing was that as these discussions developed, and we pushed deeper into people's thinking, partners started saying: 'Well this is how the founders saw it, and it worked for 150 years, so we don't see why it should change.' When we asked how they knew how the founders had seen it (given that they had died well over 100 years before), we were greeted with puzzled expressions and comments such as: 'We all knew how they saw it. Every partner talked about it when I was a junior, and I guess that when those partners were juniors, every partner talked to them about it.'

Despite the generations that had passed, these beliefs were deeply embedded in the thinking of the current partners, and that threw them into a contradictory position on strategy and culture. The folklore in Firm B was strong and powerful. People, including younger partners and senior associates, believed that they knew what the founders believed, and that this was sacrosanct. These beliefs were the bedrock of the firm, and people could not face up to challenging them.

This was a classic case of a culture (which was almost a religious belief) that had been handed down by word of mouth over many generations. The firm had prospered and succeeded for many years, and the beliefs and assumptions were absorbed into the fabric. By the time people became partners, these beliefs were deeply ingrained and never discussed. People who rejected these beliefs, or held them only loosely, left before partnership was in prospect, as the firm had made it clear to them that they were not 'cultural fits'. Furthermore, no lateral hires were made at partner level so there was a very deeply embedded culture.

The problem for Firm B was that the external world had changed significantly, resulting in the firm's culture becoming a strategic impediment. It took quite a while to work through this strategic/cultural contradiction. The internal tensions abated as people came to accept that there were different types of economic structure required by different practice groups. Some increase in delegation occurred, and a much greater focus on client and business development gradually took hold. Nevertheless, the firm never regained its pre-eminent position, and whilst it is successful today, it is in a somewhat different market position than it was 15 years ago. It is still smaller than many firms which were from its past peer group, and profitability is lower than that of those peers. However, over the last ten years, the culture has slowly adapted to the new market, and, whilst the old beliefs are still present to some extent, they have been tempered by strategic realities.

Yes, small can be beautiful but a firm cannot afford to be so much smaller than its competitors if it wishes to be seen as part of a peer group. Yes, quality will often win over size, but not if larger competitors have a compatible quality. Yes, no team is comprised of stars alone, but the stars have to work hard to maintain their star rating – it is not given as of right.

Firm B has retained its basic beliefs and assumptions, but has adapted them somewhat to market conditions. Partners also came to accept that by retaining the core parts of its culture, its strategic position in the market would be different to what it had been for 150 years. Yes, it is still a high-quality firm, but it is outside the overall market leaders. Firm B has now become comfortable with this, and is pursuing a strategy that more closely matches its adapted culture.

Can a firm change its culture?

A critical issue that emerges from **Examples 10.1** and **10.2** above is how hard it is to change the culture of a firm. When management, post-merger, says that it intends to develop a 'new culture for a new firm', one has to ask if it really knows what it is saying. Changing the deeply held beliefs about human nature and the way the world (ie the firm) works is a Herculean task. As Firm A found out, if a firm has a reasonably strong culture, trying to change it is likely to result in a massive cultural clash, unless it is managed very carefully (and even then it will be extremely difficult).

We were involved in a proposed merger between two firms. One firm's culture was based on the view that money is all that matters – pay people enough, and they will do anything. The other firm's culture was based on the belief that people will respond to systems and procedures that allow them to use their initiative and skills to the full.[15] Both firms, given their respective cultures, could comfortably operate with a merit-based remuneration system. The first firm could because it allowed management to manipulate the system to enable it to highly reward those partners who produced the most revenue, and to 'punish' those whose revenue generation was below expectation. This firm's system was not transparent. The other firm saw a merit-based reward system as an encouragement to everyone to fulfil their potential. It used a wide range of performance measures, of which revenue and profit generation were only two. This firm's remuneration system was very transparent.

The initial merger discussions between the two firms proceeded well. There was no hint of any problems until the discussions moved into the area of the reward system for the new firm, and the distribution of management information to partners. Neither side could agree on what was best. In endeavouring to find an answer, we probed deeply into the underlying thinking of the two firms. Reasonably quickly (and to our surprise) it became apparent that the problem really lay in management style. The merger therefore had all the elements of a disaster. Rather than try to reconcile the two sides, we suggested that the merger should not proceed, and both parties eventually accepted this.

The critical point is that it is not enough to look superficially at the tangible aspects of two firms (eg the reward systems), and to assume that the cultures are the same because they appear to have similar systems. The thinking behind using a certain system might be driven by an entirely different set of cultural beliefs and assumptions. In the example above, we are sure that we could have developed proposals that would have been agreed to by both sides, and the merger could have proceeded. However, the fundamental issue would have emerged post-merger, and there would have been a major organisational upset whilst the different 'cultures' battled it out. As we noted

---

15 In practice, of course, the culture of a firm tends to be more complex than this but we use these merely as examples.

earlier, major cultural clashes post-merger cause enormous disruption to the day-to-day operations of the business as well as impede any integration efforts, thereby jeopardising the objectives of the merger.

One upside in all of this for law firms is that many of them do not have a particularly strong culture due to their historical development, or, strictly speaking, because there is a diverse range of beliefs held by people in the firm which results in the organisation not having a strong set of core beliefs. This is not to say that some firms do not have a culture, but that its main elements are broad, and leave scope for a number of differing beliefs to exist. For example, a firm with a weak culture might still demonstrate certain cultural characteristics such as formality, being systems-driven and being respectful of individuals. However, within that firm people will hold a range of other contrasting beliefs. Weak-cultured firms often find that they operate with systems and processes that have changed little or, if they have changed, have only changed enough to ensure that they are supported by the majority of the firm. Any major change will need to be debated, as it is likely to throw up challenges to the different cultural factions in the firm.

Firms with a weak culture find it hard to agree on a clear-cut strategy because, again, to do so will mean they will need to promote certain behaviours that will challenge the differing sets of belief in the firm. Whilst the debates appear to be about specific issues that are on the table, in reality they are about differing cultural beliefs that influence systems and processes and, ultimately, behaviour.

The reason why many law firms have diverse cultural beliefs that co-exist is down to the historical development of competition in the legal profession. Pre-1990s, before competition really bit into the profession, a very high percentage of firms outside the very top group in each major market tended to operate as a somewhat loose group of individuals. Partners had their own clients, and often provided a range of services personally to them. Specialisation was not well advanced, and the perceived need to work in teams was absent. Firms were really just groups of individual practices sharing costs and support functions.

As we noted earlier in **Examples 10.1** and **10.2**, the culture of a firm is derived from a series of experiences learned over time. Up until the late 1980s, firms generally had little 'learning' to do. There were few crises, and the main cultural belief was that firms worked best by allowing each partner to deal with their own clients.

The advent of competition has changed all of this. Firms' profits can fall as well as rise. Firms have failed, or have almost failed, and a number have been forced to merge. Management of these firms have recognised the need for 'institutionalising' clients so that they belong to the firm rather than to individual partners, and have implemented teams of specialists to work with and develop work from those clients. Management has also sought to impose organisational constraints on individualism, and has created a much more 'managed' environment. In many firms now, partners are subject to performance assessments, and face reductions in income or removal from equity (or the firm) if their performance is judged to be below that required.

These represent enormous changes, and were fought against very strenuously by many firms. Some firms adapted reasonably quickly, which indicates that they already had a latent culture that supported the changes. Others faced enormous battles within the partnership (not always conducted in a respectful fashion), and had to compromise on many of the required changes. As a consequence, they fell behind many of their original peer group of competitors.

The firms which have moved more quickly in restructuring their internal organisation to meet the market conditions have mostly had to ask some partners to resign or, in some extreme cases, expel them. These were partners who were strongly opposed to many of the changes, and who either refused to conform or continued to actively oppose them. However, the firms which failed to reorganise as quickly tended to try and compromise in order to avoid 'losing' partners, and, in many cases, faced resignations from many of their more forward-looking partners.

In summary, over the last 15 to 20 years, the legal profession has seen a major organisational shift as firms have had to come to terms with the needs of a competitive market place. This in turn has triggered a major cultural clash in several firms that, in many cases, was resolved by forcing some people out, and, in other cases, by newcomers with different cultural beliefs 'taking over'. In the middle are firms which continue to have cultures that are quite diverse, and are still in a state of cultural, organisational and behavioural compromise.

This brings us back to the question of whether a firm can 'change its culture'. From what we have noted above the answer would appear to be 'yes', but we need to be careful.

Organisational cultures can change, that is clear. However, the people in the organisation do not suddenly take on a whole different way of thinking about human nature, and the way the world works. If one person believes for 40 years that people are basically selfish, they will find a considerable amount of evidence to support that belief, and will attempt to refute anyone pushing for openness, sharing, teamwork, a supportive environment and all of the things that go with a belief that people, at heart, will be more motivated if they work in a harmonious, supportive environment. If that person sees the tide turning against them, and that more and more people are supporting the change, they might actively resist at first, then whinge and complain as the movement towards change gets stronger, and finally might look to move to a firm that operates on the same basis as they believe it should. On the other hand, that person might be pushed out.

Individuals, particularly adults, rarely change their deeply held cultural beliefs. They might modify them somewhat or find ways to adapt behaviour to market changes without letting go of their beliefs (see Firm B in **Example 10.2**). However, will they change their cultural beliefs? Almost never.

Change in tacit assumptions

We noted above that cultures are a set of deep-seated beliefs and assumptions about human nature and how the world works, and these are translated into the way an organisation works. Over time the assumptions disappear below the surface and become what Edgar Schein[16] calls 'tacit assumptions'. These are not articulated, and, like cultural beliefs, are the hidden drivers of much of the behaviour in an organisation. Many of these assumptions are learnt over time – the history of an organisation, how it grows and develops, how it averts crises and how it survives crises or other periods of tension all become part of the set of assumptions that lead to 'the way we do things here'. These tacit assumptions are a formulation of what has made the organisation successful and will continue to do so (a recipe for success).

Whilst it is very difficult, indeed impossible, to change the fundamental beliefs embedded in a firm (without a frontal lobotomy of most people or an influx of new staff), it is possible to get a form of cultural change by changing the tacit assumptions.

An organisation that goes through a 'life-threatening' experience is probably not going to drop its embedded belief that people perform best in a hierarchical structure. What if the assumption that follows from this belief (learnt from the past history of the firm) is that all power must be contained at the top of the organisation, and that the several layers of people below the top should have little influence over key decisions?

In this situation, it might be possible to change the way decision-making occurs in the firm without challenging the fundamental belief. Evidence from the external environment as to how other firms operate, evidence that recruitment consultants have had trouble getting good recruits because of the centralised control of the firm, evidence that the firm is losing market share, evidence that clients see the firm as out

---

16 *Organizational Culture and Leadership* (San Francisco: Jossey-Bass, 1995).

of touch with their needs, when all put together might lead people to see the need for some delegation of responsibility.

This form of cultural change can occur, but it is a change in the tacit assumptions of 'how the world works' rather than in the core belief. It is a change in how the belief is put into practice, not a change in the belief itself. It takes a long time to achieve this shift, especially when the firm has lived with the belief and assumption for many years. People will need help and training. A lot of support will be required to assist people who have not had to accept responsibility before. Reward systems must not be primitive. People must feel that they will not be blamed for making mistakes (particularly early in the process).

Organisational change

Organisational change tends to occur if there is already a latent culture existing in the organisation, and this supports the change. Change can also occur if, over time, there is an infiltration of people with a different set of beliefs which become dominant. In the second situation, the organisational culture changes because of the influx of new people, not because the original members changed their beliefs. Alternatively, even when new members join, it could be a change as to how the original belief is interpreted rather than in the belief itself.

When management announces that a newly merged firm will have a new culture and set of values, it is difficult to work out what they mean. It could be that they are aware that the culture of each firm is different, but not too different, so there will be a blurring and merging of the two and a hybrid (or new) culture will be the outcome. Alternatively, maybe management detects a latent culture in each firm that already exists, and which will now be strengthened and brought more to the surface. On the other hand, there may be hidden in the announcement a message that management intends to bring in to the firm a significant number of new people with different cultural beliefs and values. However, developing a new culture when the people have not changed is impossible, unless there is an underlying latent culture that has been previously suppressed.

Similarity in systems does not equal similarity in culture

Similarity in culture cannot necessarily be established because two firms have similar systems and procedures or even structures. We noted in **Chapter 9** that when specific processes of the two firms seeking merger differ (eg one firm uses a lockstep remuneration system and the other has a performance-based system), the firms will need to explore the thinking behind the use of the process in the other firm. We will come back to this below. Our point here is that even when specific processes are the same or similar, it still might be because of differing cultural beliefs.

Example: remuneration systems

Consider a real life example in which two firms, both with performance-based remuneration systems, discussed whether to merge. They both believed that they shared a similar culture because of the remuneration system similarity. However, a deeper exploration demonstrated a fundamental cultural difference.

One firm's culture was a form of organisational liberalism. Individuals were free to grow, develop and use their skills and resources to the full. Rewards were based on the results of this because each person was free to choose their level of output. It had a minimum standard performance level, but partners could choose to operate at this level for a long period of time. Partners also had a 'safety net' in the form of income guarantees in case they had a very bad year through no particular fault of their own.

The second firm supported performance-based remuneration but for very different reasons. The underlying reason was that the firm believed that people would take advantage of others if given a chance, and so the only way to ensure that everyone 'pulled their weight' was to reward them for what they had done.

One clue that the two firms might have had differing beliefs lay in the fact that the first firm included some team and group performance measures for each partner. In the second firm, all performance measures were based on the individual.

Example: organisational structures

The formal structures of two firms can look very much alike, including role descriptions, accountabilities and responsibilities. However, questions need to be asked about how they are operated in order to test if they are in fact similar. For example, in another merger discussion we were involved in, two firms exchanged information about their structures, which on paper appeared to be remarkably similar. Again, the initial assumption was that the 'cultures cannot be too far apart if we manage the same way'. However, by interviewing a representative number of people in the two firms, we found that, despite the similarity in structures, they were managed very differently.

In one firm, the managing partner was authoritarian, and saw the world in very hierarchical terms – everyone had their place, and those 'in charge' were at the top. As such, he ran the firm, and everyone else did what they were told. In the interviews, a few grumbled, but most people accepted this approach, and thought it was the best way to operate.[17] They got on with the work, and did not have to worry about management issues. The firm had operated this way for some generations, and most partners had been with the firm for most of their careers. Hence, although there was a formal structure in place, it operated very much from the top down, and decisions actually came from just one man.

The other firm was more democratic. The firm's structure operated in practice as it was described in the information exchanged in the merger discussions. Decisions were mainly made on a group basis, and people were treated as adults. Unlike the other firm, where there was a strong belief in the need for one individual to control everything, this firm believed that trust and dialogue between people would result in the best outcome.

The interesting point was that the authoritarian managing partner of the first firm had not demonstrated his attitude or beliefs in any of the merger discussions. Whilst it was clear that he was a strong individual with firm beliefs and opinions, his need to control everything and lack of trust in people did not surface until a series of internal interviews were carried out. Needless to say, merger discussions did not proceed.

Conclusion

The key point we are making here is that two firms might have similar systems, processes and structures, but they can be underpinned by very different cultures. Likewise, two firms might have quite different systems, processes and structures, but share similar cultural beliefs. As we discussed in **Chapter 9**, it is vital that these systems, processes and structures are tested to try and understand how they actually operate in practice in each firm.

However, in order to understand the culture of two firms to see whether there is a reasonable cultural compatibility, this will not be enough. Whilst an exploration of the systems, processes and structures will start to give some hypotheses about culture, it is unlikely to probe deeply enough to even start to flesh out the patterns of cultural beliefs and assumptions that lie behind them.

Need to work from within the firm

Herein lies the problem, and an explanation as to why the issue of culture is often neglected in law firm mergers. A real sense of an organisation's culture can only be achieved by working inside a firm, and exploring the underlying drivers of attitudes

---

17 Interestingly enough, people used military and naval metaphors to justify the management style.

and behaviour with other people. Given that a high proportion of merger discussions are kept confidential (in some cases, even from partners) until near the end, the idea of hiring a consultant to explore a firm's culture is not something that management would countenance. However, given the importance of culture, there is no reason why it should not happen once the discussions look like they are getting serious. There is no need to impart to the firm that the consultant is there as part of merger discussions. Instead, their presence could be described as what it is – carrying out an organisational review with a view to understanding more about the firm's culture.

Firms which lack strong culture

Any investigation into the culture of a law firm also needs to take into account a point made above, which is that many law firms do not have particularly strong cultures.

As we explained, pre-1990s, many firms tended to operate more as a 'loose group of individuals' than as an organisation, and had been through many experiences which would have led to the embedding of cultural beliefs and assumptions in the firm. Whilst increasing competition has led to most law firms now operating more as organisations, this has not yet led to the formation of a strong culture in many. What they tend to have is a series of sub-cultures – people with different beliefs and assumptions have joined over the years, and the individual working environment has allowed these sub-cultures to co-exist.

When people in such firms are asked what their culture is, many will describe the main feature of it as 'individualism'. This might be true. However, more likely, 'individualism' is the behavioural norm that results from the existence of several sub-cultures in the firm preventing any dominant culture emerging. If 'individualism' was a strong and deeply held belief in the firm, we would expect people from it to put that into practice in their everyday lives. However, when we have tested this expectation with partners who describe their firm's culture as 'individualistic', we have found that those partners belong quite comfortably to groups and societies, and participate in team activities outside of work.

The underlying culture of these firms is therefore not about being 'individualistic' at all. Instead, individualism is more a behavioural norm carried over from the pre-competitive environment. In probing deeper into the cultural issues of many such firms, a wide variety of differing beliefs and assumptions (sub-cultures) have emerged, and the tensions between these tend to preserve the status quo in behavioural terms. As these firms have come together as organisations, many of these sub-cultures have started to clash, mostly sub-consciously. Whilst some firms have forged a strong culture over time through one of the early sub-cultures becoming dominant, others have not, and they still consist of a series of sub-cultures. Some of the extreme sub-cultures have been forced out by a set of sub-cultures that had some commonality, but not enough to create one strong culture. However, the consequence is that many of the systems, processes and structures of the firm, and the firm's strategy, have been compromised. What we mean by this is that remuneration systems, for example, have been put together to try and satisfy the differing views in the firm but, as with many compromises, satisfy very few.

These firms have been through endless debates about strategy and organisational development, and find it very difficult to reach agreement about some of the core issues that they need to address in order to sustain a level of competitiveness that matches their ambitions. Whilst it is almost never articulated, a key factor behind these debates is cultural – people holding differing beliefs and assumptions about 'human nature and how the world works', and, as a result, being uncomfortable with many of the proposals that affect how people in the firm, and ultimately the firm itself, are to work. Each group tends to see the others as unreasonable, arch-conservatives, reformers for the sake of reform, unrealistic, not facing the facts, etc. The fact is that agreement about many of the core issues about how the firm will operate and be managed is highly unlikely to happen until one sub-culture becomes dominant. In fact (and it has happened) some of these firms would have been better off if they had split into two (or even three) firms, and then merged with another, more like-minded firm. Instead, most of them have allowed their competitiveness to be eroded by living with compromises on most or all of the important factors that should shape and guide a firm.

Hence, when trying to understand the culture of a firm, it could be that there are several 'cultures', all equally strong, or that there is one culture representing the slim majority with several 'renegade' cultures surrounding it.

How to develop a cultural understanding of a firm

How then do we get a better understanding of culture, remembering that the deeper cultural issues lie, the longer it might take to surface them?

In **Chapter 9**, we explained that an attempt to understand why specific systems, processes and structures are in place should be made. This is a start, but only a start. The next steps that should be taken are somewhat more complex, and can only really be carried out by an objective outsider (or, possibly, a very recently joined insider).

Do not rely on surveys

The first step is to not rely on surveys. Culture lies deep down in the organisation, and is taken for granted by those working in the firm. Trying to identify it through surveys tends to identify behavioural issues rather than cultural beliefs and assumptions. People will use terms such as 'client-focused', 'respect' and the other behavioural norms that we noted at the beginning of this chapter. What they will have trouble with is articulating the deep-seated and hidden cultural norms in the firm.

Equally ineffective is asking people what they want the culture to be. Again, people will list attributes of behaviour, which might all be good things to have (eg teamwork, openness, etc), but if the culture 'in action' is driving structures, systems and processes that work against this type of behaviour, then the survey is nothing but a wish list, and there are no fairy godmothers to make the wishes come true.

Culture review

Use representative groups

Developing a cultural understanding of a firm is best done using several, reasonably representative groups, and working through a series of issues with them, with the consultant acting as facilitator. One group might contain fairly recent recruits, another might include long-term members, and others might contain people in between. Age group and practice group representation is also important.

Work through the issues with each group

Step 1: Identify an issue to discuss

This might be a specific system or process (eg remuneration) or it might be a behavioural norm that people see as important to institute in the firm.

Step 2: Discuss that issue

Take, for example, the issue of a performance-based remuneration system and ask people what it is about that system that people find attractive and unattractive.

Step 3: Identify the values of the firm

Capture the points that people make during the discussion, and then ask them to identify what appears from the discussion to be the values of the firm. Do not challenge these, but be prepared for the likelihood of people articulating behavioural norms rather than deep-seated values.

Step 4: Explore how these values are represented (or not) elsewhere in the firm. [18]

If people see teamwork as a value because it is recognised when it comes to remunerating people, explore with the group where else teamwork is a visible feature of the firm. Look for both consistencies and inconsistencies.

Step 5: Set out consistencies and inconsistencies

Set out both the consistencies and inconsistencies, and work with the group to identify the issues behind both. What seems to be causing the inconsistencies (eg other systems that do not support teamwork), and what issues lie behind these? Take the same approach to the consistencies.

A critical issue here is to retain a balance in the discussion between the visible or 'espoused' values, and the areas in the firm where these appear to operate and not operate. Then work with the group to explore what lies behind each set. As Edgar Schein states:

> '… the way to deeper cultural levels is through identifying the inconsistencies and conflicts you observe between overt behaviour, policies, rules and practices… and the espoused values… Identify then what is driving the overt behaviour and other artefacts [the practice]. This is where the important elements of the culture are embedded.' [19]

In his book *Beyond the Quick Fix: Managing Five Tracks to Organisational Success*, [20] Ralph H Kilman sets out a not dissimilar process to that of Schein. Kilman refers to 'culture gaps', which is the gap between how people want the firm to operate, and the way it actually does. He suggests that these gaps can be explored to see what impediments exist to implementing the new norms of behaviour. By pushing further into these areas, beyond the systems and processes, the tacit assumptions that constitute the organisational culture start to emerge.

In our work with professional firms, we find it useful to explore both consistencies and inconsistencies. What this often does is reveal the sub-cultures at work, although, at times, it reveals that one or the other is driven by a dominant (or majority) culture. Schein prefers to start these group sessions by identifying the 'artefacts' or the visible practices. Examples of these are the level of formality used

---

18 Edgar Schein describes these as espoused values in his book, *Organizational Culture and Leadership* (San Francisco: Jossey-Bass, 1995).

19 Edgar Schein, *The Corporate Culture Survival Guide* (San Francisco: Jossey-Bass, 1999), p67.

20 (San Francisco: Jossey-Bass, 1984).

in the firm, public space layout in the office, working hours, decision-making, communication, etc. For partnerships, we also include reward systems, methods of accountability, how aberrant behaviour amongst partners is handled, information flows and the transparency in information, and the relationships within the partnership.

When working with lawyers, we find that it is more effective for the group to articulate its view of the espoused values before considering the artefacts, rather than vice versa. Articulating artefacts can lead to assumed values based on those, rather than people articulating the values from a more neutral standpoint.

Step 6: Explore the tacit assumptions behind the consistencies and inconsistencies
Schein provides a useful framework for capturing the tacit assumptions in an organisation's culture[21] which is set out in the box on page 250.[22]

These are just examples but illustrate the type of information that can emerge in the group sessions as people probe behind the espoused values and behaviour, and try to understand what is really driving the way they work.

Exploring the tacit assumptions that appear to lie behind why specific actions occur or do not occur can take some time. Schein[23] suggests a process that can be conducted in four hours, but our experience with law firms is that it takes the best part of a day with each group, and then there is often a need for a follow-up meeting.

Collate feedback
Having carried out this exercise across a number of groups, the next task is to pull all of the feedback together. A pattern of basic assumptions is likely to emerge across the groups. The stronger the culture of a firm, the greater the number of assumptions around which there will be an agreed view. In weaker cultures, where there are a number of sub-cultures operating, the list of agreed assumptions will be shorter, and there will be more divergence of views. Where some of the divergences impact on core activities, it is worth taking the time to explore these further with a mixed group, and to test whether they are inconsistent (ie sub-cultures exist) or whether there is a deeper cultural issue that provides a reconciling force to the sub-cultures.

---

21 *The Corporate Culture Survival Guide* (San Francisco: Jossey-Bass, 1999), pp72-75.

22 This framework has been adapted for professional firms.

23 Edgar Schein, *The Corporate Culture Survival Guide* (San Francisco: Jossey-Bass, 1999).

Assumptions in an organisation's culture

- Assumptions about how the work is done:
    - how the work gets done, what energises people, how problems are addressed, individual or team approaches, hands-on or hands-off, systematic or ad hoc, on time or always late
- Assumptions about people and their motivation:
    - whether people are self-motivated or not, how they view success, what motivates/demotivates people, the role of ego, what the firm expects in work dedication and work-life balance, the extent to which groups self-manage, the role of intervention when there are problems
- Assumptions about the management process:
    - what is the style, what is given attention, what role do 'numbers' have, is it cost-driven or revenue-driven, where are decisions made and by whom, where is it on a micro/macro management scale, what role does responsibility and accountability have, the degree of sensitivity/empathy in management, the role of hierarchy, systems and processes linked (or not) to management's espoused policies, the overall underlying approach of management (eg paternalistic, domineering, laid-back, etc)
- Assumptions about the organisational climate:
    - the key characteristics of the internal environment – friendly, blameful, worried, polite, formal, individualistic, aggressive on performance, non-transparent, superficially open but actually not, how people progress, why people stay/go
- Assumptions about the partnership:
    - the degree to which partners act as owners, the extent of delegation, the real focus – clients or work, relationships between partners, clarity of role and expectations, extent of mentoring, coaching, etc, the degree of project management

Timeframe

In our experience, this is not a quick-fix process, although, with the appropriate dedication of resources, a significant understanding of some key cultural concepts in a mid-sized firm can be uncovered over a six to eight week period. This process can be carried out on both firms at the same time as the more tangible aspects of the merger are being discussed by the negotiation teams. However, it is not as long a process as people sometimes imagine. Of course, it is unlikely that every detail of the culture of the firm and its history will be teased out within the timeframe, but it is possible to develop a set of working hypotheses about the major cultural elements of the firm, and how they manifest themselves in practice.

If there is a need or desire to evolve a 'new' culture for the merged firm, one that shifts the impact of the cultural elements of the two merging firms relative to their cultures, there will be much more to do after this exercise has been carried out, but that can take place post-merger.

Cultural issues in cross-border mergers

Cultural differences are likely to rear their ugly head in cross-border mergers, and probably even more so than where a merger occurs within one jurisdiction. While there are endless jokes about differences in national cultures, there is some truth behind them. Nation states have different histories and have encountered different problems over many years. While it is wrong to generalise that every citizen from one country will have the same beliefs as all other citizens from that country, cultural differences between countries do exist, and can create issues in merger discussions.

This is illustrated by many of the merger discussions between USA and UK law firms. Traditionally, UK firms tended towards lockstep partner remuneration systems and US firms tended towards performance-based systems. The cultural explanation has always been that the US, being a relatively new nation state, values the individual pioneering approach to building a business more than a collective approach. People say that the UK, being a state with a much longer history of trade and commerce, values a collective effort over that of individual performance. Whether these explanations are correct is beside the point. The real issue is that when a US and UK firm start discussing merger, a difference in remuneration systems is often classified immediately as a national cultural issue that will be hard to overcome. In fact, many successful US firms are on either lockstep or part lockstep/part performance-based systems, and more and more UK firms are building a performance element into their remuneration system. Is the issue a cultural one, or does it simply reflect two legal markets at different stages of development? Once the markets start to converge, so firms will change systems and processes to suit the market, and these also converge.

A similar point used to be made about German law firms, in that they operated with much lower gearing (ie ratio of equity partners to other fee-earners) than most UK and US firms. This was often attributed to a particular aspect of German culture – that partners were very technically focused and saw their role as carrying out legal work, not managing others.

This argument overlooked two things. The first was that partners in UK and US firms were not that dissimilar up until the late 1980s, when competition between law firms increased significantly in the UK and US. Partners often had to delegate work to junior people (and, therefore, manage them) or face being uncompetitive on price. Price competition came much later to Germany, and, even today, it is still somewhat behind the UK and US.

The second point that the 'German culture' argument missed was that, due to education system requirements, German lawyers do not join law firms until around five years after their peer group in the US and UK. German firms do not have a large pool of 23 to 28 year old associates. People enter firms much later in age, and, therefore, do not want to wait a long time before becoming a partner. Someone entering a UK firm as a trainee at, say, 23 years old, could be a partner in around ten years (at 33 or 34 years old). A German lawyer, entering at, say, 28 years old, does not want to wait until they are 40 years old before getting on the bottom rung of the partnership ladder. The consequence is that German firms generally have a higher percentage of partners amongst their fee-earners than firms in many other jurisdictions.

Our key point here is one we have already made above. One should not assume that differences in the way two firms work is down to culture, even national cultures, until some examination of the issue has been undertaken. Of course, it is difficult to get German firms to increase their gearing, but is this due to cultural resistance or a systems issue that cannot be changed simply by stating the need to change? (Many German lawyers we know recognise the value in having better gearing, but are at a loss as to how to change the system that is causing low gearing.)

The other issue about cross-border merger discussions is that the 'national culture' argument can be used simply to avoid change that people find unpleasant. In a few cross-border mergers in which we have been involved, both parties were 'guilty' from time to time of using the 'national culture' objection as a negotiating tool: 'We couldn't possibly change this. Everyone does it like this.' However, this is not true. As a cross-border adviser, we were able to point out the fallacy, and then work with both sides to find a solution.

Cross-border mergers will raise issues that are a product of differences in national cultures. For example, US firms generally are more centrally managed than European firms, and this is echoed in the US business world. The US culture does focus on individuals more than most European cultures. Nevertheless, the 'national culture' argument should not be accepted at face value – it is often not true, and, in some situations, a solution acceptable to both parties can be found.

Culture post-merger

As we have argued a number of times in this chapter, it is important that the management of the two firms, and that of the subsequent merged firm, decides on how it wishes to handle issues of culture post-merger. What management often articulates as a 'new culture' or 'new set of values' are simply some behavioural norms that it believes are important for the new firm to have. However, these might be able to be achieved without any changing of the merging firms' culture. All that might be required is some changes to the organisational systems and processes, and greater attention being given to the behavioural issues by management. (It might not be an easy change, but just because it is difficult does not necessarily mean it is a change in culture.)

Example 10.3

One merger with which we were involved demonstrates this clearly. Both sets of management recognised a need for much greater teamwork in the merged firm than either firm had before. They carried out the above culture review, and there was no evidence that 'teamwork' was counter-cultural to either antecedent firm. In fact, many people in both firms were active members of teams outside of work. The two firms also seemed reasonably compatible in a couple of key cultural elements. One was a strong belief in the need for people to strive to achieve, and that the world (ie the market) offered almost unlimited opportunities for growth and development. There was also a broad belief in both firms that progress was more likely to happen if the firm encouraged participation in decisions rather than if it had an authoritarian/centralist approach or individual 'anarchy'.

Both firms had, however, operated largely through individuals in the work processes – ie individuals 'controlled' client relationships, and partners tended to work alone or with small teams of their own selection. The organisations themselves were, however, very participatory, and individuals had personal plans with high-achieving goals. Hence, in neither firm was there a bias or a belief against teamwork.

The key lesson for the management of the 'new' firm was not to rush out and announce a new culture based on a value of 'teamwork'. If they had, people within the firm would probably have questioned management's sanity or grasp on reality. As the view of most people was that they worked as a team when it was best for the business (ie managing), and as individuals when that was best (ie when doing the work), a focus on teamwork as a new culture would have been dismissed as irrelevant.

Management avoided talking about culture change and of 'new values'. Instead, it talked about the need to open up clients to a wider group in the firm than before (ie a behaviour change). It used client feedback to demonstrate very convincingly that both firms were losing revenue as a result of the individual nature of the work processes and client relationship. It also analysed the top client base of both firms pre-merger, and showed to partners that a high proportion of the top clients required services from mainly one practice area only, with 'bits and pieces' being required elsewhere. It asked consultants who knew the market place to provide data about what other firms were doing in the area of client development, in particular those firms which would be the peer group competitors of the merged firm (a somewhat different group to that of either pre-merger firm).

Management also initiated a small pilot study with four major clients, and developed a client development process that, whilst retaining the original client partner for each, provided a means by which the potential development of those clients could be identified. Over an 18-month period, more clients were brought into the process, and the use of teamwork around client development increased. There was, of course, a need for training, management support, new processes and systems, and other organisational changes to underpin the process. However, the key issue was that once people realised that acting as individuals was no longer in the best interests of the firm, there was no opposition *per se* in moving towards greater teamwork. People had to learn to behave differently, and to remember to involve others. They also needed new skills, and had to understand how the process worked. The 'behavioural change' had to be managed well, and required considerable organisational change. However, there was no cultural change involved.

What this demonstrates clearly is that even when there is no actual cultural bias against teamwork embedded in the core beliefs of a firm, people can build up tacit assumptions over time as to where teamwork fits into the firm, and where individualism produces the best results. This is the 'learnt' aspect of culture. To achieve the behavioural change necessary, people had to 'unlearn' and then 're-learn' about the new behaviour.

The terms 'unfreezing' and 'freezing' instead of 'unlearning' and 're-learning' are often used in culture change programmes, but they carry the same implications. Organisations (and indeed any system involving people) try to maintain the status quo or equilibrium. However, for a major change to occur there has to be some 'force' that substantially rocks the status quo, and leads to people questioning it. This is a part of the 'unfreezing' or 'unlearning' process.

This is the approach management adopted in this example. It built a range of evidence to create a level of discomfort about the wisdom of continuing to work the way it always had. It then gradually developed an alternative behaviour, provided support and help, and, over time, established a new behaviour. This is the subsequent 're-freezing' or 're-learning' stage. The process takes time, even when people do not have a deep-seated objection to change.

Example 10.4

Another firm with which we were involved post-merger highlighted the problem of announcing a 'new culture' without being aware of what it meant. The two antecedent firms went through discussions about merger without carrying out a culture review, and agreed to merge. The new management announced a new set of values which included teamwork, sharing and participation.

Two years later, there had been no improvement in any of these areas. People guarded their clients very strongly, there were arguments about who got the 'credit' for billings to specific clients, there was a lack of partner participation in departmental management, with the department head being seen as the person who 'did it all', marketing was still mainly done on an individual basis, associate performance reviews were carried out very late or not at all, and partner meetings tended to consist of a lot of carping and whinging as to why management 'hadn't done X, Y or Z'. Worst of all, the two firms had hardly integrated, and operated almost as separate units.

Eventually, management agreed to carry out an organisational and cultural review. Unsurprisingly, it emerged that both firms had been very individualistic pre-merger. They both accepted a hierarchical view of the world (which coincides with centralised control), and saw it as a somewhat hostile and conflict-driven place where power resided with those individuals who had the strength.

Translated into an organisational environment, it meant that those outside the central group would not accept responsibility for anything that was not under their immediate control (their 'control' was assumed to be over legal work only), and believed that strength (ie power) came from having high personal billings, and a clutch of their 'own' quality clients (even though others might carry out some of the work for them).

In addition, both antecedent firms had developed systems and processes over the years that supported these cultural beliefs and assumptions. The structure, systems and processes therefore mirrored what would be expected from an environment where people believed in a hierarchical organisation and felt the need to 'accumulate assets' (ie billings and clients) in order to give them power, and to protect them from aggressive moves by others seeking to build up their power base. In other words, it was an environment where trust between partners was lacking. There were numerous 'war stories' of the past history of both antecedent firms that supported the behaviour. For example, people in both firms recounted stories about partners who had 'foolishly' passed client relationships over to others only to have their remuneration reduced because of lower billings, and who then came under such pressure from management that they resigned.

This led to the futility of management's efforts to achieve a change in behaviour simply by exhortation. The approach to addressing this problem had to be long-term. The starting point was to adapt the systems and processes to the desired environment. A re-interpretation of performance was discussed, and whilst a sudden move away from focusing on individual performance was resisted, management was able to initially broaden it out to include collaborative and co-operative activities. Over a longer period of time, some group activities were also included.

We worked with several small groups, discussed the feedback from clients that indicated how they would instruct the firm more if they knew more people, and worked through ways in which greater collaboration and co-operation could be achieved without overthrowing the core beliefs.

It was slow work, but progress was made. Not everyone in the firm believed in the need for a controlling hierarchy, nor for the need for power in the way that it had previously been interpreted. However, they had gone along with this approach, and could live with it because the new firm (and the antecedent firms) provided other benefits (eg it was highly profitable).

Management also had to change. Despite its recognition of the need for teamwork, it was also a 'lone ranger' in its own way. Management meetings were constantly cancelled because individuals were called away on client matters, and they were mainly used as forums for people to air opinions than for work by the management group. Management praised individuals rather than teams, and it berated people who 'under-performed' on personal billings, even though some of these people had been making a significant contribution to the firm in other ways. Hence, management also needed to demonstrate teamwork behaviour, and not just tell others how important it was. This was tough for it as well, as it too valued the underlying cultural beliefs and assumptions.

Gradually some of the changes in behaviour began to stick. Small groups started to be more collaborative, and it became possible to amend the systems and processes even further. For example, management stopped circulating a weekly list of every person's chargeable hours for the previous week and year-to-date to all partners, something both firms had done for years pre-merger. Only 20% of the partners complained – the others barely noticed it.

The big change came about two years into this process. As the changes had gradually moved across the firm, a small number of partners became more and more disruptive in their behaviour, and were openly critical of the changes. It came to a head in a partnership meeting when two partners were extremely aggressive towards management, and called for a vote of no confidence. This was only supported by a handful of votes. Within the week, management asked three of the disruptive partners to resign or face a partnership vote to force them out. A real shudder went through the firm as these were high-billing partners. They resigned, and two other partners left shortly after. The firm's revenue fell a little in that year but profits improved once the profit shares of the retiring partners were discontinued. What became apparent was that the culture in the firm had been taken to an extreme. Those partners had generated revenue but not necessarily profits, and were, in effect, taking out more than they were putting in.

This gave a further boost to change, and the firm managed to achieve a significant shift in behaviour over a five-year period. However, it is important to realise that individualism still remained within the firm, and at a higher level than at many of its peer group firms. It still held the core beliefs, as did many of the people in the firm, but it was able to adapt its assumptions about how those beliefs could be put into practice. The firm still uses a performance-based remuneration system which contains a number of individual performance measures. However, it also contains a number of measures of collaborative and co-operative behaviour. Information is now distributed on a group basis, and the detail of each group member's performance is only seen by partners from that group. Whilst clients have still not been fully 'opened up' to the rest of the firm, and many of the client relationship partners are the same as before merger, the firm's top 50 clients now retain services across several practice areas.

The firm has also developed a sophisticated approach to recruitment and to partner promotions. Whilst it still looks to recruit people who have a strong individual achievement level, it also seeks people who are willing to work with others when necessary. It will not be a 'teamwork' firm as such for another generation (if ever) but there is a significantly greater level of collaboration, co-operation, participation and sharing, at least at the smaller-group level. This firm did not go though a cultural change in terms of overthrowing beliefs, but there was a cultural shift in that it adapted the assumptions that supported a reduction in individualism and an increase in forms of teamwork.

Conclusion

Achieving a significant behavioural change in any organisation (law firm or otherwise) when there are no cultural barriers is difficult. Achieving it when there are cultural impediments means that it will be a long, drawn-out process. Even then, it will be more about cultural adaptation, adapting the tacit assumptions that flow from the cultural beliefs, rather than a change in the beliefs themselves. Achieving a significant cultural shift early on in the life of a newly merged firm is a huge task given all of the other things that need doing. Management might 'liberate' a latent culture over a relatively short period of time, but a change in culture during the same period is highly unlikely.

Therefore, we stress the importance for management of a merged firm to be clear about what it is trying to achieve when it announces the requirement for a change of culture or for a new set of values. In many cases, what management is actually seeking is a change in behavioural norms.

If there is a behavioural norm that management wants to encourage, but which appears to be held back by culture, there is little point in talking of the need for culture change. It is far more effective to start by explaining what the required new behaviour is, and how it can be implemented in practice, than to talk about concepts that are not grounded in reality. Take, for example, the value of 'client focus'. If what management means by this is that they want partners to increase the time they spend with clients, it should simply say that. If it also wants partners to seek out more information about client service needs and satisfaction levels, that should be articulated as well. Management needs to follow through on this, and discuss how individual partners can make the change. It also needs to consider whether there are structural, systems or processes issues that inhibit the change.

Far too often management talks of 'cultural concepts' but never spells out what this means in terms of behaviour. By describing them in terms of cultural concepts, people do not recognise the need for the hard, detailed work of examining structures, systems and processes, and changing them in order to support the required behaviour. Yet without these changes, behavioural change will not happen. It is easier to launch concepts such as client focus under the 'culture' banner, and then beat up partners by exhortation when the change fails to materialise, blaming it on their lack of 'buy-in' to the culture change, when in fact the failure is a lack of structural and process change needed to support the behaviour change.

Dressing behavioural change up as cultural change is also self-defeating. It can create a sense of scepticism or even cynicism in the firm, rather than creating an environment that is open to changing specific behaviours. When management talks of creating 'new' values for a merged firm which include integrity and client focus, it could be implying that the antecedent firms lacked those values previously. Partners from both firms will doubt this without considerable evidence that the firms did in fact lack these in the past.

It is nonsense to speak of there being a cultural 'fit', or the need for a new culture and related values, in the absence of a cultural audit, or a similar in-depth review. Everyone acknowledges the importance of culture in making a merger effective, but to then do little about understanding what the two cultures of the antecedent firms were seems to be a reflection of poor management.

If management does understand the cultures of the two merging firms, it is better to start with the strong cultural aspects of the new firm than to trumpet the need for cultural change. By focusing on positive aspects of the merged firm's culture, and linking that to the consequent behavioural outcomes, management establishes something concrete in the minds of people in the firm.

Cultural beliefs almost never change, at least not in a short period of time. If two firms that harbour similar cultural beliefs come together, these beliefs are likely to be reinforced rather than be opened up to change.

The starting point has to be adapting the tacit assumptions that flow from the cultural belief. This can occur, as we noted above, by working with groups, producing evidence of the need for a specific type of behaviour, and working through the constraints until one can probe into the 'deeper recesses' of the issue.

An example we dealt with above was that if the world is seen as a hostile, challenging place where people are seeking to build up their power and wealth at the expense of others, then other people will do the same either defensively or aggressively. Hence, partners who refuse to 'open clients up' to others, and keep them as their own 'personal' property, are not about to change their belief because management advocates it. Rather, management needs to find a way to reassure those partners that, despite their belief, there is no danger in bringing others into the client relationship. Hence, working with them to adapt their tacit assumption of 'if I let anyone near my client they will steal them', and finding a way to allow others to work with the client, is the correct process, not tub-thumping about culture and values.

The final point for this chapter is that this all points to the fact that firms need to avoid communicating the need for culture change and new values, even when this is in fact what is required. If a culture change really is needed, firms need to either change many of the people in the firm or settle in for the long haul and a bumpy ride. It is far more effective to address the behaviour change that is required in the merged firm as this is, indeed, what it is all about much of the time. As we noted previously, behaviour can change without a change in culture. There will be a much greater response to practical discussions about behaviour than to conceptual communications about culture and values.

We noted at the start of this chapter that there tends to be one of three outcomes when it comes to establishing the culture of a merged firm:

(i)   the culture of one firm (and not necessarily that of the larger firm) takes over and becomes dominant;

(ii)   the different cultures of the antecedent firms co-exist, usually uneasily, which can produce different behaviours and responses by the same organisation; and

(iii) a true merging of the cultures occurs where the best of both cultures is managed, and the weaker parts are driven out.

One danger of the first and second outcomes is that there will be a damaging culture clash. It will be resolved in the first outcome by one firm 'winning the war', and, in the second outcome, by an 'uneasy truce'. In the third outcome, good management will reduce the likelihood of a culture clash, although there will be differences from time to time, especially in the early days of the merged firm.

Knowing which outcome is the best one for a merged firm will result from a deep and insightful understanding of the culture and supporting values of both antecedent firms. As we have argued above, this is impossible without some type of cultural audit, review or investigation prior to merger. The failure to undertake such a process in a formal manner remains one of the greatest weaknesses in law firm mergers today.

Chapter 11: 'It's not over until the fat lady sings'

The 'fat lady' will not sing in a law firm merger until both partnerships have voted for the proposal. Even then, that is only in respect of the agreement to merge – the first part of the process. The 'new' firm then needs to go through the integration process and make it work. Indeed, the 'fat lady' might need to be ready to sing a few times over the life of the merger process, from initial discussions to the achievement of objectives.

A constant theme in this book is that there is no single correct way to conduct merger negotiations, but, in terms of achieving a deal, there are some approaches which are less risky than others.

In **Chapter 4**, we discussed the approach to take with regard to the issue of communication. We noted that there might be situations where the negotiations need to be kept confidential, and only presented to partners as a complete proposal a short time prior to voting (the approach taken by Denton Wilde Sapte). We explained that this is a high-risk strategy, as partners might reject the proposal, either because they resent being 'bounced' into a decision, or because they do not have enough time to think the proposal through, and so err on the side of caution and reject it.

Our view is that if partners are brought into the negotiations as early as possible, the risk of the proposal being rejected is reduced. The ideal time to involve the partnership is when the negotiating team has laid out the business case (and views it as strong), at least in principle, and can see that there are solutions to any deal-breaking issues. Bringing the partnership on board at that point, and keeping them informed, has significant advantages. Keeping partners informed does not mean drip-feeding them with the specific details of the merger proposal one by one as they are discussed. It means informing them about the issues that the negotiating teams are dealing with, perhaps testing the waters with them about the potential options with regard to some of those issues, and seeking their input.

Take, for example, the situation where two firms are discussing a possible merger, and both operate with a single-tier management structure, but the negotiating team is thinking of recommending a dual-tier structure for the 'new' firm. It is likely to be helpful to the process if the negotiating team informs partners of the thinking behind recommending such a structure, and the pros and cons of both structures, and invites comment from the partners. What might result in a tough and emotional discussion if presented to partners as a concrete recommendation a few days ahead of voting can become a more rational debate if it is held over a longer period and is presented more as an option rather than an issue that has been decided.

This approach also allows management to engage in discussion with partners who have serious concerns about particular issues well ahead of the vote. Our experience is that many concerns that are expressed initially in a very negative manner can be turned around to be expressed more positively once people understand the background, why there is a need for change, and how the change will operate. The dual-tier structure issue is a common concern. When first confronted with the proposal to move from a single-tier to a dual-tier structure, many partners express negative views. Once the reasons for the choice are explained, and there is a discussion as to how the dual-tier structure will work, there is often a swing of opinion in favour of it. (Some might remain sceptical about it working, but they will not oppose the merger because of it.)

In this chapter, we explore three issues:

1. managing the concerns expressed by partners through the negotiation process;

2. managing the voting process; and

3. the 'prospectus' or other material to be presented to partners prior to a vote.

Partners' concerns during negotiations

We touched upon one of these concerns in **Chapter 1**, where we noted that partners sometimes oppose a merger on the basis of the resultant size of the merged firm, even though they may be ignoring the fact that they might have previously voted for a growth strategy which would have required the firm's size to increase significantly anyway. As we discussed, they are, in fact, therefore disagreeing with the original strategy. We also noted in **Chapter 1** the danger of partners looking first at the impact of merger on them personally, rather than on what effect it will have on the firm.

One disadvantage of opening up communication with partners earlier rather than later is that management will then need to be prepared to spend time discussing issues and ensuring that partners understand them, and the reasoning behind the actions of the negotiating teams. The reverse side of this is the advantage of having a well-informed partnership at the time of the vote.

Members of the negotiating team at Theodore Goddard provided regular 'surgery' sessions for partners, enabling them to come at designated times and discuss any issue related to the merger negotiations with Addleshaw Booth & Co. Paddy Grafton Green (previously senior partner of Theodore Goddard) remarked that:

> 'The surgeries were a very effective way of addressing partner concerns but also of alerting us to issues that were "floating" around in the office. We were able to head off a number of issues that could have been troublesome later on, but which disappeared once we explained what they were about.'

Many concerns raised by partners during negotiations are easier to deal with if there has already been a good and reasoned debate about the firm's strategy and its implications. In some cases, partners can be reminded of that, particularly the implications, and this then answers their questions. (It is surprising, perhaps, how people forget the context in which a merger is being pursued and put the strategy and the merger discussions into separate 'compartments'.)

This assumes that the implications of a particular strategy were explained and discussed at the same time as the strategy itself. If this did not occur, especially if the growth implications of the strategy were not explained, management should have that debate before embarking on the merger search. We have been involved in quite a number of situations where management believes partners are aware of the implications of a strategy when, in fact, that was not the case. Subsequent discussions revealed that the implications were never really spelt out or debated. Management, partly because of its deep involvement in the strategy, thought they were obvious and wrongly assumed that everyone else was aware of them as well.

This illustrates a key principle which should underpin communication with partners during the merger negotiation process. Those involved in the negotiations will have spent more time than anyone else in considering the issues, thinking about the options and matching the options to the merger business case in order to get the 'best fit'. Partners, however, will receive the result of all of this discussion in a much more truncated communication process.

It is vital that management remains patient when partners raise concerns and react negatively to certain aspects of the negotiating process. Lawyers are lawyers, and are trained to question in order to test the evidence. Often, when partners raise concerns about what is emerging in the negotiating process, they do so in a critical fashion, with their 'lawyer hat' on. Management, often under pressure due to the timeframes involved in the negotiation process and the need to deal with other issues on the agenda, as well as the fact that it has already explored the issue in some depth, responds in a way that can be interpreted as 'you are such a nuisance raising this' or by treating the concern with derision. All that does is put a good lawyer on the offensive, resulting in the partner then pursuing the issue with vigour.

Management needs to be able to stand back and 'walk' people with concerns through the firm's strategy and its implications, and explain why the negotiating teams see specific options as viable in the context of the merged firm and the business case and what it means for the particular firm and its partners. Put another way, it is critical that management adopts a very facilitative role during the communication and discussion process. This is another area where an appropriate strategic adviser can assist. An objective outsider is often better able to facilitate such discussions than someone who is, at the negotiation stage, committed to the deal and under pressure in terms of the time available to deal with the concerns that are raised.

The critical issue is that if management is to open up communication with the partnership during the negotiating process, it must be prepared to devote a significant amount of time to it. While there are significant advantages in doing so (eg by opening up communication early rather than late it will help to secure the vote), there is also a serious downside if these discussions are not handled well.

There are three general categories of concerns that are expressed once partners are aware that a merger is being seriously considered by management:

1.   the 'specific issue' group;

2.   the 'right firm' group; and

3.   the 'do we have to' group.

We noted earlier that some partners approach the issue from a personal viewpoint, rather than one that looks at the benefit to the whole firm. These people can be found in any of the three categories.

The 'specific issue' group
People who raise concerns about specific issues are usually the easiest to deal with. By and large, they have accepted the deal in principle but have concerns about individual

aspects emerging during the negotiations. In most (but not all) cases, these are not concerns that will lead to a negative vote but are, nonetheless, important.

For example, a possibility of a change to the structure of the business units (departments) can create concerns. If one practice group has operated in the past as a stand-alone business unit, but consideration is then being given to grouping it with another practice group (or groups) to form a department in the 'new' firm, this often results in questions to management.

As noted above, management needs to 'walk' partners through the thinking, explain why this is an option, and what that option is intended to achieve. If possible, management should add that any such proposals, even if adopted, are not 'set in stone', and will be reviewed for effectiveness after a given period. (Such a review of many of the structural and systems changes in the merged firm should occur in any case after a year or so.)

The 'right firm' group

This group can be more difficult to deal with. There will be some who will ask 'is this the right firm?' when they are initially told of the firm with which the discussions are being held, but who will be satisfied with the choice once the reasons for it are explained in the context of the business case.

There will, however, be others whose concerns are more emotive and subjective, and are not so easily convinced. We touched on some of these issues in **Chapter 3** and so do not intend to repeat them here. The key point is that many of the issues raised are based on rumour or one-off events that happened in the past (eg 'I was once on the other side of that firm in a deal and they were awful'). There is no point in simply ignoring or denying the concern – an attempt must be made to provide evidence to counter it. It may be that other partners have had good experiences with that firm or that press reports or directories (eg the *Legal 500*) provide a counter view. Management might also want to ensure that any partner expressing such a view is given the opportunity to meet some people from the other firm, and to 'organise' such a meeting so that the partner is given a good impression of it.

There is a third type of concern which falls under the 'right firm' category, coming from those partners who simply express their belief that the firm chosen is the wrong firm but do not produce any reason for their view. These are the hardest partners with which to deal. No matter what is put forward to convince them otherwise, they refuse to change their minds. Some people in this group are actually members of the third category (the 'do we have to' group) in the sense that they cling to a view that, if they are to merge, it will be with a firm so far out of their firm's reach that it would be impossible – what they are really saying is that they will not merge. Others from this group are likely to vote against the merger, and management therefore needs to be sure that they are a small minority, and to seek to counter any negative influence they might have on others.

The 'do we have to' group

The third category is also difficult to deal with if there have already been extensive discussions with partners about the firm's strategy and implications of a possible merger. (Where such discussions have not already occurred, it will be reasonably easy to convince some members of this group of the benefits of the merger, assuming the business case for it is strong.) The partners in this category divide into two groups. One group is, in fact, opposed to merger on almost any ground, and will not be convinced. The second group consists of partners who are nervous about the impact of a merger, fear being moved out of their 'comfort zone', and would rather the whole issue went away. In general, these people will come around once they are explained the strategic issues facing the firm (again), why the merger seems appropriate, and its implications for the partners.

It is very useful in these circumstances to indicate the implications for partners of developing the firm's strategy without a merger, and to then compare it to the merger situation. In most cases, the implications are no worse under the merger and might even be better than if the firm 'stands alone'. The key point to explain to these partners is that it is the implementation of the agreed strategy that is going to take the partners out of their 'comfort zone' and not the merger per se. Whatever the strategy implementation process, life will not continue as before. Provided management is prepared to spend time discussing the issues with these partners, most eventually see the benefits of the merger and will come around.

Managing the voting process

Out of the communication process could emerge a minority which is opposed to the merger and remains sufficiently unconvinced to vote against it. Management therefore needs to seek out partners who are respected opinion-formers and ensure they are on-side early in the process. These people can then spend time with the 'waverers' and the 'over my dead body' partners, and try to establish a dialogue. Having someone outside management talk with the opponents of the deal can carry some weight, especially with the 'waverers'.

We have been involved in many mergers where this process of communication and discussion results in 100% of the partners supporting the transaction, even though many did not from the start. There might have been different degrees of enthusiasm amongst those partners, but the critical point was that there were no opponents. This is quite an important point for psychological reasons. Even having 10% of the partnership opposed to a transaction that requires a 75% majority can leave some partners feeling worried that they are, in effect, voting to force some people out (which, of course, they are not, but they feel that might be the consequence). It can also mean that a partnership will be going into a merger knowing that there are some people who are opposed to it but who might remain at the firm and not make the effort required for the merger to succeed.

Management needs to keep its ear to the ground and assess the likely opposition that is emerging. There might be a point at which it is clear that the opposition is a small minority and will not affect the vote. Management could find it worthwhile at that point to discuss the issue with the minority, and to see whether they are prepared to 'give way' and vote with the majority or abstain.

A more difficult situation arises where a 75% majority vote is required to merge, and the opposition appears to represent around 30%. Should 30% be able to prevent the other 70% doing what they want to do, or is a 30% opposition too high to take into a merged firm, even if the issue could be forced through? There are some partners in firms who believe strongly that management should not 'play politics' and should simply state the arguments and stand back. However, this fails to address the problem that, in situations where the opposition is a significant minority, in our experience, politics always comes into play. For management (the driver of the merger) to stand back and let others engage in 'politics' seems somewhat self-defeating.

There is no one solution to this problem. Clearly, if management believes strongly in the merger, it should be prepared to lobby those in the opposition group who are most likely to change their mind. It might even appeal to some of the opposition to vote in favour of the merger solely on the grounds that it would realise the intentions of a significant majority. We are even aware of several situations where the vote took place and was lost by a couple of percent (when a 75% majority was required). Management called the partnership together, announced the result, and asked whether, in light of the circumstances, another vote should be taken. It was agreed, (this time with a required majority of 50%) and the vote for the merger passed the 75% requirement.

The issue here is the belief that management has about the merger. It should not be putting it to the vote if it does not see significant benefits of the merger for the firm.

Having spent a large amount of time and (probably) money, it would seem strange that management should not do all it can to secure a vote in favour of the merger. In our view, it is rare to find a situation where this is not the case. We would go even further to say that once management believes that the merger is right for the firm, it should do all it can to secure a vote in favour – to not do so raises questions about management's own beliefs about the benefits.

In terms of the voting process itself, the partnership agreement of many firms will set this out. If it does not, our preference for a mid- to larger-sized firm is for a secret ballot to be adopted, with each partner being given one vote. It is also desirable to have a scrutineer present (possibly from the firm's auditors). The vote should be held on the same day and at the same time for each firm, and partners should be given sufficient time to vote (eg between 9am and 6pm). In the event that there are time differences between jurisdictions, these should be taken into account.

Our preference is to allow 24 hours from closure of voting to announcement of the result, which gives management in both firms time to assess the situation and to compare the results.

The prospectus

One of the questions most often asked of us by management in a merger transaction is what information should be given to partners ahead of the vote and, in particular, the extent to which the papers should go into detail. There is also the process by which the information is distributed.

No matter what type of communication has already taken place in the run-up to the vote, we always recommend that a detailed prospectus covering all issues relevant to partners about the transaction be prepared. An executive summary of the prospectus should also be drafted, containing a synopsis of the business case, some key data about the 'new' firm and comments about its strategic positioning, and highlighting any substantive change that will happen to either firm as a result of the merger negotiations.

The prospectus and executive summary should be the same for both firms (other than where there is a need for one firm to focus more on an issue than the other). For example, if the proposal is for the merged firm to have a dual-tier structure, and one firm already has such a structure in place but the other has a single-tier structure, there will need to be more in-depth comment on this issue in the prospectus to the latter firm's partners than to the former's.

We also recommend that an oral presentation is given first, which should be mainly based on the executive summary, together with an opportunity for questions and discussions. The prospectus can then be handed out at the end of the presentation. Where a firm has partners in more than one location, it would be ideal if they could all be brought to the one place for the presentation. If this is not logistically possible, management should seek to deliver the presentation at each location within the shortest space of time possible (ideally within 24 hours). Where this is not possible, it would be best if a representative from the management team went to each of the locations and the presentation be made by videoconference.

The key point in all of this is to ensure that management is seen to be driving the merger proposal, there is a consistent message communicated, and all partners receive the presentation within a short period of time. This latter point is of crucial importance – once partners start to hear snippets of information from other partners second-hand, it can result in them making assumptions that could then influence their view, even before hearing the presentation.

Prospectus contents

In **Chapter 4**, we set out a (non-exhaustive) list of items that would normally be covered in merger negotiations. The prospectus should set out the findings of the due diligence process in respect of these items as well as the recommendations. The findings should be included so that partners from each firm are aware of the impact of the recommendation on their own firm.

The opening section of the prospectus should cover the business case in some detail and include the strategic vision for the 'new' firm and the key objectives. Either as an introduction to this section, or as an appendix, it would be helpful to set out a short (recent) history of both firms, as well as details of each of their current strategies.

At **Appendix 4**, we have listed as a pro forma the issues that usually need to be included in the prospectus. For each item, especially those in Section II, it is helpful to provide a short summary of the findings, along with what is being proposed for the 'new' firm (as noted above).

It is extremely useful if the contents of each section are assembled as the negotiations and due diligence process are conducted. This is especially so if a number of task forces are being used in the due diligence. Each task force should be asked to provide its report to the negotiating teams in a way that facilitates it being inserted into the prospectus. While there will be different writing styles adopted by each task force, once all the reports are in, it is relatively easy for one person to go through the prospectus and apply a consistent editorial style. This approach also means that the negotiating teams will be able to see the prospectus developing, and will recognise whether there are any gaps, cross-referencing or other work that needs to be done prior to its completion. One person should be appointed as the 'custodian'/editor of the prospectus, along with an 'editorial board' consisting of one partner from each of the firms involved.

CHAPTER 12: CONCLUSION

We have tried throughout this book to provide guidance to those firms which are contemplating a merger, and to provide a reference source for those which see the need to merge at some stage in the future. Where possible, we have endeavoured to indicate what we believe to be the low-risk approaches to the process (whilst still recognising that firms might choose higher-risk approaches based on their particular needs).

In our view, mergers between law firms will continue, and become a 'way of life', as has been the case in the corporate sector. As we illustrated in **Chapter 1**, the UK legal profession is still highly fragmented, even within the largest 500 firms (in terms of number of fee-earners), with almost 70% of those firms having less than 100 lawyers, and only 4% having more than 500. In terms of the percentage of lawyers in the size bands, of the total number of lawyers in the largest 500 firms, 26% are in firms with over 500 lawyers, and 32% are in firms with less than 100 lawyers. **Table 12.1** below shows this on a different basis for five major European jurisdictions, based on the largest 25 firms in each jurisdiction. (We recognise that there is some distortion created by the presence of international firms who might compete effectively with local firms despite having significantly less lawyers in the jurisdiction, and also by the presence of one exceptionally large firm in a couple of markets. Nevertheless, even allowing for these two points there is a significant gap between the two groups.)

The implications of **Table 12.1** are, we believe, clear. The difference in size between firms who are, to a large extent, competing for similar types of work from

Table 12.1: Comparative size of firms in major European markets (no of lawyers)					
	France	Germany	Italy	Spain	UK
Average size of largest five firms	611	375	214	567	1,400
Average size of firms 21-25 in size	82	97	51	46	452
Ratio (top to bottom)	7.5:1	3.9:1	4.2:1	12.3:1	3.1:1

Source: The European Legal 500 (2004)

similar clients will lead to more mergers throughout these, and other, European jurisdictions. Smaller firms, who wish to remain 'full service', will find it increasingly difficult to compete for better-value work and for more sophisticated clients when their direct competitors are three times their size. A well-managed large, full-service firm has major competitive advantages over a much smaller full-service firm trying to compete in the same space.

The situation is not all that different in the US, although the scale is somewhat greater than in Europe. As **Table 12.2** demonstrates, the AmLaw 200 is heavily populated between 200 and 500 lawyers with 55% of firms in those bands. Only 5% of firms are over 1000 lawyers and a further 18% over 500 and up to 1000 lawyers.

Table 12.2: Number of firms by size in the USA

Number of lawyers	Number of firms	Percentage of total
Over 1,000	10	5
801-1,000	12	6
601-800	25	12.5
401-600	39	19.5
201-400	86	43
200 and less	28	14
	200	100

Source: AmLaw 200 (2004)

It is not surprising that there is considerable merger activity in the US as well as in Europe.

Mergers between law firms are likely, therefore, to increase in the longer term. Although there might be a rise and decline in the number of mergers as an inverse to the economic cycle for law firms (more mergers when demand is low, less when demand is high) there will be an upward trend over time due to the fragmentation in all major legal markets.

Smaller firms do, of course, have other options. Some will choose to narrow their focus and become more specialist rather than 'full service'. This will allow them to compete effectively in terms of critical mass within their chosen areas of specialisation, without increasing in overall size to that of the larger full-service competitors. Some will seek to expand through rapid organic growth.

Others will choose not to merge but to remain full service and accept a downward shift in market position. Some, of course, will not choose it but it will happen anyway.

In the longer term, there are no other strategic options within a domestic market. At the cross-border level of competition (eg within Europe) some firms will choose to merge and use the total size of the firm as a way of off-setting being smaller domestically. Others will seek to form exclusive alliances that represent mergers, but where local management, profit-sharing and partnership arrangements are independent of each other. In these cases, firms will need to carry out a very similar exercise to those who merge. The steps set out in this book provide guidance to such firms.

Firms do not have to merge but, to reiterate a point made in **Chapter 1**, competition in legal markets leads to consolidation (as it does in any market). Firms who choose not to merge will face the need to grow organically in order to keep pace with rivals or to change their desired strategic positioning in the longer term. Handled well, and approached in an appropriate way, a merger is not to be feared, and nor should it be seen as a 'desperate' option. As we have endeavoured to demonstrate throughout this book, merger can be a very effective way of implementing a strategy, and need carry no more risk than any other option for implementation.

APPENDICES

APPENDIX 1: ISSUES TO CONSIDER IN IDENTIFYING MERGER CANDIDATES – SUMMARY GUIDE

We noted in various places in the text a number of key issues to be considered in identifying merger candidates. We thought it worthwhile to set out in summary the range of issues that need to be considered in a majority of merger searches, even though a definitive list that would meet the needs of every firm is not possible.

The initial identification of potential merger candidates has to rely on evidence that is available externally from a variety of sources. For a start, there are the websites and marketing materials of firms now available in many countries. Within the UK and US, there is a significant amount of financial data available on the largest firms (see for example the *Legal Business* 100 and Am Law 200) and more valuable information is available on the UK's largest 500 (see the *Legal 500* directory). Information on smaller firms is more difficult to obtain, but it can be gathered by researching the legal press, speaking with recruitment agencies and headhunters and from people within one's own firm. New recruits are often useful information sources – their previous firm might be a possible target and they would be able to provide some information about it without breaking any confidences. New recruits will often have explored opportunities with several firms before making their choice and, in the process, picked up some interesting information.

The key criteria that can assist in selecting merger candidates can be divided into two groups: the first is the 'must-haves', ie characteristics that must be present. [A]n example is that a mid-sized firm seeking to develop a strong commercial law positi[on in] the market is likely to have a commercial law focus as a 'must-have'. It is highly u[n]of to find a small private client firm as suitable, no matter how profitable and suc[cess]et of is in its own market niche. Hence the 'must-haves' assist in developing an i[nitial] occur as candidates, comprising those who best meet the 'must have' test. The [second] lly, want criteria, the 'good to haves', are important, but are where some trade-offs[ ]t these are the selection narrows down. For example, the firm seeking to merge mig[ht] candidates in a merger partner that is located already in several specific jurisdicti[o]ns, whereas the 'good to haves' not 'must-haves'. It might eventually find that the b[est]ons, whereas the terms of the 'must-have' lack a presence in one or more of these lo[cations] firms who are in the desired locations are somewhat weaker on the 'must-haves'. If location is a 'good to have', then it will be of secondary importance.

The three core 'must have' criteria are:

1.   present strategic position and apparent strategy;

2.   culture and behaviour; and

3.   economic structure.

Location of offices, or at least the main office, could be a 'must-have'. For example, a firm seeking to develop in London will want to ensure that all candidates have a strong London position: there is little point merging with a firm that has good offices in, say, Leeds and Newcastle but nothing in London. Hence the main office could be a 'must-have' whereas other offices could be 'good to have' (or even a negative factor).

Structure is another issue that is usually a 'must-have', although not always. In a number of searches for merger partners, the management of the search firm has ruled out candidates who met a number of other criteria but whose management structure was vastly different to that of the search firm – it was thought likely to be too difficult to reach agreement on a structure that would be acceptable to the search firm. In other cases, however, structure is seen as a 'good to have'.

Within the 'must-haves' some firms emphasise culture over strategy, while others have a reverse emphasis. The first group want a firm with an acceptable, strategic position and strategy, but believe that culture is the most important issue – the view is that if the culture is right then any shortfalls in strategy can be overcome, but differences in culture could result in an ineffective merger.

The contrary view is that the business case for merger will be built around the combination of the two firms' business strategies. Partners are unlikely to vote for a merger where there are significant strategic shortcomings with the proposed merger firm, no matter how good the culture is. (We use culture here in a wider sense and refer to the discussion in **Chapter 10**.)

While this position, somewhat who acted for whom, the identification of a potential candidate's strategic position, some idea as to the types of clients it works with and the work done with these clients is also important. This strategic position, somewhat more difficult to obtain than a sense of a firm's overall market position, information can often be gathered the legal press, from data available as to who acted for whom M&A transactions and from general market 'gossip'.

In setting out the 'must-haves', we seek to divide the main criteria into subsets. This is particularly important when it comes to ranking firms in terms of how they meet the criteria. It also forces the search firm to be specific. So, instead of stating that a candidate must have a similar strategy to that of the search firm, we identify the several characteristics that would demonstrate a similar strategy. Hence the main headings of strategic positioning and strategy, culture and structure would contain a number of sub-criteria that would enable a judgement to be made as to whether a potential candidate meets the overall requirements under each criterion. For example, in a recent merger search we used the following categories in order to collect information about prospective merger candidates:

- Strategic positioning and strategy:

    - core client types
    - directory rankings – core practice areas
    - recognised leading practitioners
    - international capability
    - direct competitors
    - perceived position in terms of high to low value suppliers
    - perceived competitive capabilities

- Culture and behaviour:

    - degree of autonomy versus tight management control
    - degree of self-discipline in pursuing strategy versus strong central direction
    - degree to which performance management is a focus inside the firm
    - significant external profile raising (or not)
    - degree to which the partnership is collegiate
    - degree of teamwork versus individuality
    - degree to which tough decisions are made versus advance compromise

- Economic structure:

    - reputation for aggressive pricing (or not)
    - reported leverage
    - number of equity to other partners

- perceptions about charge rate levels
- reputation in regard to salary levels
- perceptions about the firm's focus on revenue growth or cost-cutting
- average revenue, cost and profit per equity partner and per fee-earner (if available)

- Organisational structure:

  - single- or dual-tier structure
  - key decision-makers
  - process for making key decisions
  - extent of management delegation to practice groups
  - extent of delegation by partners to central management
  - role of key support service personnel in structure
  - regularity of partner meetings

The 'good to haves' would normally include:

- Strong support infrastructure that complements that of the search firm

- Leases due for expiry within a short time period (where an unwanted duplication of premises is likely)

- A pool of effective managers within the partnership

- Partner remuneration system (can be a 'must-have')

- A partnership age structure that complements that of the search firm (can be a 'must-have')

- A good reputation amongst recruitment agencies and headhunters (as a firm that manages recruitment well and about which good feedback is received from recruits)

- An appropriate level of technology already operating inside the firm

All of this information is available from the various sources listed earlier for some firms and some of it is available for others. In many cases, the 'evidence' will be built up from a sense of perceptions by people and by collecting samples of data from other sources. In our experience, it is possible to draw up a reasonably accurate profile of any medium to large-sized firms in any of the more sophisticated legal markets in the world, even though some have much less published data than in the UK or US.

APPENDIX 2: PRO FORMA ECONOMIC STRUCTURE

We find that firms often exchange a huge amount of financial information during merger negotiations, much of which might be of interest to finance directors but which is irrelevant to understanding the economic structure and key financial performance indicators of both firms.

What we have found very useful is to summarise the relevant data into a relatively simple report that highlights the key variables. This allows comparisons to be made between the two firms and also provides an understanding of each firm's performance in financial terms over a defined period (which we usually suggest should be at least three years).

The following pro forma sets this out in three schedules, and we have found that most lawyers find it easy to understand. The first schedule sets out the basic data and key variables. The second schedule analyses performance on a per fee-earner basis down to profit, and then converts this to a profit per equity partner. The third schedule covers work in progress and debtors.

The pro forma can be used for a firm as a whole, for a practice group/service line, for an office, or for any particular sub-group which is defined as a profit centre. The example is for one firm over a three-year period and this would normally be followed by a similar analysis for each profit centre, all aggregating to the numbers of the firm as a whole. An explanation of each line follows the example.

The key variables on which to focus are leverage (Line 11), the hourly rate recovery (Line 14), utilisation (Line 19), the hours recovery (Line 17), the cost multiple (Line 20) and the cost-income ratio (Line 21). The basic data on which to focus are the actual hourly rate (Line 13), billed hours per fee-earner (Line 18), revenue per fee-earner (Line 22) and revenue per equity partner (Line 23). Significant differences in any of these items between two firms considering merger should be investigated closely even if the profit per equity partner is similar.

This pro forma has been adapted by many clients as a part of their management information system. It can be prepared monthly for each profit centre and contain a monthly actual and budget column plus the same year to date. In the event that there are variations in the revenue and profit being generated, this report allows easy identification as to where the issues are.

Pro Forma
Schedule 1: Summary economic structure – aggregate data

Line	Item		Year 1		Year 2		Year 3	
			£k	%	£k	%	£k	%
1	Revenue		20,600	100	21,650	100	25,415	100
2	Direct costs		7,700	37	8,500	39	8,825	35
3	Contribution		12,900	63	13,150	61	16,590	65
4	Overheads		8,550	42	9,800	45	10,895	43
5	Net profit		4,350	21	3,350	16	5,695	22
6	No of equity partners		14		16		17	
7	Profit per equity partner	£k	311		209		335	
8	Add back notional salaries	£k	175		175		175	
9	Earnings per equity partner	£k	486		384		510	
10	Total fee-earners		84		90		95	
11	Leverage (1x)		5.0		4.6		4.6	
12	Average standard hourly rate	£	197		198		205	
13	Average actual hourly rate	£	185		192		203	
14	Rate recovery: write-up/(down)	%	<6>		<3>		<1>	

Note that some calculations will not be precise in the schedules due to rounding.

Explanatory notes
First Schedule
Line 1: Revenue
The actual revenue earned in the year, calculated by adding or subtracting the net change in work in progress (valued at realisable selling values) from the amount billed in the year.

Line	Item		Year 1	Year 2	Year 3
Schedule 1: Summary economic structure – aggregate data (continued)					
15	Recorded billable hours	Hrs	130,200	132,750	143,450
16	Actual billable hours	Hrs	111,350	112,500	125,400
17	Hours recovery: write-up/(down)	%	<14>	<15>	<13>
18	Billed hours per fee-earner	Hrs	1,326	1,250	1,320
19	Utilisation	%	82	78	82
20	Cost multiple		2.67	2.55	2.88
21	Cost/income ratio		1.27	1.18	1.29
22	Revenue per fee-earner	£k	245.2	240.5	267.5
23	Revenue per equity partner	£k	1,471	1,353	1,495

Line 2: Direct costs

Salary and related costs of fee-earners. Must also include a notional salary for partners because they have contributed to revenue and there must be an associated cost. (Failure to do so can distort comparisons where there are differences in leverage). Notional salaries can be calculated from market rates for in-house lawyers and tested against the salary paid to senior associates in the firm. (Note: some firms include secretarial salaries here as well. We prefer to retain these in overhead.)

Line 3: Contributions

Line 1 less Line 2.

Line 4: Overheads

All overhead costs associated with the business. An analysis of specific categories of costs (eg property) and specific items (eg rent) should be on a separate sheet and not listed here.

Pro Forma

Schedule 2: Summary economic structure – per fee-earner/per equity partner

			Year 1	Year 2	Year 3
	Per fee-earner				
24	Standard available hours	Hrs	1,610	1,610	1,610
25	Utilisation	%	82	78	82
26	Actual billable hours	Hrs	1,326	1,250	1,320
27	At average standard hourly rate	£	197	198	205
28	Revenue at standard	£k	261.2	247.5	270.6
29	Rate recovery: write-up/down	%	<6>	<3>	<1>
30	Actual revenue	£k	245.2	240.5	267.5
31	Direct costs	£k	91.6	94.4	92.9
32	Contribution	£k	153.6	146.1	174.6
33	Overheads	£k	101.8	108.9	114.7
34	Profit	£k	51.8	37.2	59.9
	Per equity partner				
35	Leverage (+1)	£k	6.0	5.63	5.59
36	Profit	£k	310.8	209.4	335.0
37	Add back notional salaries	£k	175.0	175.0	175.0
38	Earnings	£k	485.8	384.4	510.0

Line 5: Net profit

Line 3 less Line 4. Shows the true profitability of the business, assuming the partner notional salaries are reasonably accurate. It demonstrates the earning power of the business after paying partners an appropriate reward for their work.

Pro Forma

Schedule 3: Summary economic structure – work-in-progress and debtors £k

WIP	January	February	March	April	May	June	July	August	September	October	November	December
WIP at start	3,200	3,400	3,200	3,100	3,000	3,100	3,150	3,000	2,850	3,100	3,450	3,750
Less:												
Billed in month	2,400	2,100	2,200	2,150	2,050	2,150	1,950	1,850	1,650	1,750	1,850	2,450
Sub-total	800	1,300	1,000	950	950	950	1,200	1,150	1,200	1,350	1,600	1,300
Plus:												
WIP input	2,600	1,900	2,100	2,050	2,150	2,200	1,800	1,700	1,900	2,100	2,150	1,700
WIP at end	3,400	3,200	3,100	3,000	3,100	3,150	3,000	2,850	3,100	3,450	3,750	3,000
No of days	34.0	32.0	31.0	30.0	31.0	31.5	30.0	28.5	31.0	34.5	37.5	30.0
Debtors												
Debtors at start	4,600	5,200	5,600	5,600	5,250	4,700	4,250	4,100	3,850	3,400	3,350	3,500
Less:												
Paid	1,800	1,700	2,200	2,500	2,600	2,400	2,100	2,100	2,100	1,800	1,700	1,400
Written off	–	–	–	–	–	200	–	–	–	–	–	–
Sub-total	2,800	3,500	3,400	3,100	2,650	2,100	2,150	2,000	1,750	1,600	1,650	2,100
Plus:												
Billed in month	2,400	2,100	2,200	2,150	2,050	2,150	1,950	1,850	1,650	1,750	1,850	2,450
Debtors at end	5,200	5,600	5,600	5,250	4,700	4,250	4,100	3,850	3,400	3,350	3,500	4,550
No of days	52.0	56.0	56.0	52.5	47.0	42.5	41.0	38.5	34.0	33.5	35.0	45.5
Combined no of days	86.0	88.0	87.0	82.5	78.0	74.0	71.0	67.0	65.0	68.0	72.5	75.5

Line 6: Number of equity partners

Based on full time equivalent for the year. Where there are salaried partners they should be treated as non-partner fee-earners. The same applies to fixed-share partners: their profit share will need to be added to their salary and treated as a salary cost.

Line 7: Profit per equity partner

Line 5 divided by Line 6.

Line 8: Add back notional salaries

Add back to Line 7 the amount included at Line 2.

Line 9: Earnings per equity partner

Equal to what is recorded in the partnership accounts when multiplied by Line 6.

Line 10: Total fee-earners

Based on full-time equivalents. Some firms include trainees whereas others leave them in overhead. We tend to exclude them because their fee earning is often low and erratic. Include equity partners.

Line 11: Leverage

Line 10 less Line 6 divided by Line 6. The ratio of non-equity partner fee-earners to equity partners.

Line 12: Average standard hourly rate

Derived by calculating all of the hours in revenue (Line 1) at their standard billing rate and then dividing revenue at these standard rates by the number of hours. Indicates the average hourly rate that would have been achieved given the mix of fee-earners who did the work, if there were no write-offs or write-ups and standard billing rates.

Line 13: Average actual hourly rate

Revenue (Line 1) divided by Line 16, actual billable hours.

Line 14: Rate recovery

The percentage of the standard rate (Line 12) by which the actual rate (Line 13) either exceeds or is lower.

Line 15: Recorded billable hours

Shows the actual time recorded against client matters. Should not include time that was considered a waste or which were never intended to be charged.

Line 16: Actual billable hours

Shows the actual hours constituting revenue (Line 1). In effect this time, multiplied by Line 13 equals revenue (Line 1).

Line 17: Hours recovery

Indicates the percentage by which Line 16 was under or over Line 15. Derived by subtracting Line 16 from Line 15 and dividing the sum by Line 15.

Line 18: Billed hours per fee-earner

Line 16 divided by Line 10. Provides quantification of the average hours per fee-earner included in Line 1.

Line 19: Utilisation

Indicates the percentage of available hours that was billed to clients in Line 1. Requires a standard definition of available hours. In the UK we use 1,610 hours per annum being seven hours per day, five days a week for 46 weeks in the year. It is assumed that the six weeks between 52 and 46 are represented by vacation, statutory holidays, etc. This will vary country by country. Do not include overtime as 'available' as it is variable and prevents any comparisons over time. In the event that people put in more hours than the standard of 1,610 hours, this should be reflected in additional billable or other time.

Line 20: Cost multiple

One of the most valuable key performance indicators. Results from dividing Line 1 by Line 2. Shows the amount of revenue generated from each £1 of fee-earner salary cost. In the example, the firm provided £2.67 in Year 1, £2.55 in Year 2 and £2.88 in Year 3. Provides a reliable reflection of trends in profitability subject to overheads being under control.

Line 21: Cost/income ratio

Similar to the cost multiple but includes all costs. Result of dividing Line 1 by the sum of Lines 2 and 4. Shows the percentage that profit (Line 5) exceeds costs and is the converse of the percentage that profit represents of revenue. (Put another way, in Year 1 the net profit is 27% above total costs and 21% of revenue.)

Line 22: Revenue per fee-earner
Line 1 divided by Line 10. Assuming costs are under control, driving up this number will add directly to profits.

Line 23: Revenue per equity partner
Line 1 divided by Line 6. Also derived from Line 22 multiplied by Line 11 plus one. (The leverage number must be increased by one as it does not include partners who are also fee-earners. Provides a measure of the revenue that partners, on average, must generate from their won work and that of others, in order to achieve the required levels of profit per equity partner.

Second Schedule
Line 24: Standard available hours per fee-earner
See note to Line 19 above.

Line 25: Utilisation
Taken from Line 19.

Line 26: Actual billable hours per fee-earner
Line 18.

Line 27: At average standard hourly rates
Line 12.

Line 28: Revenue at standard
Line 26 multiplied by Line 27.

Line 29: Rate recovery
Line 14.

Line 30: Actual revenue
Line 22. Also Line 1 divided by Line 10.

Line 31: Direct cost
Line 2 divided by Line 10.

Line 32: Contribution
Line 30 less Line 31. Also Line 3 divided by Line 10.

Line 33: Overhead
Line 4 divided by Line 10.

Line 34: Profit
Line 32 less Line 33. Also Line 5 divided by Line 10.

Line 35: Leverage (+1)
Converts Line 34, profit per fee-earner to Line 36, profit per equity partner. Multiplies Line 34 by Line 11 plus one. Hence, in Year 1 Line 35 is six which is five (as per Line 11) plus one. As noted before, this is because the 1:5 ratio of leverage does not include partners in the figure five but they are also fee-earners.

Line 36: Profit
Calculated as Line 5 divided by Line 6. (More precise calculation of Line 7.) Also as Line 34 multiplied by Line 35.

Line 37: Add back notional salaries
As per Line 8.

Line 38: Earnings
A more precise calculation of Line 9.

Third Schedule
The numbers recorded here would come direct from the main accounting system. Key points to note are:

1. Work in progress must be at realisable selling values and brings a proportion of profit into account. It should, therefore, only include work that has been commissioned by clients.

2. Controlling the input to WIP so that only genuine billable work is included assists in the end of month valuation.

3. The calculation of 'No of Days' for both WIP and debtors represents the number of days of revenue contained in each. It is vital that a standard be set for the number of days. In the example, 250 days has been used, which is the number of normal weekly working days in a year less statutory holidays. Some firms use 365 days (being the total days in a year). Whichever is used, it must be consistent if comparisons are to be made.

4. Calculating the revenue per day during a year before the actual revenue for the year is known creates a slight problem. We tend to use the budget revenue for the year although this will require recalculation in the event that a significant difference between actual and budget emerges. An alternative is to use the aggregate revenue for the year to date, along with the proportion of days to that point. In the example, revenue for the three months to March was £6.6m (calculated as the three months' billings of £6.7m less a decline in WIP of £100,000 from 1 January to 31 March). Based on 62.5 days (25% of 250) the revenue per day is £105,600; hence the number of days revenue in WIP for March would be 29.4 rather than the 31 days shown in the example. (The example was based on £25m revenue and 250 days, being £100,000 per day). Using the latter method will require a re-calculation, every month, of the previous months number of days if a proper comparison is to be made.

5. The combined number of days is arrived at simply by adding the number of days for WIP to those of debtors. The total indicates the length of time between the month in which work is done and the cash is received. Hence, in the example the firm is running at over 80 days in the first four months, which represents 16 weeks (ie five days a week). This improves in the middle of the year such that by September it is down to 55 days or 13 weeks. It rises again, however, in the latter months of the year and reaches 75.5 days (or 15.1 weeks) in December. The reasons for this pattern should be explored in the merger negotiations.

Appendix 3: Issues to be agreed for the 'new' firm

(i)   Status of non-equity partners and equity criteria.

(ii)   Partnership agreement, including:

- partnership/management decisions;
- retirement;
- expulsion;
- entry to partnership; and
- any others.

(iii)   Tax reserves and tax position:

- how they will be managed.

(iv)   Management and support role definitions.

(v)   Management style issues:

- how major decisions are to be taken.

(vi)   Property leases to be taken into the 'new' firm.

(vii)   Outstanding claims under the professional indemnity (PI) policy, treatment of claims and future PI policy.

(viii) Professional advisers (including bankers, accountants, etc).

(ix)   Assets and liabilities to be assumed by the 'new' firm.

(x)   Treatment and valuation of work in progress.

Appendix 3. Issues to be agreed for the 'new' firm

(xi)   Ongoing non-productive costs (eg annuities).

(xii)   Cost of personnel not joining the 'new' firm.

(xiii)   Future liabilities incurred but not yet due (eg lease contract pay-outs, etc).

(xiv)   Other balance sheet issues.

(xv)   Integration of IT systems:

   • how it will occur.

(xvi)   Management information systems:

   • information to be distributed and to whom.

(xvii)   Performance management systems.

(xviii)   Business planning/budgeting processes.

(xix)   Staff remuneration, grading, etc.

(xx)   Support staff management roles and selection of candidates.

(xxi)   Membership of international alliances/associations (if any).

(xxii)   Marketing policies.

(xxiii)   Personnel policies.

(xxiv)   Client management procedures.

(xxv)   Dates of financial year.

(xxvi)   Annual financial budget and cash flows:

- last three years and projection.

(xxvii) Training and development programme/policies.

(xxviii) Policy in regard to trainees.

Appendix 4: Pro forma prospectus agenda

Section I: Business rationale (for the firm and each major practice area)

Introduction: short history of each firm and their respective strategies.

(i)   What will be the strategic focus of Newco:

- client type
- work type
- value/volume positioning
- competitive edge?

(ii)   With whom will it be competing in three to five years?

(iii)   What will be the economic shape of Newco on day one? What are we seeking to achieve over three to five years?

(iv)   Who will be the core clients of Newco and what competitive issues exist with these?

(v)   Possible areas of client conflict?

(vi)   In what way will each firm be more competitive with the merger than without it?

(vii)   What will be the structure of Newco and how will it be managed?

(viii) What are the key objectives for the internal environment of Newco?

Section II: Primary issues

(ix)   Capital structure and firm's borrowings policy.

(x) Equity partner remuneration system and drawings policy (including benefits).

(xi) Status of non-equity partners and equity criteria; remuneration systems.

(xii) Partnership deed (key clauses – attach copy as appendix):

- partnership/management decisions
- retirement
- expulsion
- entry to partnership
- others.

(xiii) Tax reserves and tax position.

(xiv) Name of Newco (taking into account local Bar requirements).

(xv) Management and support role definitions.

(xvi) Management style issues:

- how major decisions will be taken along with percentages required?

(xvii) Property leases – current status and issues that arise in forming Newco.

(xviii) Outstanding claims (PI) and treatment of claims; future PI policy.

(xix) Professional advisers (including bankers, accountants, etc) for Newco.

(xx) Assets and liabilities to be assumed by Newco.

(xxi) Treatment and valuation of WIP.

(xxii) Ongoing non-productive costs (eg annuities, leases for unoccupied premises).

(xxiii) Cost of personnel not joining Newco.

(xxiv)   Future liabilities, incurred but not yet due (eg lease contract pay-outs etc).

(xxv)   Other balance sheet issues.

(xxvi)   Integration of IT systems.

(xxvii)   Management information systems:

  •   information distributed and to whom.

(xxviii)   Performance management systems.

(xxix)   Business planning/budgeting processes.

(xxx)   List of all partners and fee earners by category and practice area.

(xxxi)   Staff remuneration, grading etc.

(xxxii)   Support staff management roles and selection of candidates.

(xxxiii)   International alliances/associations.

(xxxiv)   Marketing policies.

(xxxv)   Personnel policies.

(xxxvi)   Client management procedures.

(xxxvii)   Dates of financial year.

(xxxviii) Annual financial budget and cash flows: last three years combined and projection for Newco.

(xxxix)   Training and development programme/policies.

(xl)   Policy in regard to trainees.

Subject index

---

* For individual firms featuring in the case studies, see the **Index of law firms** on p309.

INDEX OF LAW FIRMS

* Denotes firms featuring in the case studies in this book.

* Denotes firms featuring in the case studies in this book.